DEREK WRIGHT

# The Psychology of Moral Behaviour

PENGUIN BOOKS

Penguin Books Ltd, Harmondsworth,
Middlesex, England
Penguin Books, 625 Madison Avenue, New York,
New York 10022, U.S.A.
Penguin Books Australia Ltd, Ringwood,
Victoria, Australia
Penguin Books Canada Ltd, 2801 John Street,
Markham, Ontario, Canada L3R 1B4
Penguin Books (N.Z.) Ltd,
182–190 Wairau Road,
Auckland 10, New Zealand

First published in 1971
Reprinted 1973, 1975, 1976, 1978, 1981

Made and printed in Great Britain by
Hazell Watson & Viney Ltd, Aylesbury, Bucks
Set in Linotype Plantin

PELICAN BOOKS

# The Psychology of Moral Behaviour

Derek Wright was educated at Bembridge School, and –
after serving for three years in the Army Intelligence
Corps – at Keble College, Oxford, where he studied
English. He then taught for a few years at a grammar
school, during which time he took an M.A. in education at
Birmingham University, studying part-time. This was
followed by three years working with maladjusted
adolescents in London while at the same time taking a
degree in psychology at Birkbeck College. He then became
a lecturer at Culham College of Education, where he was
responsible for a supplementary course for experienced
teachers in the education of backward and maladjusted
children. In 1962 he moved to the Department of
Psychology at Leicester University, where he has since
remained. His main teaching and research interests lie in
the fields of child development and the psychology of
religion. He is one of the authors of the Penguin text
*Introducing Psychology: An Experimental Approach.*
He is married, with three children.

For
JUNE

# Contents

# Preface

The purpose of this book is to introduce the reader to the psychological study of moral behaviour, and in particular to the empirical or behaviourist approach within it. That is to say the content is generally limited to a discussion of data which have been obtained under more or less controlled conditions and which it is in principle possible for others to check. This is in no way to imply that the armchair, the clinic, the psychoanalyst's couch, the novel, and everyday experience are not valuable sources of our psychological understanding of morality; it is only to say that this is one kind of book rather than another. Commitment to the empirical approach means that assertions have to be confined to those that research can substantiate. This has not stopped me from speculating however; indeed many of the discussions that follow go well beyond the evidence. I hope that I have made clear, implicitly if not explicitly, when I am reporting fact, when I am drawing reasonable inferences, and when I am engaging in speculative fancy.

One feature at least may be judged in need of defence. The reader will find that the bibliography is fairly exhaustive, and that some pages are quite thickly littered with names and dates. And he may well feel a trifle exasperated to discover that many of these references are to articles in obscure and inaccessible journals. There are several reasons for this. Any book of this kind is a record of a journey through the literature on the subject. Whereas some readers will be content simply to sit at home and read about the strange places visited by the author, other more adventurous spirits may be drawn to make the same journey themselves. So, in order to help them, the full details of the itinerary are given. And there is always the hope that someone, somewhere, will be stirred into doing research in this field as a result of reading the book. I should want to make his task as easy as I can.

But there is another reason. It is an accepted practice for people to make money out of writing books in which they spend most of their time describing other people's research. This is not as parasitic as it might seem, for the author usually adds something of his own and, put at its lowest, he may save others some heavy reading. But it is only right that he should give his sources, so that the reader knows where the real credit lies. And if some writers are less than zealous in this respect, it behoves the author of a book on morality to set an exemplary standard.

I owe many debts to many people: to my friend and colleague, Wladek Sluckin, for carefully reading the whole book, and for being a constant support to morale; to Julia Vellacott for removing the worst stylistic blemishes; to Ann Robinson, Robert Thomson and David West for reading parts of the book and challenging me to new thoughts; and to Brian Foss, best of teachers, who encouraged me to write the book in the first place.

# CHAPTER 1

# Introduction

It is now widely recognized, both in ordinary conversation and in social science, that games provide an illuminating analogy or model for other more 'serious' social activities. We talk of the political game, the game of commerce or scientific research, and even of the game of warfare. Berne (1966) has taught us to look on any relationship that has become stereotyped and repetitive and in which ulterior motives are at work, such as those that can occur within marriage, as a form of game; mental illness, criminality and religion have all been called 'life games'.*

The reasons why we find the analogy satisfying are doubtless as many as there are distinguishable features of games. For instance, a game is to a large extent cut off from the rest of life; it constitutes time taken out of the ordinary business of living. In calling an occupation or marriage a game we may be simply pointing to the fact that these often become separate compartments in a man's life. Games are also competitive challenges to an individual's skills that offer the rewards of winning or coming first; politics and scientific research are challenges to skill which offer the rewards of status, power and fame. Games are artificial, invented activities that are not judged to be serious, though they are taken seriously while being played. A great many human occupations may strike us as similarly invented, and as not being completely serious.

But the most important feature of a game is that it is an activity in which actions are governed and controlled by rules. Without rules, and without obedience to them, there can be no game.

* See for example Szasz (1961) and de Ropp (1969).

The rules define the moves open to the players, they are binding on all of them, and they mark off one game from another. It is this feature of games that has excited the interest of social scientists; for a great deal of human behaviour consists in obedience to rules of one kind or another. 'Man is a rule-following animal,' says Professor Peters.* Just as it is impossible to understand a chess player's behaviour without knowing the rules of chess, so we cannot fully explain the conduct of a politician or a husband without taking account of the rules of politics or marriage.

I am, of course, using the concept of a rule to cover a wide range of phenomena. In addition to formulated lists of what people should and should not do, it refers to unwritten, and even unformulated, customs, traditions, conventions and norms. Our behaviour is constantly being steered by rules of this kind. But rules are not like the natural laws studied by scientists, for they can be broken without being invalidated. Indeed we often do not become aware of a rule until we have broken it. Though rules are man-made, we cannot usually point to a moment when they were invented, and though we must all more or less agree to follow rules if they are to be effective, we are seldom actually asked whether we accept them. With such trivial exceptions as a newly marketed game or a newly formed club, rules to a large extent grow and develop on their own. There may come a time when they have to be explicitly framed and institutionalized, but as often as not this is merely to make fully conscious a rule that is already tacitly accepted.

In a career, or even in a game like football, people quite often learn to conform to a rule before they are fully aware of what it is. The classic example of this kind of 'ignorant' rule-following is speech: children learn to speak grammatically long before they learn the rules of grammar. Though in some sense the product of man's intelligence, rules are seldom the fruit of conscious and deliberate reasoning; tuning in to the rules operative in any social setting is an intuitive art.

*See Peters (1958).

## Moral Rules

Without drawing any precise distinctions we can all recognize the difference between at one extreme the conventional rules of dress or eating and at the other those concerned with keeping promises, honesty, respect for the rights of the individual, and sympathy for those in need. Whether or not the former ever deserve to be called moral, the latter always do.

Morality is not a game or activity among others, marked off from them by the nature of its rules. Perhaps we should call it a metagame. If we find the rules of a particular activity uncongenial or impossible to keep, we can, at least in principle, contract out and play a different game. However uncongenial and difficult moral rules may be to keep, we cannot contract out of the metagame they define. Moral rules are foundational in the sense that they are concerned with the maintenance of, for instance, trust, mutual help and justice in human relationships. Unless these exist in some measure it becomes virtually impossible to continue any social activity. Moral rules form the yardstick against which we evaluate the rules of any particular activity. It is therefore not surprising that, though conventions and customs vary widely from one society to another, basic moral principles apparently do not.

The more we study moral codes the more we find that they do not differ on major points of principle and that the divergencies that exist are partly due to different opinions about empirical facts, for example about the effects of certain types of conduct, and partly to differences in social and economic organization that make it appropriate to apply the fundamental rules now in one way, now in another. (Nowell-Smith, 1954)

The *concept* of a moral rule forms part of a network of related concepts which together make up what can be called the language of moral obligation. A sample of some of the key concepts in this language might include good, right, rights, wrong, ought, duty, virtue, guilt, responsibility, sin, blame, and so on. Analysis of the meaning of these terms, the logic of their usage, and the grounds for making assertions with them, all lie within the province of the moral philosopher. But language is inseparable from experience.* Men not only say they have obligations to others, they *feel* a sense of obligation; they not only recognize that they are guilty of breaking a moral rule, they feel guilt and remorse. Perhaps the most distinctively moral experience we have is the conflict between inclination and duty that we express in the words 'I want to but ought not to', and 'I ought to but do not want to'. This kind of experience is one of the mainsprings of religious activity, for one of the purposes of the religious discipline of life, it is said, is to train the personality so that this conflict is resolved by turning obligation into that which is desired. Both the conceptual framework in which they are formulated and the experience which goes with them mark out moral rules as distinctively different from, for example, the rules of tennis, grammar or etiquette.

One final point: the rules of games like tennis or the conventions of etiquette usually prescribe what should be done in specific detail with rulings for various contingencies that may arise. This tends to be true also for unwritten customs and norms. Moral rules, on the other hand, at least when stated in a way that commands universal agreement, are abstract and general principles of conduct that have to be applied to all kinds of concrete situations. There are many occasions when their application is too obvious for serious dispute (e.g. much theft and murder); but notoriously there are many others when it is fiercely controversial (e.g. extramarital intercourse and abortion). The legality of these activities can be settled by judicial arbitration, their morality however cannot.

## The Nature of Moral Behaviour

No discriminable class of actions can be labelled moral as such; for whether or not an action is morally evaluated depends on the

* cf. Wittgenstein's remark that 'to imagine a language means to imagine a form of life'.

context in which it occurs. It is its relationship to a moral rule which justifies us in calling behaviour moral. As a conveniently loose and informal definition of the subject-matter of this book, I propose the following: *moral behaviour consists of all the various things people do in connection with moral rules*. Before all the objections to this crowd the reader's mind, let me spell it out in detail.

First of all, of course, people keep the rules and break them. And here we must remember that moral rules are positive as well as negative; they command us to be generous and altruistic as well as forbidding us to lie or steal. Then because the behaviour is rule-related, people are apt to congratulate themselves if they conform and blame themselves if they deviate. Moral rules not only serve as guides to future behaviour but also provide the basis for post mortems on past behaviour.

People also construct moral ideologies. That is, they announce their commitment to moral beliefs, and they attempt to defend these beliefs by arguments of various sorts. They make moral judgements in the light of their beliefs and try to show others that they are correct. They preach and give moral instruction to the young.

Finally we cannot escape some involvement in how others keep moral rules. Put at its lowest, if others break certain rules we may suffer; hence we take steps to deter them by ensuring that offenders are punished, either legally or socially. But for most people there is much more to it than this. When moral rules are broken, or at least certain of them, they feel indignation and anger; they *want* to see the offenders punished and find it difficult to tolerate the possibility that they may get away with it. If they can they punish the offenders themselves by verbal rebuke, social ostracism, or even physical assault if feeling is very intense. These punitive feelings towards offenders are enlarged and strengthened by sympathy for and protest on behalf of those who have suffered at their hands. Certain offences, such as the ill-treatment of children, incest and sadistic cruelty, seem to provoke vigorous moral condemnation in most people. Beyond these, however, people tend to specialize in the offences which make them indignant. Some feel strong moral revulsion against sexual immoralities and aberrations and fulminate against theft and vandalism; others are relatively undisturbed by these but find their anger violently stirred by economic injustice, lack of freedom and deprivation of rights.

All these kinds of behaviour fall within the purview of this book, though they will not all be given equal attention. There has been much less research into some of them than into others. But though they are all related to moral rules, it is not implied that the relationship is one of conscious deduction from rule to behaviour. Quite the contrary. Just as people may speak grammatically without knowing it, so they may be generous or sympathetic without realizing that they are also being virtuous (at least at the time – looking back afterwards it is difficult to resist a quiet glow of self-satisfaction!). Feelings of remorse and guilt are often disproportionate to the gravity of an offence as consciously judged. Moral judgements are dictated more by emotional response than by deliberate reference to a moral rule; indeed we sometimes find it difficult to rationalize our judgements afterwards in terms of any moral rule.

Moral rules and ideals are, I have said, man-made; they are the fruit of cultural rather than biological evolution. In the past this has been taken as evidence of a sharp antithesis between the moral and the biological. Moral rules, it was thought, were imposed from above by reason or divine decree upon a recalcitrant human nature. It was morality which redeemed man from his nasty and brutish animal nature, though it usually needed supernatural assistance to do so. Probably because we only become vividly conscious of moral rules when they conflict with inclination, we tend to think that in conforming to them man demonstrates his superiority to other species.

It is now abundantly clear from the labours of the ethologists that other species have developed very effective social controls for inhibiting intraspecies strife, regulating sexual behaviour, looking after young and defending territory against enemies. The control of antisocial impulses, guilt and altruism all have their behavioural counterparts in other species. Heroic self-sacrifice in the service of his fellows is not the prerogative of man. The mechanisms underlying these behavioural analogies of morality have evolved biologically; they derive from the genetic constitution common to the species. The consequence of this genetic programming is that under normal conditions the presentation of a given stimulus produces the appropriate 'moral' response whether the animal 'likes it or not'. It has been observed for instance that if a chimpanzee is eating and he sees another chimpanzee begging for food, he is compelled to give some of his food away even though he shows clear signs of anger and irritation at the same time (Hebb and Thompson, 1968). Of course environmental conditions and individual learning play their part in the development of these controls. The higher the animal in the evolutionary sense the more these genetically determined mechanisms can be disrupted by adverse environment factors during development; moreover in the higher mammals specific attachments or bonds usually formed early in life play an increasingly important role. Yet the fact remains that the 'morality' of other species is primarily instinctive.*

The influence of genetic constitution upon social behaviour is very much less specific in the human species than in any other. Human infants are, as we all know, extremely malleable and undergo a long period of socialization before they become fully mature moral beings. Yet we cannot discount the possibility that genetic predisposition facilitates the development of moral controls. We probably underestimate the extent to which we conform to moral rules spontaneously and without realizing the fact. Then there is surely a strong biological basis for the universally protective and altruistic response that human adults have towards their young, and that males have towards females with young. Consider too the way in which submissive acts such as apology and confession tend to disarm the aggression of others. This also has its counterpart in other species.

If human morality builds upon biological predisposition at one end, it certainly goes a lot further than just specifying the

* For a vivid and provocative discussion of the ethological perspective on human morality, see Lorenz (1963).

conditions for species survival at the other. Human beings extend the scope of their moral rules into areas of 'private' life where the social consequences of behaviour, whether good or bad, are to say the least unclear. The justification for this enlargement of moral concern is usually sought in religious beliefs or in some conception of the 'ideal moral man'. Moreover morality for many people encompasses man's relations to other species and to God as well as to his fellows.

## The Empirical Study of Moral Behaviour

Although it appears that always and everywhere men have been interested in moral problems, it is only comparatively recently that empirical studies of moral behaviour have been carried out. Indeed most of the work to be reported later was published after 1950. There seem to be at least two reasons why psychologists have tended to neglect the topic. First, it has been generally assumed that moral behaviour can be adequately explained by applying to it those fundamental laws of human behaviour that are discovered through the study of learning, perception and so on. Studying these laws in a moral context adds nothing new. Secondly, the controlled experimental study of moral behaviour faces formidable practical and ethical limitations. It has simply not been found possible to achieve the same experimental rigour that has been attained in other areas of psychology. Yet despite these handicaps a fairly substantial body of evidence has accumulated in which certain patterns are now beginning to emerge.

The adoption of an empirical approach towards moral behaviour has certain consequences. At the risk of taking the reader over familiar ground, some of these must be briefly mentioned.

It may demand some readjustment of perspective. In one sense we know a great deal about moral behaviour, for it is part of our daily experience. But in the sense of having knowledge based upon independent and reliable evidence, we are extremely ignorant. We must not be surprised if some of the results of empirical studies strike us as obvious. It is sometimes said of the psychologist that he goes to elaborate lengths to prove what we already know. This criticism is largely irrelevant for even if the psychologist shows that a commonsense assumption is correct (and sometimes he can show that it is not), progress has been made; for what was once a matter of belief based upon personal experience is now knowledge based upon evidence.

Secondly, the empirical approach deals with *variables*, or ways in which people differ in their behaviour. As can be seen from the discussion above, one can conceive of a number of dimensions along which people's moral behaviour might vary. In practice I shall be concerned with five variables – or rather five clusters of variables. These are *resistance to temptation*, or the capacity to refrain from morally reprehensible behaviour when motivated to engage in it, either in the presence of others or alone; *post-transgressional responses*, or the way people behave and the emotions they express after they have violated a moral rule of some kind; *altruism*, or sympathetic behaviour intended to benefit others; *moral insight*, or the kinds of reasoning that people engage in to defend and justify their moral judgements and beliefs; and *moral ideology* or the actions people believe to be right and wrong, their degree of commitment to these beliefs, and the function such beliefs serve in their personalities.

Thirdly, these variables have to be reliably and validly measured. This means that we must be sure that the measures used really do measure what they purport to measure, that they do not change from one occasion to another, and that the results derived from them are only minimally if at all influenced by the personality of the person administering them. As we shall see, many of the measures devised so far in this field are vulnerable to criticism on one or more of these counts.

Fourthly, every empirical study has to be limited to a comparatively small sample of people drawn from one particular cultural and social setting. Strictly speaking we can only generalize the results of a study to the population of which the sample is representative. This raises a problem, for though the existing evidence has come from countries as diverse as Scandinavia,

Israel, Australia, India, and Korea, and from primitive as well as advanced societies, the great bulk of it is drawn from the United States. Can we conclude that the results of an experiment on middle-class American children will apply to Chinese, or even English children? There is no easy or general answer to this because it depends on the nature of the study and the nature of the cultural differences. All that can be said in general terms is that the further a generalization is extended beyond the population sampled in the original study the weaker the confidence we can have in it. But unless we know of a cultural difference that would invalidate it, and until the necessary cross-cultural checks have been made, it is not unreasonable to make such generalizations provided we are duly cautious and tentative.

Finally, the conclusions we draw from an empirical study depend upon its design. The most common design in the studies to be reviewed is *correlational*. This design tells us whether the particular moral behaviour variable is associated with a variable of another kind, such as intelligence, personality or type of home background. Correlational studies do not allow us to infer causal relationships, however, though sometimes they do provide grounds for preferring one speculative causal interpretation to another. If the claim we are advancing specifies a causal relationship, it must be grounded in an *experimental* design. The point about an experiment is that the experimenter *induces* variability in one variable, and then sees whether this is followed by variability in another, under conditions in which variability in the second variable could be attributed to no other cause than the variability in the first.

Each of the five aspects of moral behaviour listed above will be dealt with in turn. The ultimate goal is, of course, to understand how and why people differ in their moral behaviour, and we shall see just how far existing empirical evidence takes us towards this. Broadly speaking, the evidence relates to the *correlates* of moral behaviour, such as intelligence, personality, religious commitment, age and sex difference, the *immediate conditions* which influence behaviour, such as whether other people are present, whether they will ever learn what has happened, and the immediate incentives at work, and to the *long-term antecedent conditions* associated with moral behaviour such as family background and parental discipline and example. In the present state of research there can be no final answers to the questions we may ask, but certain trends emerge, and even when the evidence is inconsistent it may help us to understand the problems better.

## Character

So far we have assumed that moral behaviour is essentially a matter of making, defending, following and breaking rules. It is of course much more. The moral differences between a Nazi concentration camp commandant and St Francis of Assisi are not satisfactorily encompassed in the statement that the former broke the rules and the latter kept them. Morality is not just a matter of rules but also of dispositions or traits. Certain characteristics like humility, integrity and compassion are judged good and worthy of cultivation, whereas others like habitual malice, arrogance and contempt for others are condemned.* The extremes of human wickedness and goodness contrast so sharply, especially when exhibited by the same person, that to attribute cosmic force to these qualities is an easy step for the human imagination.

There are levels of human moral aspiration, experience and behaviour which psychology, and particularly the empirical approach within it, has not yet begun to penetrate. But we can inch a little closer to these mysteries by considering not differences in behaviour but differences in character. The concept of character overlaps so much with that of personality that the two are often used interchangeably. They are both equally abstract and general. But some differentiation is possible. For our purposes character can be defined as those attitudes and dispositions within an individual which relate to the behaviour that is the subject of moral

---

* cf. Oscar Wilde's remark: 'But while I see that there is nothing wrong in what one does, I see that there is something wrong in what one becomes.'

evaluation in his society. It is personality viewed from the point of view of moral rules. Empirically this gives rise to two groups of questions.

We can first ask whether the various dimensions of moral behaviour are associated with each other. For example, is severity and rigidity of moral judgement correlated with a certain kind of moral reasoning, or is a relatively strong capacity to resist temptation related to particular kinds of post-transgressional response? Material relevant to these questions will be discussed in the chapters dealing with the different moral variables.

Secondly, we can concentrate on the different patterns or profiles which individuals obtain on all the moral variables. To take a crude example, one person's profile might be strong resistance to temptation, weak post-transgressional anxiety, average on measures of altruism and sympathy, relies upon authority in his moral reasoning, and is dogmatic and rigid in his moral beliefs. Others would have different profiles. We can then ask whether certain profiles are typical, whether there are discernible character types, and if so what are the functional relationships between the different aspects of moral behaviour for each type. Unfortunately the evidence at present is far too fragmentary and incomplete to allow any clear answers to these questions. However, a number of somewhat speculative character typologies have been proposed by psychologists, and though they vary a good deal in detail, they also have much in common. Since they are insecurely rooted in evidence, they must be regarded as approximate and provisional. They are like grossly oversimplified maps of a complex terrain which provide little more than a directional orientation. But they are a beginning. They will form the substance of chapter 9.

All empirical study must be guided by ideas and expectations; some kind of theorizing however naive and rudimentary is inescapable. In its comparatively short life psychology has spawned a rich profusion of technical concepts and theoretical systems. Among these are four distinctive traditions of thought which have obvious relevance to moral behaviour, and which together have guided much of the research. In the next chapter I shall give a short outline of these four perspectives. Although I shall be referring to them as theories it should be emphasized that they are really more like ways of looking at all behaviour than precisely defined theoretical systems designed to produce rigorous explanation. I shall take up some of the main ideas in each that seem most relevant to moral behaviour. No serious student of the psychology of moral behaviour can afford to ignore these viewpoints, for each takes up and elaborates a basic, common-sense explanation of why we restrain ourselves in the interests of morality. The *social-group approach* starts from the idea that we are well behaved because others expect us to be and would be shocked if we were not; and the *psychoanalytic approach* from the notion that we are good because our consciences make us so. It is also claimed that people are good because they have been suitably disciplined in their upbringing and surrounded by the good example of others. The processes involved in such moral training are analysed in the *learning-theory approach*. Finally it can be argued that to behave morally is simply to behave rationally and sensibly, that acting morally is an aspect of intelligent adaptation to our social environment – this is the view of the *cognitive-developmental* approach, which draws attention to the importance of intelligence in moral control.

Though the account given of these theories is far from exhaustive and precise, it is more detailed than is strictly needed to follow the discussion of the empirical material later. But it is important that the reader should have some sympathetic understanding of the attitudes involved in these theories, that he should see their plausibility, and also that he should appreciate the limitations and relativity of each. One advantage of playing along with the languages of all four theories is that we realize how essential and how inadequate each is.

# CHAPTER 2

# Some Theoretical Perspectives

It is a truism that what people do in public may not accord with what they do in private. In other words, the individual's moral behaviour is shaped not only by his character and inner controls but also by his immediate social context, the nature of his relationships to other people and the social pressures at work on him. The first theoretical perspective, the *social-group approach*, treats moral behaviour as a function of social control or control by others. It is essentially a sociological point of view, though the focus here will be upon its psychological implications. However, no account of moral behaviour would be complete without mention of it.

## The Social-Group Approach

The distinctive feature of this approach is that the system taken as the object of study is not the individual person but two or more persons in relationship. The individual is defined as the occupant of a position in a group and his behaviour viewed as the outcome of the forces at work within the group. Though the behaviour to be explained is that of individuals, the explanatory concepts used refer to characteristics of the social systems to which the individuals belong. Groups, especially large institutionalized ones, retain their identity despite changes in their membership; and there is a sense in which people can feel themselves to have relationships to groups which are distinct from, and may take precedence over, their relationships to particular members. There is therefore some validity in a point of view which conceives the individual's behaviour as a function of social structures.

Two of the basic concepts in group theory are *norm* and *role*. The term 'norm' is used descriptively and dynamically. Descriptively it is a way of behaving, thinking, feeling or believing which is relatively uniform among the members of a group. But for the individual member this uniformity among the others becomes a force compelling him to fall in step too. It does so because of the tendency for actual conformity to generate the expectation of conformity. Dynamically, then, a norm is the force or pressure brought to bear upon each member of a group by virtue of the fact that the rest expect him to behave in a certain way. Though we all acknowledge the existence of this force, experimental evidence suggests that we frequently underestimate its strength (see Hare, 1962).

Norms develop spontaneously in a group, they are related to the group's purposes, and their positive function is to facilitate the achievement of these purposes. They vary from unvoiced assumptions to, in formal groups, a list of rules. Continuing membership of a group requires some conformity to its norms; to violate these norms is to court group sanctions such as collective disapproval, ostracism or expulsion from the group.

All norms are rules, in the sense implied in the last chapter, but not all rules are norms. A moral rule is a norm when the members of a group agree in expecting each other to keep it. Thus the rules governing the treatment of other people's property are norms in a great many groups in society. Norms also control what people *say* about moral rules; in one context the norms may require the constant expression of impeccable moral sentiments, in another the adoption of an overt, cynical amorality. On the other hand a rule may not be a norm. A trivial example is the rule restricting the speed of vehicles in built-up areas in Britain to 30 m.p.h.; manifestly the norm sets the limit about 10 m.p.h. faster. It is not uncommon for the members of a group to accept formally that a certain kind of behaviour is always wrong (such as lying or premarital sex) but actually to live by a norm that is much more indulgent ('you can't expect people to be perfect').

And of course it can happen that the norms of a group not only permit but prescribe actions contrary to moral rules; thus a youth may steal because it is the only way to maintain status in his peer group even though he regards stealing as wrong.

The term 'role' refers to the norms associated with a particular position in a group. It is the set of expectations that members have about how a particular individual will behave. An obvious illustration is the committee, where there are norms common to all members and also norms specific to the positions of chairman, secretary and treasurer. A role is a part played within a group. In a highly formalized group like an army or a police force, the norms applying to particular roles are explicit and encompass most areas of behaviour so that there is little room for the expression of personality differences between occupants of similar roles. In informal groups there may be plenty of room for the individual to carve out the kind of role he wants to play.*

An individual's moral behaviour may be quite extensively shaped by his social role. The clergy are expected to engage in a great deal of moralizing and provide living examples of moral rectitude. Theft is a more serious offence in a policeman than in others. The double standard of sexual morality has traditionally allowed the male role more latitude. When people take on the role of parent they are apt to discover a new concern with moral issues since they are partly responsible for their children's moral education. Different roles carry with them special obligations; examples might be the academic's duty to truth or the social worker's commitment to alleviate distress.

People do not always conform to the requirements of their norms and roles. The sociologist is interested in why norms are violated at one time or place rather than another, and he seeks his answer in terms of variations in social structure. For example, it seems that deviation from norms is increased when norms lack clarity and universal acceptance, when people are deprived of access to legitimate means of attaining desirable cultural goals, when they are not integrated into social institutions which impose sanctions for deviation from norms, and when they belong to

* For a full account of role theory, see Sarbin and Allen, 1969.

subgroups with deviant norms. The psychologist, on the other hand, is interested in why people vary in their conformity to norms within the same social structure, and he seeks his answers through an analysis of the processes of social influence and through the study of individual differences in personality and character.

A number of the elements which go to make up the process of social influence have been identified. Some of these will be discussed later in various contexts. Only four of the more important ones will be mentioned here.* The first is *social facilitation*, or the tendency for an individual's performance of a well-established pattern of behaviour to be enhanced when others are watching him or doing the same thing in his presence. This tendency has been offered as part of the explanation of crowd behaviour, and it has been attributed to the fact that the presence of others intensifies motivation and general level of arousal. The second is *effect dependency*, or the fact that our self-esteem is dependent upon the approval and acceptance of others. The third is *information dependency*, or the fact that, when uncertain what to do, we frequently have to make use of information that others, deliberately or inadvertently, supply us with. Finally, when he is a member of a large and unstructured group, the individual is likely to experience *responsibility defusion*, or *loss of identity*. This is a condition in which his sense of himself as a separate person is temporarily weakened or lost.

These, and other, aspects of social influence all represent ways in which individuals may differ from each other. But perhaps most important of all is the fact that sometimes people actively resist group pressures because they have morally evaluated the group's norms and found them wanting. It is generally agreed that the higher reaches of moral development are shown precisely by those who stand out against the group in defence of their moral judgements.

Social-group theory has attempted to assimilate moral independence through the concept of a *reference group*. It is argued

* For an account of the experimental evidence bearing upon each, see Jones and Gerard (1967).

that the norms that are operative for an individual may not be those of the groups to which he actually belongs, but rather those of the groups to which he aspires to belong or thinks he ought to belong. Independent moral behaviour is seen as remote conformity to the reference group. And of course this reference group may be the moral leaders of mankind or the community of saints.

It is hard to refute this interpretation of moral independence, since it is always possible to postulate some reference group for the independent person. But it is difficult to see how reference groups can generate the same kind of pressures towards conformity as the immediate social context, and it does not explain why some people are controlled by remote reference groups and others are not. (For an excellent discussion of this issue, see Jahoda, 1959.)

Finally, people exercise moral restraint on occasions when it must seem to them that the possibility of others knowing how they behave is negligible. There is no way of explaining this except through processes of inner moral inhibition and self-control. The label usually given to these processes is the *conscience*. Before turning to the remaining psychological theories, all of which deal with processes of self-direction, it is worth taking a closer look at this term.

## The Conscience

In the previous chapter I mentioned the language of moral obligation. In contemporary western society a pivotal concept in that language is *conscience*. This is a rich and complex notion. What makes it of special interest here is that in some of its usages (e.g. 'I would like to but my conscience won't let me') it seems to imply a rudimentary psychology of moral experience and behaviour. A convenient way of drawing out some of these implications is to trace the development of the term in the English language.*

* The following account is based upon Lewis (1960) and the Oxford English Dictionary.

*Conscience* derives from the same root as *conscious*, namely *conscio,* or 'I know together with (someone else)'. Its origin is therefore the notion of sharing knowledge with someone. From shared knowledge in general it became 'sharing a secret', and then the sharing of a guilty secret. The person with whom I share the knowledge becomes the potential witness against me, the person who could make me ashamed. But people argue and debate with themselves; they have the trick of thinking as if they were more than one person, as if there were another point of view within them which they can interact with. 'And of course this shadowy inner accomplice has all the same properties as an external one; he too is a witness against you, a potential blackmailer, one who inflicts shame and fear' (Lewis, 1960).

So far then *conscience* is the personified function of remembering, with the strong implication of remembering misdeeds and therefore of feeling shame and guilt. The next major step in the development of the word came when it acquired in addition the meaning of internal lawgiver. It became the name of that part of me which tells me what is right and what is wrong. And finally, through association with the sense of obligation generated by the recognition of what is right and what is wrong, it became the source of the impulse to do good and of the aversion from doing wrong. Now conscience is partially autonomous, for feelings of guilt, the impulsion to do good and the recognition of what is right are to some extent outside conscious control—we cannot help them. These facts of experience, in the Christian cultural setting anyway, together with the acceptance of certain systems of religious belief, led not only to the personification of conscience but to its virtual deification. It became the voice of God in man, his representative implanted in the soul.*

From the psychological point of view we can sum up the theory that seems to be implied in the concept as follows. Con-

---

* In a survey commissioned by the Independent Television Authority (1970), people were asked the question 'How do you think a person knows what is right and what is wrong?'. In all, forty-three per cent answered *conscience, inner self* or *God,* twenty-eight per cent *upbringing,* sixteen per cent *commonsense,* and thirteen per cent *instinct.* What is interesting is that conscience was distinguished from the effects of upbringing.

science is an inner entity or organ of the mind, usually personified, which has certain distinctive functions. These are to enable the individual to discriminate right from wrong; to generate an impulse to act in the right way and avoid acting in the wrong way; to observe and record the individual's actual behaviour; and to blame or approve him after he has acted. It appears to be assumed that these functions are all mediated by the same 'part' of the personality; the various forms of moral behaviour are all expressions of the same 'mental organ' which operates with some degree of autonomy, but which also leaves the individual a measure of choice over whether or not he 'obeys' it. Since they are 'organs of the mind' it tends to be assumed that all people have consciences; thus evangelical moralists tend to think of their task as one of awakening the dormant consciences of the wicked rather than of helping them to acquire consciences they did not previously possess.

Making explicit commonsense assumptions is a perilous undertaking, for there is no way of checking how accurate we are. It is open to anyone to deny that the account given above represents his understanding of the term, or that ordinary usage commits him to any psychological theory. Yet the impression is inescapable that people do use the notion of a partially autonomous, inner moral agency to explain both their own experience of moral compulsion and conflict, and their observations of the moral behaviour of others.

Insofar as there is a psychological theory involved in the concept of conscience, it is indisputably a primitive one. For a more sophisticated version we must turn to psychoanalysis. Freud and his followers have taken up the idea of a 'mental organ' or 'psychic structure' responsible for moral control and direction, christened it the *superego*, and developed a very elaborate theory to account for its nature, growth and functioning.

## The Psychoanalytic Approach

Today anyone who sets out to give a brief and accurate outline of psychoanalytic theory and in particular its bearings upon moral behaviour faces a number of discouraging considerations. In the first place, the main outlines of the theory are widely familiar; there are many introductory accounts, some excellent (e.g. Hall, 1954; Stafford-Clark, 1965), and there is already a classic exposition of moral behaviour from the psychoanalytic point of view (Flugel, 1945). Then secondly, in his own theoretical discussion Freud made skilful and imaginative use of metaphor and personification. These are initially a considerable help to the reader, but when we study the theory more carefully they become an impediment. Many of the concepts are comprehensible and acceptable at a relatively superficial level of definition but reveal ambiguities and obscurities on closer analysis (examples might be the concepts of pleasure, instinct and mechanism). Thirdly, Freud was seldom satisfied with his theoretical formulations and was constantly revising them. Since his death his followers have further refined and extended the theory, giving rise to a number of controversies which are unresolved and probably unresolvable. In such a situation any account that goes beyond a series of quotations from Freud's work is bound to be in some degree an individual interpretation. Finally, the theory did not arise in the context of experiment and controlled observation, but is based exclusively on 'clinical experience'. As a result its relation to the empirical material we shall be looking at later is uncertain and ambiguous. Nevertheless, despite all these difficulties, the theory cannot be ignored. Its influence on research in this field, even though indirect, has been considerable, and it draws attention to certain aspects of moral behaviour and development that other theoretical perspectives neglect.

A human being is a structure in motion. The *id* is the generic term for the energies in the system, and they are always present in a given *quantity*. The id is what distinguishes the system at rest from the system at work. At the physical level it may be thought of as a quantity of energy, at the physiological level as a quantity of excitation in the nervous system, and at the psychological level as a quantity of 'psychic energy' which may be subjectively experienced as tension, discomfort and 'unpleasure', or as a demand for mental work. The quantity of energy, excitation or tension in the system is raised by stimulation and lowered by its removal. This stimulation may be external or internal and somatic. Once induced by stimulation psychic energy is mobile and displaceable, and is ultimately discharged through motor activity and mental work. The most interesting psychologically of the forms of psychic energy are the instincts and among these the instincts of sex and aggression. 'An instinct', says Freud,

differs from a stimulus in that it arises from sources of stimulation within the body, operates at a constant force, and is such that the subject cannot escape from it by flight as he can from an external stimulus. ... And, we picture it as a certain sum of energy forcing its way in a certain direction. (Freud, 1933)

The somatic sources of the sexual instinct are the erotogenic zones of the body, and the energy generated by them is called *libido*. Libido is therefore one kind of id energy. The somatic sources of the aggressive instinct are obscure. Indeed Freud frequently writes as if he conceived aggression as not somatically based at all, but as that mobilizing of energy from all sources which occurs both when an individual is faced with intense and noxious external stimulation which he cannot for some reason escape, and when behaviour directed towards the satisfaction of a somatically based instinct is frustrated by some external obstacle. Libido and aggressive energy are invariably fused. However, despite the fact that they are always in practice fused, the conceptual distinction between libido and aggression is important for understanding the psychoanalytic account of moral development.*

The two main structural concepts that Freud uses are the *ego*

* There is no doubt that Freud's instinct theory is fraught with problems, and it is significant that some psychoanalysts are now recommending that it should be abandoned (see Bowlby, 1969).

and the *superego*. The *ego* can be defined as a *hypothetical, acquired, psychological structure through which psychic energy is discharged in work*. To understand it properly, however, we must look at both its nature and its functioning.

The elements that make up the ego structure are sensations and perceptions (those inside the body as much as those outside) and the memory traces left by these perceptions. In the course of development two things happen to these percepts and memory traces. First they become *cathected*, or charged, with small quantities of energy from the id. As the discharge of instinctual energy in action is always accompanied by perceptions of some kind, these percepts have quantities of the instinctual energy tied to them through association. For example, since libidinal satisfaction for the young child is accompanied by perceptions of the mother, small quantities of libido become tied to the memory images of her. It is in this way that the ego draws off energies from the id for its own use. Secondly these percepts and memory images become progressively synthesized, first into a number of 'ego-nuclei' (see Glover, 1968) and then into the full ego structure. Two factors are held responsible for this synthesis, the ordered nature of the world which means that some percepts always go together, and an innate 'synthesizing capacity' which the organism is presumed to possess. The term 'ego' refers to both this synthesizing capacity and the existing organization of memory traces and percepts. A primary aspect of this structure is the distinction between self and others. On the one hand, as Freud put it, 'ego is that part of the id which has been modified by the direct influence of the external world acting through the perceptual-conscious' (Freud, 1927). On the other hand it is a 'body ego', the mental or cognitive representation of the surface of the body and of bodily sensation. The ego's capacity to discriminate between the self and the rest of the world depends on the way these two kinds of percepts are organized within it.

The functions of the ego have never been exhaustively catalogued, but certain of them are clear. It is the organ of adaptation to reality in the service of the id. Its main function is to carry out the wishes of the id and to control and direct behaviour so that the fullest possible gratification is achieved. Because of the energy it has acquired from the id through cathexis, the ego is able to delay behaviour in the interests of fuller satisfaction later, to think ahead and to plan, and to bring about a temporary redistribution of energies within the system by fantasy. It is the seat of consciousness, though of course it is not always conscious, and no individual is ever conscious of all the contents of his ego.

However, the exigencies of living in civilized societies demand not only the postponement of instinctual satisfaction but also the radical modification of instinctual needs and sometimes their permanent inhibition. To quote the classic psychoanalytic example, the male child has permanently to suppress his wish for sexual intercourse with his mother and his desire to kill his father. Which brings us to the last major structural concept.

The superego is a substructure developing out of the ego. It has two primary functions. The first, or *conscience*, function is to suppress, neutralize or divert those instinctual forces which, if acted upon, would violate the moral rules of society. The superego is not itself an original source of energy. It is a structure which serves as a channel whereby aggressive energies from the id are fed back into the system. Thus id energies are used to counterbalance and suppress other id energies. By contrast the *ego-ideal* function of the superego is to hold before the ego those positive ideals of behaviour that society judges worthy of cultivating. The ego-ideal is what the ego aspires to become. In both its functions the superego represents the voice of society, and particularly the voice of the parents, within the individual's own personality.

The nature of these two functions of the superego can be brought out more clearly if we consider how they are acquired. The basic mechanism involved is *identification*. This is the process whereby the individual adopts the attributes of others, primarily his parents, and comes to behave *as if* he were they. Identification can take either of two forms, one producing the conscience, the other the ego-ideal.

The mechanism said to underly the formation of the conscience is *identification with the aggressor*. The situation that gives rise to it is essentially as follows. The child is punished or frustrated by an adult, usually the father, so that his own aggression towards that adult is strongly aroused. But if he expresses this aggression towards the adult, or displaces it onto others, he will be punished even more severely. The child is trapped. The only way of coping with his aggression is to turn it in upon himself. And he does this when he identifies with the aggressor and adopts towards himself the same punitive attitude that the adult adopted towards him. The percepts and memory traces of the adult, and especially his verbal prohibitions and rebukes, split off from the rest of the ego structure to form a separate agency through which the child's own aggression can be directed inwards upon himself. It is important to note that the strength of the child's conscience depends not upon the intensity of the adult's aggression towards him, but upon the intensity of his aggression towards the adult. The child's aggression may be provoked by adult behaviour that is not particularly aggressive. According to Freud this separate agency is finally established at the time of the resolution of the oedipal conflict about the age of five. Thereafter it becomes a permanent channel through which aggression which cannot be expressed outwardly can be directed inwards. Whenever a forbidden impulse arises, the aggressive energies of the superego are immediately evoked to keep the ideas associated with the impulse from consciousness. If they are not strong enough to prevent the forbidden ideas entering consciousness, then they act to prevent the ideas being implemented in action. If the impulse does break through into action then the full aggression of the superego turns upon the ego in the form of guilt and remorse. In Freud's words:

A portion of the external world has, at least partially, been abandoned as an object and has instead, by identification, been taken into the ego and thus become an integral part of the internal world. This new psychic agency continues to carry on the functions which have hitherto been performed by the people (the abandoned objects) in the external world: it observes the ego, gives it orders, judges it and threatens it with punishments, exactly like the parents whose place it has taken. (Freud, 1949)

The more severe the conscience, that is, the harsher the restrictions it imposes, and the greater the quantity of aggression channelled inwards through it, the higher the general level of tension in the system. The only way in which temporary relief from this tension can be achieved is by creating conditions under which this superego aggression can be turned outwards on to someone else. The condition most conducive to this is the presence of someone else who is plainly guilty of the actions which the individual wants to do but is inhibited from doing. He can then, with the connivance of his own superego, seek out and punish the sinner; for a brief time ego and conscience are one. It is thus that psychoanalysis accounts for the peculiar ferocity with which righteous people can punish sinners.

The mechanism responsible for the development of the ego-ideal has been called *anaclitic identification*, and the motivation behind it is libidinal attachment, or love. Since libido is limited in quantity, the more love a child has for his parents, the less he has for himself. This disequilibrium is accentuated when the loved person is absent, and is felt as painful. The child re-establishes equilibrium by incorporating into himself the cathected images of the other person, in other words, by thinking, feeling and acting as if he were the other. Anaclitic identification is a way of restoring self-esteem.

However, as the ego-structure matures, so the child's sense of the difference between himself and others is sharpened. The simple incorporation of images of the other into the idea of himself becomes more difficult. A compromise is then adopted. The images of the other form a differentiated structure which represents not what the child thinks himself to be, but what he thinks he would like to become. The other is internalized but as something the child aspires to become. This compromise is a way of restoring equilibrium without doing violence to the child's sense of reality. Though the parents form the primary content of the ego-ideal, subsequent attachments contribute to it; successive anaclitic identifications leave a sediment in the form of values and goals.

These two forms of identification have been described separately. In practice, however, it is very doubtful whether either ever occurs on its own. In families where the parents are highly punitive and the child minimally attached, there is usually plenty of opportunity for the child to avoid his parents or to displace his aggression onto others rather than upon himself. On the other hand, strong attachments to parents always involve some measure of covert hostility towards them as well. In normal families it is precisely the child's attachment to his parents which constitutes the main inducement for him to internalize the aggression they provoke in him. The attachment keeps him close to his parents, and the fact that he loves the people he wants to hurt acts as a powerful motive for directing his aggression upon himself. It is thus that both the conscience and the ego-ideal are based upon the same people, and both arise out of the same ambivalent relationships.

This account of the psychoanalytic theory of moral behaviour is oversimplified, and much has been left out.* As a theory it is extremely vulnerable to criticism – indeed as far as empirical psychology is concerned it is now mainly of historical interest. Its value for us lies in the fact that it draws attention to the importance of both aggression and attachment in moral development, and it leads to certain general expectations of an empirical kind. Some of these are as follows:

(a) Since both resistance to temptation and guilt are a function of the same structure, the conscience, it is to be expected that those who resist in one situation will be likely to do so in others, and that those who are good at resisting temptation will feel more intense guilt on those occasions when they do succumb. In other words, measures of resistance to temptation should be positively associated with each other and with measures of guilt.

*Psychoanalysts are far from being in complete agreement over the detail of the theory. See Spitz (1958); Beres (1958); Hartmann and Loewenstein (1962); Hartmann (1964); Nass (1966); and Malmquist (1968).

(b) The theory suggests that the strength of an individual's conscience is largely settled by the age of about five years. Though ideas about right and wrong will develop, capacity to resist temptation will not change much after this age.

(c) Since the main authority figure in the family is father, and since boys identify much more with their fathers than girls do, it is to be expected that boys will have stronger consciences than girls (see Freud, 1950).

(d) The crucial function of aggression in the conscience suggests that those with strong consciences are more likely to condemn others severely for their misdeeds than those with weaker consciences.

(e) The nature of the identification processes is such that the conditions in family life most likely to produce children with strong consciences are first that there is a close affectionate bond between parent and child, and secondly that the parents set high standards and consistently express displeasure when the child fails to live up to them.

## The Learning-Theory Approach

It can be argued that an approach to moral behaviour that *starts* by conceiving it as the functioning of a hypothetical mental structure such as a conscience or superego is misguided. Instead we should recognize at the outset that moral behaviour is learned, that the training procedures and learning processes involved do not differ in principle from those found in other sorts of behaviour, and that if we understand how moral behaviour is acquired there is no need to trouble ourselves with hypotheses about mental structures.

Though there have been few studies of the learning of moral behaviour, there is now an abundance of experimental evidence in the general field of learning, and interest in the subject shows no signs of waning. Analysis of learning processes has reached a high level of refinement and subtlety, and the resulting body of knowledge is formidably complex. I can only touch lightly on the fringes of it.*

Basically, parents shape their children's behaviour in three ways: by punishing them, by rewarding them, and by the example they set. Put more technically, parents are sources of negative and positive reinforcement and they serve as models. Negative reinforcements include verbal rebuke, sarcasm, smacks, isolation, stopping privileges, and withholding affection; positive reinforcements include praise, smiles, hugs, gifts and attention; and modelling can be symbolic in the form of verbal descriptions of how children ought and ought not to behave as well as actual. All the time parents are reinforcing their children in one way or the other and setting an example, and their deliberate employment of these techniques for the purposes of training their children constitutes only a small part of the total influence mediated in these ways.

We shall now look briefly at a few of the main findings from the experimental study of these influences. Their application to aspects of moral behaviour will be postponed to later chapters. The immediate effect of punishment is to produce one or other of those physiological responses which are associated with the feelings we label fear, pain and anxiety. These terms are not synonymous since the experiences they refer to are subjectively distinguishable and it is probable that they have different physiological bases; but they are all similar in being disagreeable. Since the differences are not important at the level of discussion here, the term anxiety will arbitarily be extended to cover them all.

Activity that culminates in punishment tends to be inhibited. However, experiments on animals and children suggest that a number of factors may modify this inhibitory effect.† For example, consummatory acts like eating and copulation are very readily suppressed by punishment, though this suppression is

---

*For extended accounts of the application of learning principles to moral behaviour the reader is referred to Bandura and Walters (1963); Bandura (1969a); Eysenck (1964); and Aronfreed (1968; 1969).

†For reviews of this evidence, see Church (1963); Solomon (1964); and Walters and Parke (1967).

accompanied, not surprisingly, by considerable tension. On the other hand, punishment tends to be rather less effective in suppressing behavioural sequences that have been well learned because they have previously led to rewards of some kind; indeed it has been found that under certain circumstances, not only does punishment fail to weaken such behavioural sequences, it actually strengthens them. In short, the effects of punishment are not simple. Behaviour is most effectively suppressed, however, if the punishment closely follows the forbidden behaviour in time, and if the individual is taught to make an alternative, incompatible response for which he is rewarded.

Anxiety is easily conditioned; that is, neutral stimuli present at the time a punishment is given themselves come to evoke anxiety. And this conditioned anxiety tends to be long-lasting, though if these stimuli are later persistently associated with pleasurable experience, the conditioned anxiety will gradually disappear.

The importance of timing in punishment is brought out in an experiment by Solomon and his associates (Solomon, Turner and Lessac, 1968). Puppies were punished either just before they began to eat forbidden food, or just after they had eaten some of it. After being trained in one of these two ways, they were all tested by being made hungry and by being left alone in a room with the forbidden food. Those puppies who had been punished just before eating held out much longer against the temptation to eat than those who had been punished after they had eaten a little. However, once the early-punished animals had started eating, they showed little sign of anxiety, in marked contrast to the second group who displayed all the usual signs of doggy guilt. These differences are explained by assuming that the first group of puppies were conditioned to respond with anxiety to all those stimuli which occurred during the approach to food, and the second group to those occurring after food had been eaten.

This experiment has been offered as evidence that resistance to temptation and guilt are not functionally equivalent but are learned through the differential timing of punishment. Punishment that is consistently administered just before misdeeds will result in high resistance to temptation but weak guilt when transgression does occur, whereas the converse will be produced by punishment that consistently follows the wrong act and the satisfaction the wrong act brings. But though a similar effect of timing has been found in experiments on children (see Aronfreed and Reber, 1965, and Walters, Parke and Cane, 1965), it is obvious that in the normal family the training of children is complicated by the fact that parents reason with their children.

Let us suppose that a child is caught in the act of taking money from his mother's purse and is punished by verbal rebuke or a smack. The consequence will be that the other stimuli present, such as the sight of the mother's purse, its touch, will become conditioned to evoke anxiety in the child; he will be just a little more hesitant about touching it next time. But it is most unlikely that this conditioned anxiety will last, for there are bound to be plenty of occasions later when the sight of the mother's purse is associated with pleasure, as for example if the child obeys a request to fetch it and is rewarded for doing so. In this way all the other conditioned stimuli will lose their anxiety provoking power – with one exception. If the mother, at the time of punishing, labels the child's act as stealing, explains what she means by the term, and gives reasons why it is wrong, then for the child the whole notion of stealing, and particularly the idea of 'me stealing', will become associated with anxiety. Now this association is not likely to be weakened on subsequent occasions; on the contrary it will be strengthened. Later, when the child is alone and tempted to steal, it is the inescapable knowledge that the act is one of theft that arouses the inhibiting anxiety. It follows that the timing of punishment will be somewhat less important, though not unimportant; the question now is which of the two ideas 'I am about to steal' and 'I have stolen' is most strongly associated with anxiety.

The effect of rewards is to increase the probability of the rewarded behaviour occurring again. It is through reward that habits of prosocial behaviour such as being generous and helpful are established. Again experiments on animals and children have revealed many of the principles involved.

Unusual and complex patterns of behaviour can be taught by the method of 'successive approximations'. The technique is to reward consistently the response that is nearest to the one desired. In this way the animal's or child's behaviour is progressively shaped in the direction we want. It is probable that unconsciously we are all the time shaping each other's behaviour in this way. In the early stages of building a new habit, progress is greatest if every correct, or near correct, response is rewarded. But learning that results from regular reward is apt to be lost quickly if the reward ceases. More stable learning is achieved by shifting slowly from a policy of rewarding every response to one in which rewards are intermittent and occasional. Conditioning applies to rewards as well as to punishments; neutral stimuli associated with rewards become rewarding, though the effect tends not to last. Finally children learn to reward themselves. Having discovered the principles underlying his parents' use of praise, the child comes to praise himself in a similar way. Thus the recognition that an act is 'good' can be its reward.

We learn a great deal simply by watching others. Experiments have demonstrated what we know from everyday observation, namely that new forms of behaviour can be quickly learned by watching someone else demonstrate them, that there is a characteristic amount of learning of this kind that people can take in at one time, that seeing someone else punished for an action has a deterring effect on the observer, and that seeing someone else rewarded for an action tends to increase the probability that we will do it in the same situation. An interesting series of experiments has shown that self-control is influenced by example (Mischel, 1966): the subjects watched a model who chose a delayed and more satisfying reward over an immediate and less satisfying one, or who set himself high standards in a task, and their own behaviour was modified in the same direction.

Finally people can be conditioned by watching others. Berger (1962) has shown that if a subject watches a model punished by an electric shock every time a buzzer sounds, he will later on respond to the sound of the buzzer with clear signs of anxiety. In other words, people can develop conditioned anxiety without themselves being punished. Other experiments have shown that a subject's anxiety can be reduced by watching a model behave in a relaxed and easy way in the presence of stimuli that evoke anxiety in the subject. It is probable that this vicarious, emotional conditioning can be mediated symbolically. When a mother qualifies people or places with adjectives that have strong emotional connotations in the presence of the child, it is likely that he will be conditioned to feel these emotions in relation to these people and places later on. Racial prejudices may be transmitted this way.

## The Cognitive-Developmental Approach

So far we have glanced at three quite distinct conceptions of moral behaviour. Social-group theory sees moral man essentially as a conformist who complies with the expectations of others out of an imperative need to be accepted by them. According to Freudian doctrine, moral man is pictured as a lonely and rather helpless ego struggling to satisfy the insistent demands of an amoral id without angering the watchful and punitive parents (who are now permanently installed within his own mind) in a real world that is, in the last analysis, totally indifferent to his welfare. Moral development is forced upon the reluctant child; he acquires moral control as an almost desperate defence against intolerable conflict. According to learning theory, the child is trained into morality in much the same way as circus animals are trained to do tricks. Moral man is little more than a complex network of conditioned responses and learned habits.

Plainly these points of view fail to do justice to man as an originator of moral ideas and judgements. None of us is entirely moulded and shaped by others; in greater or lesser degree we are all independent sources of intelligent action and thought. Instead of being a sign of more or less 'blind' obedience, moral behaviour can also be interpreted as one aspect of the active and intelligent creation of community with others.

At this point a number of related theoretical traditions

could be drawn upon. For instance, it would be interesting to explore the consequences for our understanding of moral behaviour of the use of servomechanisms and computers as models for physiological functioning (e.g. Young, 1964) and for behaviour (e.g. Miller, Galanter and Pribram, 1960). It would be a stimulating exercise to discuss moral behaviour in the language of genetic and environmental programming, and of storage and translation mechanisms. Moral rules can be thought of as instructions given to a central, controlling computer, or as basic plans which get expressed in various behavioural strategies. Or again, moral training can be viewed as the establishment of a kind of homeostat or self-regulating mechanism within the individual (the super-ego in another guise). We could then raise the question of the adaptive efficiency of different 'settings' of this homeostat in different environments. Even the study of psycholinguistics is not without its suggestive implications for moral behaviour (see Miller and McNeill, 1969).

But, however attractive these speculative openings are, we cannot pursue them here. Instead there is one theoretical perspective, developed in isolation from those just mentioned but having affinities to them, which must be taken further: that is Piaget's theory of the development of intelligence.* Piaget's theory is important because it is really a general theory of behaviour from the point of view of intelligence rather than a theory about what intelligence tests measure, because it therefore helps us to think of moral behaviour simply as the manifestation of intelligence, and because the application of his approach to moral behaviour has generated a lot of research. What follows is a summary of a few of the more important concepts in his general theory; discussion of its specific application to moral development will be given in later chapters.

A piece of behaviour is to be conceived as an event occurring between the individual and his environment. It is at one and the same time, the *action* of the individual upon the environment and the *action* of the environment upon the individual. From the

* For a detailed account of Piaget's theory, see, in addition to Piaget's own numerous works, Flavell (1963) and Baldwin (1967).

individual's point of view, his action is thought of as the functioning of an underlying *cognitive structure* to which Piaget gives the label *schema*. No action is only the functioning of a schema, since it is also shaped by the environment. Likewise, though schemata are conservative in the sense of being relatively lasting structures, yet they are constantly being modified as a consequence of functioning.

Piaget's interest lay in the properties of schemata that can be inferred from studying behaviour, and more particularly, in the *developmental changes* in schematic organization that can be inferred from developmental changes in behaviour. It is important to note, however, that he extended the concept of an action in two ways. First, looking, listening and attending are all actions. Secondly, an action may be internalized and representative. Thinking and remembering are actions, and since their content is always the symbolic representation of the outside world, they can be judged by the same criteria of adaptive efficiency that apply to overt, muscular actions.

The goal of action is adaptation, and adaptation is defined as a state of equilibrium between the actions of the individual and those of the environment. Intellectual development is in the direction of ever more complete and stable equilibria with the environment, both social and physical. Maintaining equilibrium means being able to anticipate and compensate for the actions of the environment (in Piaget's phrase, for 'environmental intrusions'). Since doing and knowing cannot be separated in Piaget's theory, it follows that the capacity to act adaptively is bound up with the attainment of knowledge of the world.

Piaget was a genetic epistemologist. That is, he studied the way the child's knowledge of the world develops, the way he constructs a representative model in his mind which corresponds accurately to features of the external world. Three phases of this development are of special interest to us.

It is during the second year of life that actions become internalized as thought. From then until the age of about seven the child is in the *pre-operational* stage, the pervasive characteristic of which is *egocentrism*. In calling the child egocentric,

Piaget does not mean that he is self-centred in the ordinary sense. What is meant is that the child sees and thinks about his world from his own point of view and is unable to conceive that there are other perspectives. He assumes that his understanding of a situation is *the* understanding of it. He thinks intuitively, and in images rather than in concepts; he is unable to think about his thinking and discover his own inconsistencies and contradictions. Above all his thought is completely dominated by those features of the environment that he is perceiving or noticing at the time; in Piaget's term his thought is *centred*. Since he cannot liberate himself from immediate perception he is unable to compensate for the distortion that perception introduces into his judgements.

Piaget has repeatedly demonstrated how his egocentrism prevents the child from solving many simple problems. More relevant here are the social consequences. Because he cannot conceive that from someone else's point of view a situation may look different, the child is not capable of genuine cooperation with others, and in his efforts to communicate with others he seems unaware of the possibility that he may be misunderstood and therefore does not take steps to ensure that he has been understood.*

At around the age of seven years a development occurs in the child's intelligence which is of the utmost importance; he enters the stage of *concrete operations* and begins to be capable of *operational* thinking, an event which signals the decline of egocentrism. His thinking now begins to be free from perceptual dominance, and he can realize that his perception of a situation may be different from what he knows is really the case. In solving problems he is able to vary two or more relationships simultaneously and in a compensatory fashion. In the sphere of interpersonal relationships he can recognize that other points of view exist and that therefore his own is relative, and he can

---

* It should be noted that Piaget's use of the concept of egocentrism is more complex than is suggested here. In addition to a main egocentric phase in childhood, it is expected that the child will start egocentrically and grow out of it at each of the main developmental stages, including adolescence.

regulate his actions in the light of this recognition. Communications to others are governed not only by the ideas he wishes to impart but also, and at the same time, by his awareness that the listener does not share his knowledge and may misinterpret what he says. The child is able in some measure to 'take the role of the other'.* In Piaget's words: the child

no longer confuses his own point of view with that of others. He is able both to dissociate his point of view from others and to co-ordinate these different points of view. ... True discussions are now possible in that the child shows comprehension with respect to the other's point of view and a search for justification and proof with respect to his own statements. (Piaget, 1967)

Concrete operational thinking has its limitations. As the label suggests, it is confined to the concrete and actual. The final stage in intellectual development comes in adolescence with the attainment of *formal operations*. The child's thought can now be hypothetical and abstract. He is able to think, not only of the actual relationships and events he has experienced, but also of possible relationships and events that might occur. This kind of thinking goes beyond facts in order to understand facts better. Instead of being wholly immersed in his actual social relationships the adolescent is able to reflect on human relationships in general, to classify them and to construct principles and ideals for ordering them.

It is in the sphere of moral reasoning and judgement that Piaget's theory has so far been most fruitfully applied. He himself has written a monograph on the topic, and this has in turn inspired a good deal of research. This will all be discussed in chapter 7. We should also expect his theory to bear on other aspects of moral behaviour. There are situations in which we might suppose that someone with a fully developed capacity to 'take the role of the other' would show more moral self-control and altruism than someone in whom the capacity is less developed. So far, however, no attempts have been made to test this. Piaget's theory, particularly in its account of the devel-

* For a series of experiments illustrating this change in social awareness, see Flavell (1968).

opment of operational thinking, helps us to see how all aspects of moral behaviour can be founded, not upon obedience to authority, nor upon submission to group pressure, but upon the need to reconcile and balance our own point of view with that of others. Furthermore it enables us to take account of the individual's moral creativity – his capacity to work out his own moral guidelines, irrespective of the rules of authority or the norms of his social groups.

The major limitation is the absence of any adequate treatment of emotion and motivation. Piaget does say something about them. For instance he asserts that emotions are initially impulsive and follow one another singly, but that in the course of development they become organized into systems analogous to operational thinking, that is, systems in which emotions compensate each other in some kind of equilibrium. An example might be when anger at someone else's rudeness is balanced by sympathy based upon an awareness of the stresses that made him rude. Such a coordination of emotional structures can obviously become a relatively enduring feature of an individual's social relationships, making possible responsible and considered action. To the extent to which emotions are so organized, 'they emerge as regulations whose final form of equilibrium is none other than the will' (Piaget, 1967). But these speculations are not expanded and no evidence is offered for them. We are left to wonder just how emotional responses and cognitive structures are linked. Commonsense suggests that strong emotion will disrupt operational thinking by making the individual concentrate on only one aspect of the situation (what Piaget calls perceptual centring). If so, what are the developmental conditions which will minimize the likelihood of this happening? Questions of this kind will have to be faced if the full implications of Piaget's thought for social development are to be explored.

A final word. In the following pages I shall be, in the main, reviewing the results of empirical studies. No attempt will be made to show, in any systematic fashion, how the evidence supports or disconfirms the theories I have described. Indeed, as I have tried to show, they are not so much testable theories as grand designs or ways of conceiving all behaviour. Their value for us lies in the way each complements the others by drawing attention to aspects of the nature and development of moral behaviour that they neglect, and at the same time provides a language for studying these aspects. Each has inspired a good deal of research which will remain after the theories have themselves been modified out of recognition. And it is to that research that we must now turn.

# CHAPTER 3

# Resistance to Temptation

Whatever we judge the purposes of morality to be, whether to promote harmonious social relations, to foster personal maturity, or to fit us for the kingdom of heaven, it will inevitably demand of us that we refrain from doing some things we want to do, and refrain when there is no one else around to stop us. The Christian religion, and especially its Protestant varieties, appears to have made this aspect of morality a central focus of concern, so that temptation situations have come to be accepted as *the* tests of moral strength. As with all tests, some people pass, others fail, though all are presumed to fail sometimes. Everyday experience would suggest that people vary widely in their capacity to resist temptation. At one extreme are those who are scrupulous about keeping to the rules, and who are constantly alerted against sin in themselves and others; at the other are those whose approach to living is more easy-going, and who appear to find almost any temptation irresistible.

If the psychologist wants to measure these differences, he has two main courses open to him. He can ask people about their transgressions under conditions in which most of the obvious reasons for lying are removed; or he can try to construct actual tests in which subjects are tempted to transgress, and in which their behaviour can be recorded. Self-report measures will be discussed later in the chapter. We shall first concentrate on the experimental tests. A further possible measure, namely society's classification of an individual as delinquent or non-delinquent, will be taken up in the next chapter.

## The Experimental Measures

The purpose of these measures is to differentiate people according to their capacity to inhibit morally reprehensible behaviour. To this end, situations have been devised in which the subject is given a strong incentive to act in a way which violates some commonly accepted moral norm under conditions in which, from the subject's point of view, the risk of being found out is minimal. In fact, through various subterfuges, the experimenter does find out, though the subject normally remains unaware of this. The situations are intended to simulate everyday occasions of temptation as closely as possible.

Incentives that have been frequently used are passing an exam, material or monetary reward, and, in the case of very young children, playing with an attractive toy. The unacceptable behaviour has usually been cheating, though sometimes stealing small sums of money or lying. When very young children are the subjects, the offending behaviour is usually disobedience to an adult prohibition, for example, not to touch a certain toy because it belongs to someone else. An example of a test that has been used extensively is the ray-gun game (Grinder, 1961). Subjects shoot at a target for points, and are awarded attractive prizes if they achieve a certain score. However, the game is so programmed that it is impossible to gain this score without cheating. At a certain stage in the game, the experimenter goes away on some pretext and leaves the subject to do his own scoring.

Situations of this kind are a far cry from serious, adult moral conflict, when career, family and friends may be at stake. For obvious ethical reasons there are limits to the kind of moral conflict that can be deliberately imposed upon subjects for experimental purposes, especially when they must remain ignorant of the fact that it is their morality that is being tested or the test loses its value.* A further limitation is that the

* The reader may feel that any test of this kind goes beyond the ethically permissible limits in psychological experimentation. The issue is too complex to be discussed here. But before the reader makes up his mind, he should acquaint himself with what actually happens by reading the experimental reports.

subjects used in most experiments have been children or young adults.

In an experiment all subjects are put through the same temptation procedure. Some yield, some resist. Can we conclude that the former have less self-control? Obviously this could be the case. But equally obviously they might differ in the extent to which they find the incentive really tempting, or in their subjective assessments of the risk of detection. It is to control the effects of such differences that experimenters take steps to ensure that the incentive really is attractive to all subjects and to make the risk of detection appear negligible. Nevertheless the meaning of these measures remains problematic, and I shall discuss it again later. Suffice it for the moment to say that the tests do approximate to everyday temptation situations.

## The Generality of Resistance to Temptation

The question we must ask first is whether resistance to temptation is a general characteristic or whether it is specific to a particular test situation. If a person resists on one test, is he likely to do so on others, where the incentives and conditions are somewhat different? In other words, are individual differences on one test positively correlated with differences on another? The major, and classic, study which bears on this question was reported by Hartshorne and May (1928), and involved more than 10,000 school children and over twenty measures of cheating, stealing and lying. The correlations between these tests were low, and fairly close to zero; but they were almost all positive. In other words there was a slight but consistent tendency for performance on one test to be related to performance on another, though the strength of this association varied from one pair of tests to another.

The small size of these correlations together with their variability still leaves the issue somewhat ambiguous. The results could be interpreted in terms of similarity between the testing situations or as evidence of the generality of the disposition to be honest in the subjects. Hartshorne and May themselves favour the former interpretation, and conclude that their results do not support the view that there is a general trait of honesty. People are honest in a particular situation because they have learned to be honest in it and not because they are honest people. Some later students of the problem have been inclined to endorse this conclusion. For example Kohlberg (1963a) writes: 'The data raise the question as to whether there are any psychological dispositions that can usefully be conceived as "conscience" or "internalized standards"', and 'If there is little consistency from situation to situation involving the same standard, we cannot assume that conforming behaviour is determined by the standard and not by situational forces.'

On the other hand it has been forcibly argued that the results do support the assumption of a general trait of honesty (Eysenck, 1960), and subsequent work tends to support the claim. Maller (1934) and Burton (1963) both reanalysed some of the Hartshorne and May data using more sophisticated statistical methods and concluded there was a general trait of honesty which was relatively independent of situational factors. A study by Brogden (1940) offers further support. Nelson, Grinder and Mutterer (1969) tested eleven-year-old boys and girls on six measures of resistance to temptation. The intercorrelations were all positive (varying between 0·05 and 0·55) and further analysis clearly supported the notion that there is a general disposition to be honest. A similar degree of consistency was found by Sears, Rau and Alpert (1966), who gave six tests to children of four and five, and by Nelson, Grinder and Biaggio (1969) who tested 100 thirteen-year-olds. Finally Grim, Kohlberg and White (1968) report a small positive association between two measures of cheating at the age of six years, and a much more positive association between these measures, and between both and a measure of lying, at the age of twelve.

The conclusion to be drawn is clear: it *is* meaningful to talk about a general disposition of moral restraint, but in any temptation situation this is only one of a number of dispositional and situational factors at work, and its role in accounting for individual differences may be relatively minor. Only when research has succeeded in controlling these other factors effectively will differences in moral restraint emerge more clearly.

There is another way in which we can frame our question about the generality of resistance to temptation. Instead of asking whether there is consistency across different tests we can ask whether performance on these tests is related to self-control in other situations which do not involve moral rules. Moral self-restraint may be a manifestation of a more general capacity to inhibit impulse.

Certain aspects of behaviour have been found to go together, and they have been collectively subsumed under the label of *ego-control*. They include persistence and sustained attention in a boring activity, careful and accurate performance in simple motor tasks like tracing mazes and drawing circles, an extended time perspective so that the individual characteristically plans ahead and brings past experience to bear upon the present, and a readiness to do without an immediate reward in favour of a greater one in the future. As we shall see in the next chapter, delinquents tend to manifest less ego-control than non-delinquents. And a few studies have related this trait to the experimental tests of moral restraint.

In one experiment (Mischel and Gilligan, 1964) subjects were given a measure of cheating, and a month later in a different context offered a choice between a small, immediate reward and a delayed, larger one. Those who chose the delayed reward were significantly less likely to have cheated and, if they had, were more likely to have held out longer before yielding to temptation. Brock and DelGiudice (1963) gave subjects an opportunity to steal small sums of money, and later required them to tell imaginative stories. Those who stole wrote stories involving a shorter time span than those who did not steal. Grim, Kohlberg and White (1968) gave children, in addition to measures of cheating and lying, a number of tests of their capacity to keep attention focused upon a rather boring task (pressing a lever when a light came on). There was a clear association between the moral and non-moral tests, and analysis suggested that the correlations found between the three moral measures could be explained on the assumption that what they measured in common was the same capacity as that of the tests of attention. In the studies both by Hartshorne and May, and by Sears, Rau and Alpert resistance to temptation was found to be related to impulse control in situations that did not obviously raise moral issues.

These results are of great interest. They imply that self-control in morally tempting situations is a function of some more general control factor rather than of a specifically moral form of inhibition. In psychoanalytic terms, resistance to temptation may be an ego function rather than a superego function.

## Some Correlates of Resistance to Temptation

I have mentioned some evidence that points to a connection between ego-control and moral inhibition. It is time to look at the relations between moral restraint and intelligence, sex, age and personality.

### (A) INTELLIGENCE

One of the findings that emerged most firmly from the Hartshorne and May study was that the more intelligent subjects were more honest. This remained true even when the different socioeconomic levels of the home backgrounds of the subjects were taken into account. Not many later studies have looked at intelligence, but among those that have, most have come up with a similar result (e.g. Terman and Odin, 1947; Graham, 1968). Some have found no association (e.g. Brogden, 1940) but none a negative relation.

A variety of speculative interpretations can be offered. For example, the intelligent may be less motivated to transgress. Since they are more likely, in general, to be able to achieve rewards by socially approved means, they may be less tempted to cheat or steal. However, the converse of this could be argued: because the intelligent are more accustomed to being successful they may be less able to tolerate failure and therefore more tempted to cheat when this is the only way to achieve success. More plausibly, perhaps, the intelligent may take more features of the testing situation into account; they may see more possibilities of being found out, and may be more ready to suspect a trap. Then there is at least the possibility of some intrinsic connection between intellectual activity and self-control. Much intelligent behaviour demands foresight and planning, and therefore the postponing of action to permit adequate reflection. Some of the measures of ego-control have in fact been found to be associated with intelligence, especially the tendency to prefer a delayed reward over a smaller, immediate one (Mischel, 1966). But in the absence of fuller evidence the discussion must remain inconclusive. Perhaps all that can be safely said is that the findings point to the importance of cognitive factors in moral restraint.

## (B) SEX DIFFERENCE

It is often said that girls have stronger consciences than boys. Certainly the delinquency rates are much lower for girls. On experimental tests, however, this greater virtue is not so evident. Hartshorne and May found no overall difference between the sexes, though girls cheated less on some tests and more on others. They interpret the pattern of their results as indicating that girls are more strongly motivated to *appear* good, and therefore are more likely to be dishonest when this is the only way of maintaining or gaining the approval of others. The studies of Crandall and her associates* confirm this interpretation. These investigators constructed a children's social desirability scale in which subjects have to respond with 'true' or 'false' to a number of statements. These are so phrased that subjects are tempted to present a socially acceptable image of themselves but only through being palpably untrue. An example would be the subject who responds with 'true' to the statement 'I have never felt like saying unkind things to anyone', or 'When I make a mistake

---

* Crandall (1966); Crandall, Crandall and Katkovsky (1965); and Crandall and Gozali (1969).

I always admit I am wrong.' Over a large sample of children in the United States and in Norway, it was found that girls were significantly more likely to present a favourable image of themselves at the cost of departing from the strict truth. Most other studies that have compared girls and boys on experimental tests of cheating have failed to find any differences between the sexes.* However, when sex differences have been found they nearly always favour the girls.† Examination of the experiments strongly suggests that such sex differences as are found are primarily due to the fact that the attractiveness of the incentives used is not the same for both sexes.

## (C) AGE

An adequate test of the relationship between age and moral behaviour would have to be longitudinal, with the same subjects tested at successive ages. This has not been done. However, different subjects at different ages have been contrasted. Over the age range from six to seventeen, no convincing age differences have been found. The great bulk of the studies reveal no general tendency for children to get more or less honest as they grow up, though Kanfer and Duerfeldt (1968) found a decrease in cheating with age and Feldman and Feldman (1967) a small increase. Of course the meaningfulness of age-level comparisons can be questioned, for it is to be expected that the significance of a temptation situation will vary with age. However, since a number of different kinds of test have failed to yield age differences, it does establish an initial presumption that this kind of behaviour is not related to age, at least over the age range sampled.

There is some evidence of a different kind of age change, however, and one which may in the end prove more interesting. In the Hartshorne and May study, though older subjects as a

*E.g. Burton, Allinsmith and Maccoby (1966); Grinder (1962; 1946); Grinder and McMichael (1963); Silverman (1967); Walsh (1967); Shelton and Hill (1969); and Cocking (1969).

†E.g. Brock and DelGiudice (1963); Medinnus (1966a); Sears, Rau and Alpert (1966); and Ward and Furchak (1968).

group were no more nor less dishonest than the younger ones, there was a tendency for them to be less variable, that is, to be either more consistently honest or more consistently dishonest. Then there was the finding of Grim, Kohlberg and White (1968) that persistent attention in a boring task was much more closely associated with moral restraint in older than in younger subjects. The inference to be drawn is that, insofar as there is a developmental change, it is in the direction of greater consistency and stability rather than of greater virtue.

## (D) PERSONALITY AND TEMPERAMENT

Apart from the evidence that moral restraint is related to impulse control in non-moral behaviour, there is little direct evidence of its relation to personality and temperament. However, it is likely that temperament plays its part, and this is a convenient point to introduce the personality theory which bears most directly upon the matter, namely that elaborated by Eysenck and expounded in numerous publications (e.g. Eysenck, 1964, 1968; Eysenck and Eysenck, 1969).

The basic claim of this theory is that a great many of the ways in which people's personalities vary can be accounted for by assuming two underlying, independent dimensions of personality. The first of these is labelled *neuroticism* and by this Eysenck means a basic dimension of difference between people in the stability of their nervous systems, varying from at one end those who are highly excitable to at the other end those who are stable and placid. The second is the familiar *extroversion–introversion* dimension. What Eysenck is claiming is that a great deal of an individual's behaviour can be predicted from knowing his positions on these two dimensions. And it is held that his position on them is partly determined by hereditary factors.

Hereditary differences result in certain variations in the functioning of people's nervous systems. Differences in cortical functioning are said to be related to extroversion–introversion. Extroverts are characterized by a relatively low level of cortical excitation or arousal, and introverts by a relatively high level (strictly, they differ in 'excitation–inhibition balance'). Since one of the main effects of cortical activity is to inhibit the activity of lower centres, it follows that extroverts will be more impulsive and less controlled in their behaviour. A further consequence is that they will learn conditioned responses slowly and unlearn them quickly by comparison with introverts, and they will be less sensitive to pain. In personality extroverts will be stimulus-seeking and sociable, impulsive, unreliable and quick-tempered, whereas introverts will be reserved, controlled, reliable and cautious. The dimension of neuroticism is said to correspond to differences in the stability or lability, of the autonomic nervous system, that part which mediates emotional responses. People high on neuroticism will have emotional responses that are easily triggered and volatile; those low on it will be much calmer and more emotionally sluggish.

No direct predictions follow as to whether people will resist temptation in particular circumstances, for this depends on their moral training. But since those high on neuroticism and extroversion may be expected to have benefited less from their experiences (they have more need for controls and yet learn control less easily), it is to be expected that, unless their moral training has been unusually persistent and thorough, they will be less able to resist temptation than those who are both introverted and low on neuroticism. Exactly this was found in an experiment by Keehn (1956). In a sample of children aged eleven and thirteen those high on both neuroticism and extroversion cheated significantly more than those low on both dimensions. Eysenck's picture of the introvert is similar to someone who has high ego-control in the sense used earlier, and there is empirical evidence of a link between the two dimensions (see Kipnis, 1968).

## Situational Factors

The fact that performance on one moral test is only moderately related to performance on others indicates that situational factors are very important. So far, however, not a great deal of attention has been given to its features.

The importance of risk of detection is brought out in an experiment by Kanfer and Duerfeldt (1968). The subjects, who were children, had to guess numbers between one and 100 that were drawn at random from a box. They did not tell the experimenter what their guesses were; they simply recorded whether they had guessed correctly or not. A reward was offered for a high number of correct guesses. If a child reported that he had obtained a total of correct guesses which was well above what could be expected by chance, it was inferred that he had cheated. Under one condition subjects made mental guesses and only recorded whether they were correct or not. Under the other condition, subjects wrote their guesses down on a slip of paper before hearing whether they were correct or not. In this second condition they were assured that the slips of paper would be thrown away without being looked at; but clearly, from the subject's point of view, the risk of detection should they cheat was higher. Subjects in this second condition cheated much less; but as the experiment progressed and they saw that their slips of paper were really thrown away, their cheating steadily increased. Hill and Kochendorfer (1969) provide another demonstration of how cheating increases as risk of detection decreases, and other experiments have shown that cheating is related to the subject's estimate of the risk of censure if he were found out (Rettig and Pasamanick, 1964; Rettig and Suiha, 1966).

It will be remembered that, according to Piaget, the egocentric child's thinking tends to be centred on, or dominated by, one thing at a time, and he cannot take into account several considerations simultaneously. It would seem to follow that in the temptation situation, the young child would be more influenced by whatever consideration was uppermost in his mind at the time. O'Leary (1968) gave six-year-old boys a simple task in which there was incentive and opportunity to cheat by breaking a rule. He found that cheating could be substantially reduced by the simple expedient of requiring the subjects, as part of the task, to say the rule aloud each time before doing it.

It could be inferred from Piaget's theory that this expedient would be less successful with children who had attained the capacity for operational thinking.

As is to be expected, the stronger the incentive to cheat the more the cheating that occurs. Mills (1958) varied the monetary rewards that could be gained by cheating and found that this led to differences in amount of cheating. Children are more prone to cheat on a test of achievement if they are told that their peers have done markedly better than they are likely to do. This effect is the greater the more generally anxious the subjects are about school achievement (Hill and Kochendorfer, 1969; Shelton and Hill, 1969). Temptation situations, it may be presumed, evoke moral anxiety. If the general anxiety level of the subject is reduced, then the intensity of this moral anxiety will decline also, and we may expect that he will be more likely to succumb to temptation. Schachter and Latané (1964) gave one group of female students a drug, which, unknown to them, had the effect of generally lowering anxiety level. These subjects cheated more than a control group which had been given a placebo.

The influence of motivational factors which arise less directly from the temptation situation has also been investigated. Aronson and Mettee (1968) temporarily induced high or low self-esteem in students by giving them flattering or derogatory feedback from a personality test. Low self-esteem increased the incidence of dishonest behaviour in a subsequent test and high self-esteem reduced it in comparison with a control group that was given no feedback at all. In other words, you weaken a man's self-control in morally tempting situations by damaging his self-esteem, and you strengthen it by increasing his self-respect. Self-control and thinking well of oneself are connected. In an ingenious experiment Stephenson and White (1968) provoked a sense of mild frustration and injustice in ten-year-old boys, and thereby increased the likelihood of their cheating. This suggests that dishonest behaviour can be a covert and indirect form of protest against being treated unfairly.

Moral restraint may also be influenced by observing the behaviour of models. A number of experiments have shown that being in the presence of someone else who violates a prohibition has a disinhibiting effect and makes a violation by the observer more likely (see Blake, 1958). Observation of a deviant model may also have a disinhibiting effect on a subject when he is on his own afterwards. Stein (1967), using nine-year-old boys as subjects, created a situation in which the subject was tempted to abandon a dull task entrusted to him for a more interesting alternative occupation. Those who first watched a model yield to this temptation were more likely themselves to yield when on their own later, than others who watched a virtuous model or no model at all.

In addition to the short-term effect of another's example, we can ask whether social influences of a more general kind have a detectable effect upon resistance to temptation. For example, it is often claimed that membership of religious organizations and commitment to religious belief confirm and brace the conscience. As far as the experimental measures of resistance to temptation are concerned, existing evidence does not endorse this claim. Hartshorne and May found that regular church attenders were indistinguishable from those who never attended. Certain other considerations strengthen this negative conclusion. There is abundant evidence that girls are more religious than boys (e.g. Wright and Cox, 1967a), and that religious commitment changes with age, especially during adolescence (Argyle, 1958); yet, as we saw, there is no convincing evidence of parallel variations in moral behaviour.

Of course it could be argued that adolescents are hardly likely to have much investment in their membership of such adult organized groups as churches, and would only really be influenced by their immediate circle of friends and by their parents. Hartshorne and May did find some evidence of differences between schools, and between classes within the same school, that could not readily be explained in terms of intelligence or socio-economic level. They deduced that the morale of a child's friendship group can affect his behaviour 'in private'. Moreover they also found that children who stood high in their teachers' esteem, and who presumably therefore were under some pressure to live up to this high opinion, cheated less at school, though they were just as likely to cheat at home.

Two studies indicate that current parental influence can affect behaviour 'in private'. Pearlin, Yarrow and Scarr (1967) reported that children whose parents put great emphasis upon achievement at school cheated more in tests of achievement. Piliavin, Hardyck and Vadum (1968) selected two groups of boys, one of which consisted of those who claimed that it mattered very much to them what their parents thought of them, and the other of boys who were indifferent to parental opinion. The latter cheated much more in an experimental test.

## Child-rearing Antecedents

There can be few people who doubt that moral behaviour depends on upbringing; but unless we know what kind of upbringing produces what kind of behaviour we are helpless to do anything about it. Unfortunately the practical difficulties in the way of effective research are so considerable that little if anything is yet firmly established.

In the first place, it is people's more or less enduring moral dispositions that are shaped by early family life, and tests of resistance to temptation are only moderately successful in measuring these. Then in measuring home conditions we have no alternative but to rely upon what parents tell us, and what their children remember. Because we can control the conditions under which we interview them, we can be reasonably sure that most parents will be as accurate and truthful as they can; but inevitably their accounts of their own practices and attitudes will be edited by selective remembering, by guilt feelings, and by the desire to appear 'good' parents. Several studies have shown that mothers often change their accounts from one interview to the next. And, as has been pointed out many times, having found an association between parental practice and child behaviour it is often impossible to infer which is cause and which effect. Indeed the highly complex nature of the continual interaction between parents and child is such that we may be tempted to despair of ever unravelling the important threads in it.

Nevertheless parents do differ in their general attitudes and policies, and since these are sustained over a number of years it is to be expected that they will produce discriminable differences in the children. Though we may have reservations about parental report, it is not valueless.

So far only three studies have tackled the problem of relating experimental tests of moral restraint to information from parental interviews, namely those by Burton, Maccoby and Allinsmith (1961), by Grinder (1962), and by Sears, Rau and Alpert (1966). In the first and third the children were between the ages of four and five when all the data were collected; in the second parents were interviewed when the children were five and the moral-behaviour tests were given when they were eleven. In each study the interview material generated a great many measures of parental behaviour, but very few of them were found to discriminate between honest and dishonest children, and those that did failed to present a very coherent and meaningful picture.

If there is one condition which is confidently thought to be essential for moral growth it is maternal love. None of the three studies found any relationship between maternal warmth and affection and resistance to temptation as measured by these tests. This does not mean that such affection is unimportant. In the three samples studied there is every reason to think that most if not all the mothers were firmly attached to their children. What it indicates is that beyond a certain basic minimum, differences in maternal affection are not important in producing differences in moral behaviour. As we shall see in the next chapter, when there is no maternal affection the consequences for moral growth are serious.

Turning to the positive findings, it is noteworthy that the three studies agree in presenting a different pattern of antecedents for the two sexes. We shall therefore consider them separately.

(a) Boys: Burton and his associates found that honest subjects had taken longer over bowel training, achieved daytime dryness later, and had mothers who were strict over weaning but relaxed over general cleanliness, made little use of reasoning, used physical punishment more, and left their sons alone when they misbehaved. In Grinder's study the mothers of 'good' boys set high standards for neatness, and the boys themselves took relatively long over achieving bowel control. Use of physical punishment and reasoning were unrelated. In the Sears study no measure of maternal behaviour was found to be important. But unlike the other two, Sears included a number of measures of paternal behaviour, and some of these were quite strongly related to moral behaviour. Honest boys were relatively closely attached to their fathers and distant from their mothers. The fathers were highly ambivalent towards their sons, being strongly attached and somewhat hostile at the same time, and they believed strongly in the importance of teaching right and wrong. Congruent with this, Mackinnon (1938) reported that dishonest male students said that they had felt a preference for their mothers over their fathers when they were young, and presumably were less attached to their fathers. In the same study it was the dishonest subjects who reported that their parents had made frequent use of physical punishment, a direct contradiction of the Burton finding.

(b) Girls: In the Burton study 'good' girls were found to be late in achieving daytime dryness, to have shown relatively little anxiety over learning about sex differences, and to have mothers who tended to use as their sanctions scolding and physical punishment, and to make little use of reasoning. In Grinder's study they achieved bowel control early, and suffered high maternal pressure against masturbation. The Sears study again drew attention to the importance of father. Honest girls had fathers who were relatively distant, critical and dissatisfied with their daughters, and who ridiculed them a lot. Both parents urged their daughters to be independent, but the mothers were more responsive to them, and reasoned with them.

The contradictory nature of these results, together with the fact that in each study a great many aspects of child rearing bore no relation at all to moral behaviour, creates an impression of total inconclusiveness. However, there are perhaps four suggestions that emerge. First, relationships to childhood antecedents are more likely to show up if moral behaviour is measured by a series of tests rather than by one (in this respect the Sears study is in the strongest position). Secondly, it seems probable that the pervasive attitudes of parents will prove more important than the specific practices they adopt. Thirdly, in samples from 'normal' families where maternal attachment and concern will not vary much, the father's role becomes more important. And fourthly, the antecedents of moral behaviour are likely to be different for the two sexes.

## Self-Report Measures

So far we have limited ourselves to experimental tests of resistance to temptation. These measures have the inestimable advantage of clearly separating those who transgress from those who do not and of controlling the conditions under which transgression occurs. Moreover since the subject does not know in advance that he will be faced with a moral decision he cannot reflect at leisure whether to be honest or not, nor can he discuss the matter with others. Their major limitation is that they sample only minor misdemeanors.

The alternative method open to the psychologist is to ask people in interviews and questionnaires whether and how often they have committed certain acts. This method has the advantage that we can ask about many forms of behaviour which could not be made the substance of an experimental test. Its obvious drawback is that we cannot be certain that the replies are true. Efforts are always made to remove any incentives to lie by making clear that the survey is for research purposes and that anonymity is guaranteed. It is probable that under these conditions most people will try to be truthful. In fact there is some evidence that people who say they do, or would, cheat, are actually more likely to when tested (Christenson, 1938; Brogden, 1940), and that when people are interviewed twice they tend very much to stick to their original admissions (Clark and Tift, 1966). The more serious problem is again the selective effects of memory. People who like to think of themselves as virtuous may simply have suppressed the memory of their misdeeds, or may be reluctant to see them as wrong even when it is plain to others that they are. There is no means of knowing at present how much misrepresentation of this kind goes on, and this brings an element of uncertainty to all studies using this method.

There is another problem. In discussing the experimental tests no reference was made to whether or not the subjects judged the actions wrong. This was partly because the relationship between moral belief and action will be taken up later, but also because surveys have shown that an overwhelming majority of people of all ages in the societies sampled in these studies regard cheating in exams, stealing and lying for personal gain as wrong. Many of the types of behaviour asked about in surveys, such as premarital sexual intercourse and gambling, are much less universally condemned. Whereas we should expect people who do not think such actions wrong to engage in them more often, so we should expect them to be more ready to admit doing them if they have.

At this point it will be helpful if we follow Middleton and Putney (1962) and draw a distinction between *antisocial* and *anti-ascetic* actions. Antisocial acts are those the ill effects of which are felt primarily and most directly by others. Stealing, physical assault and lying for personal gain fall into this category. Anti-ascetic acts are forms of individual self-indulgence the undesirable consequences of which, if any, are felt mainly by those who engage in them – consequences such as personal deterioration and ill health. Examples are forms of 'immoral' sexual behaviour, drunkenness and drug-taking. Many acts are hard to classify, and in any case the distinction is a slippery one and unlikely to survive close scrutiny. But it has a surface plausibility, and, what is more important for the moment, there is much closer agreement over the wrongness of antisocial acts than over anti-ascetic ones (see, for example, Middleton and Putney, 1962; Wright and Cox, 1967b). Though most surveys have ignored the distinction, I shall not.

## (A) ANTISOCIAL BEHAVIOUR

A number of inventories of possible misdemeanours have been compiled (e.g. Nye, 1958; Gibson, 1967). These lists usually contain a few anti-ascetic items but they are predominantly composed of antisocial ones. Most were designed for the adolescent age range. Characteristically the antisocial items vary from 'nuisance' behaviour such as frequent disobedience of parental authority and truancy from school at one end to serious theft and armed assault at the other. Several facts emerge from the use of these inventories:

(i) The items themselves can be shown to form a scale (Nye and Short, 1957). This means that subjects who admit serious offences nearly always admit trivial ones as well and this suggests that there is some kind of dimension along which individuals can be placed according to the seriousness of the offences they are prepared to commit.

(ii) The great majority of subjects admit one kind of offence or another. This is especially true of 'nuisance' acts; but a surprisingly high proportion confess to behaviour which would have serious consequences were it detected. All the males in a sample of prospective teachers said they had been members of gangs that had at some time broken the law (Crane, 1958), and about half a sample of grammar-school boys admitted acts that would have resulted in their being classified as delinquent had they been caught (Gibson, 1967). More than half a sample of university students reported stealing from hotels and restaurants, and the loss of books from university libraries through theft is notorious. Among a number of American universities the proportion admitting cheating on examinations varied from a third to over a half (Harp and Taietz, 1966). In a survey of about 1,000 school children aged nine to fourteen in Norway and Sweden, Elmhorn (1965) found that 89 per cent admitted petty illegal offences, 39 per cent ordinary theft, 17 per cent breaking in, and 14 per cent wilful damage to property. Just over 63 per cent of a large sample of Polish children aged twelve to thirteen confessed that they had taken other people's property (Malewska and Muszyński, 1970).

(iii) It is not my intention in this book to trespass on the concerns of the sociologist, but it is worth looking briefly at the vexed question of social class and delinquency. There is abundant evidence that those officially labelled delinquent in society tend to come from the lower classes. In contrast, many studies have found that delinquent acts reported by 'non-delinquents' are either unrelated to class, or that the relationship is tenuous and complex.* However, these surveys have been conducted mostly in the United States; in England it appears that middle-class subjects are significantly less likely to admit delinquent acts (McDonald, 1969). McDonald also found that, independent of class, grammar-school children reported fewer offences than those in secondary modern schools, and that, independent of both class and type of school, the academically successful were better behaved than the unsuccessful. Other features of social structure such as ethnic grouping, norm consensus and degree of access to legitimate means for obtaining the culturally defined goals, have all been found to be related to reported deviant behaviour (Jessor *et al.*, 1968).

(iv) There is an overall tendency for girls to report fewer antisocial acts than boys. Closer examination of the data reveals that as far as 'nuisance' behaviour and minor delinquencies are concerned they are indistinguishable from boys; but they are far less likely to have committed the more serious offences.

(v) Evidence on the relationship between religious commitment and reported antisocial behaviour is somewhat conflicting. In the study by Nye (1958), based on a representative sample of adolescents in a medium-sized American town, regular church attenders were less antisocial, though irregular attenders and non-attenders did not differ. Early religious influence was apparently unimportant, for length of time belonging to a church was unrelated to misbehaviour; what counted was the adoles-

*Nye (1958); Dentler and Monroe (1961); Christie, Andenaes and Skirbeck (1965); Clark and Wenninger (1962); and Empey and Erickson (1966).

cent's current involvement in a religious group. McDonald (1969), however, could find no association at all between church attendance and antisocial behaviour, and nor could Middleton and Putney (1962). However, Nye's inventory did contain rather more serious items than those used in the Middleton and Putney study, though not more so than McDonald's. We may tentatively conclude that high, current commitment to a religious group may reduce the incidence of serious antisocial acts, but that it has no influence over the occurrence of milder delinquencies.

Studies of the home conditions associated with self-reported misbehaviour have relied on the subjects as sources of information about the home. The major contribution of this kind is Nye's survey, and its main findings will be briefly summarized.

Taking general features of family life first, it is plain that whether a home is 'broken' or not matters much less than the quality of the relationships that exist among its members. Delinquent subjects saw their parents as unhappily married and frequently quarrelling, and their own relationships to their parents tended to be characterized by mutual rejection. They also felt that their own values on such matters as religion and right and wrong were widely different from those of their parents. In contrast, the better behaved drew a picture of their homes as places where attachments were strong, where mutual involvement in each other's activities was high, where members did many things together, and where there was relatively high agreement between parents and children over important values.

Nye's results certainly support the view that it is the general cohesiveness of the family unit that matters in the long run rather than the specific disciplinary techniques adopted by the parents. Thus it did not matter whether parents were strict or not, or whether they used corporal punishment or not; but it was important that they were seen to be fair. The more delinquent subjects saw their parents, and especially their fathers, as generally unjust and inconsistent. The example set by the parents, and again especially by the father, was of significance; badly behaved subjects were much more likely to see their fathers as dishonest people.

Nye concludes that the father's influence is more critical than the mother's as far as antisocial behaviour is concerned. He argues that 'though the role of the mother is no less crucial in relation to delinquent behaviour', mothers are less varied in their attitudes and behaviour towards their children, and 'form a more homogeneous group both in their definition of their duties and obligations of their status and in their fulfilment of the parental role'. It is also clear that delinquent behaviour in girls is rather more affected by the quality of home life than it is in boys. Girls satisfy more of their needs in the family, are likely to think of themselves as future home-makers, and tend to be under closer parental supervision. Consequently disruption of these family ties has more far-reaching consequences.

There is little other evidence to compare Nye's results with, but what does exist is generally in agreement. Jessor *et al*. (1968), for example, report that girls deviate less because they are more closely integrated into family life and consequently have less opportunity to be antisocial outside the home. Malewska and Muszyński (1970) found that children who admitted stealing were more likely to have parents who were intolerant of their needs and uninterested in them. These parents were also more violent in the sanctions they administered for misbehaviour – they easily lost their tempers, hit their children and shouted at them. In contrast, parents of children who did not report stealing were more inclined to use persuasion than compulsion in getting their children to behave well, and they were more affectionate and praised their children more.

## (B) ANTI-ASCETIC BEHAVIOUR

Anti-ascetic acts are forms of pleasurable self-indulgence which are not necessarily harmful to others, but which for various reasons are judged wrong by many people. The most obvious example is sexual 'immorality', and since it has received the greatest attention in surveys, we will focus on it here.

It has been repeatedly found, both in the United States and in England, that fewer 'immoral' sexual acts are admitted by women than by men, and by regular church-goers than by the non-religious.* But it is clear that these differences in the reported incidence of such behaviour, and particularly of premarital sexual intercourse, coincide with differences in its moral evaluation. Women adopted a stricter moral tone in evaluating sexual behaviour than men, and the religious of both sexes than the non-religious (see Wright and Cox, 1967b).

In the study by Middleton and Putney the authors took account of this difference in moral judgement and calculated the proportions of subjects who, judging an action wrong, nevertheless admitted doing it. The differences between the religious and non-religious subjects then disappeared. The non-religious were not more likely to report violating their own standards, but their standards tended to be different. The sex difference, however, remained. Men are more likely to say they have violated their own standards than women. There are at least four possible explanations. It could be due to the 'double standard'; women think the behaviour wrong for both sexes, but somehow more wrong for women. Women may be more ashamed to admit such behaviour even on an anonymous questionnaire. It could be that women have weaker sex drives and are therefore less tempted. Or it could be that girls are subjected to stronger pressures against 'immoral' sexual behaviour in their upbringing. There is probably some truth in each explanation.

There is some ground for thinking that anti-ascetic and anti-social behaviour are related. In Schofield's survey of over 1,800 unmarried adolescents, sexually experienced boys were more likely to have appeared in court than the sexually inexperienced, and the greater the experience the greater the number of court appearances.

Schofield also obtained a great deal of information about the home backgrounds of his adolescent subjects. Sexually experienced people were not more likely to come from broken homes, or from one social class rather than another. Typically they came from families with low cohesion where parents made little effort to control their behaviour and showed little interest in

* For example: Kinsey *et al.* (1948; 1953); Chesser (1956); Middleton and Putney (1962); and Schofield (1965).

their activities. They themselves tended to reject parental values, to be strongly identified with their peer groups, and to be anxious to conform to the norms of those groups. They had a permissive and indulgent attitude towards moral issues and were primarily bent upon having a good time. As in the Nye study, family relations are more important for girls than for boys. Girls have to be more completely dissociated from their families, and to get on less well with their parents (and particularly their fathers) if they are to engage in premarital intercourse.

The main difference between teenage boys and girls who have sexual experience is that the girl is more influenced by her family. She must overcome these family pressures and derogate her family loyalty before she can be persuaded to agree to premarital intercourse. (Schofield, 1965)

Self-report measures are at some remove from actual behaviour and are therefore cruder and less reliable indices of it than the experimental tests we dealt with earlier. The offences sampled include many that were probably committed in the presence of other members of peer groups, or at least with their connivance. They are actions which often require some planning and forethought, and the individual has sometimes to search actively for a situation in which he can commit them. It is therefore hardly surprising that the studies reviewed, of both anti-social and anti-ascetic behaviour, leave no doubt about the paramount importance of current group loyalties. If the adolescent is integrated into a cohesive family, he is much less likely to be guilty of delinquencies or to be sexually experienced. This will be partly because his values will be closer to those of his parents, partly because he will be strongly motivated to live up to what they expect of him and partly because he will simply have less opportunity to engage in such behaviour.

This is not a startling conclusion. But it implies that differences in reported transgression can be better predicted from a knowledge of an adolescent's current social attachments than from a knowledge of the strength of his conscience. It also implies that early family life is important for moral behaviour less because of its shaping influence upon the individual's personality than because it lays the foundation of family cohesion later on. If the parents have little interest in their child, and tend to be cool and rejecting towards him, then he will seek compensatory attachments in his peer groups. If the norms of these groups permit delinquent and 'immoral' sexual behaviour then he can be expected to engage in it. We must, however, guard against the assumption that strong family attachments necessarily lead to better behaviour in the child. If he is very dependent upon parents who set unrealistically high standards for him, the resulting stress may well force him into all kinds of deceitful subterfuges in order to keep their approval.

## The Nature of Moral Restraint

Behaviour in a temptation situation is the outcome of a decision process which is in turn influenced by the complex interaction of three sets of variables. There is first the set of relatively enduring personal characteristics the individual brings to the situation. These include his moral beliefs, his capacity for self-restraint, his susceptibility to the attraction of the temptation, his intelligence, his general dependency upon the good opinion of others, his self-esteem, and so on. Secondly, there are the actual social and physical features of the situation, for example the nature of the incentive, whether other people are present or not, and the probability that others will learn what happens. Thirdly, there is the individual's wider, current social context, that is, his present group loyalties, the norms of these groups and the sanctions they apply to deviant members. These three types of variable are not independent of each other, for, though the second and third are to a large extent external to the individual and can be described without reference to him, their influence upon his behaviour depends upon how they interact with his dispositions.

The problem now is what conceptual framework best fits the braking mechanism that resists the temptation. The social-group theorist points to the constraining effect of knowing how others expect us to behave. Whereas this effect is presumably at its strongest when others are present, the evidence indicates that it can operate when the individual is alone; deceit is inversely related to the risk of discovery. Whether or not the risk of detection can, from the individual's point of view, ever entirely be eliminated is debatable; it can be argued that it cannot, for the individual himself knows what he has done and there is always the possibility that he may betray himself to others. We may suppose that the greater the dependence upon social approval, the smaller the risk the individual is prepared to take. The fear of other people's censure is a powerful motive, but it is not by itself sufficient to explain the evidence.

Psychoanalysis locates the braking mechanism in a single, specifically moral agency within the personality which functions with some measure of autonomy. The moderate and variable correlations between different measures of resistance to temptation are hardly encouraging to, though they do not strictly disconfirm, this view. The clear indications that moral restraint is associated with ego-control variables, that it is sensitive to variations in self-esteem and is weakened by a sense of grievance, and that it is reduced by the deviant example of others, all militate against the idea that it is the function of a differentiated and autonomous structure. The expectation that boys will have a stronger conscience than girls is plainly not fulfilled. On the other hand, the failure to find evidence that strength of conscience increases after the age of about six years is what the psychoanalyst would expect.

The evidence from self-report studies indicates that the conditions said to result in identification are in fact those associated with moral restraint. However, it does not follow that therefore the effect of these conditions is mediated by the mechanism of identification. There are at least two reasons for thinking otherwise. First, the evidence points to the importance of attachment and parental control as *contemporaneous* rather than antecedent conditions. There are two senses in which the term 'identification' can be used. For the psychoanalyst it is a mechanism of personality change; but it can also be used simply to refer to any relationship that is compounded of attachment, admiration and the desire to emulate and protect. The evidence supports the view that moral restraint is a function of the individual's current identifications in this second sense, but not of a moral agency produced by the *mechanism* of identification. Secondly, according to psychoanalysis, the identification that produces moral control also results in sex-typing, especially in boys; so far the evidence fails to support this (see Sears, Rau and Alpert, 1966; and Medinnus, 1967).

Finally psychoanalysis maintains that moral inhibition is due to in-turned aggression, in contrast to learning theory which attributes it to fear and anxiety. The material in this chapter offers no basis for choice. However, some psychoanalysts (e.g. Flugel, 1945) have gratefully fastened upon the results of the study by MacKinnon (1938) as offering support for the psychoanalytic view. In this experiment student subjects were given an exam in which cheating was the only way of succeeding. The situation provoked aggression as well as putting honesty to the test. MacKinnon noted that the honest subjects characteristically directed their aggression towards themselves by blaming their own stupidity, pulling their hair, and so on. Dishonest subjects in contrast directed their aggression outwards, blaming the examiner, kicking the desk, and breaking their pencils. This is an intriguing observation. But because the honest were aggressive towards themselves it would be naive to conclude that it is therefore their in-turned aggression that makes them honest; it is as plausible, in fact more so, to argue that it is some self-controlling factor which is responsible both for their honesty and for their in-turned aggression. Properly understood, however, Freud's metatheory should not lead us to expect MacKinnon's results. For on that theory, in-turned and inhibiting aggression is energy which has been diverted away from *any* kind of motor expression in order to prevent other motivating forces from being acted out. As such, the theory is surely beyond the reach of empirical test. But despite this, and despite the fact that the concept of anxiety is generally more useful in this context, Freud's emphasis upon the intimate connexion between morality and aggression is not to be lightly dismissed, and I shall return to it later.

According to learning theory, behavioural inhibition, whether moral or not, occurs when a stimulus feature of the situation elicits a strong anxiety response. The stimulus may be intrinsic to the behaviour, such as a muscular sensation; it may be an external component of the situation; or it may be the subject's intellectual reaction to the situation, the meaning he sees in it. The anxiety itself inhibits both by directly interfering with the behaviour and by providing a motive for doing something else. This interpretation of behavioural inhibition is supported by a massive body of experimental work. More important, the theory has been shown to work; children have been induced to resist temptation in the laboratory by applying it (e.g. Aronfreed, 1963; Aronfreed and Reber, 1965).

Learning theory is not developmental; it specifies the conditions under which behavioural inhibition can be acquired whatever the age of the subject. But it is possible to infer certain general conditions in upbringing which should lead to the more or less consistently honest person. They are first that parents should use anxiety inducing sanctions (the theory is silent over what these are). Secondly, the parent should explain fully the reasons for the sanctions at the time they are administered. Thirdly, the parent should be consistent so that earlier learning is not undermined by later. Fourthly, the child should be surrounded by models of correct behaviour, or models who, when they transgress, are punished in some way. The evidence in this chapter is altogether too uncertain for us to know whether these conditions do in fact obtain in the histories of honest subjects.

There is no doubt about the significance of the part played by intelligence in resistance to temptation, both in terms of general intellectual level and in terms of the way situations are understood, risk is assessed, and so on. But the precise delineation of this role is a task for the future. Meanwhile we must point out the limitations of an explanation based exclusively upon intelligence. There appears to be no age-related change in moral restraint during the period when intelligence is most rapidly developing.

The cognitive theorist can justly reply both that greater intelligence does not necessarily mean greater virtue but only that the reasons for being virtuous are better, and that the situations in which greater virtue might be expected to follow from greater intelligence have not yet been explored. Yet children can learn to resist temptation before they have any understanding of the reasons for resisting, and in everyday experience we find that changes in outlook such that we now judge an action permissible that we previously thought wrong do not immediately free us from inhibitions over performing it (anti-ascetic actions provide the best examples). Anxiety conditioning cannot be ignored. But the learning and cognitive-developmental approaches can meet in the conception of an ideal process of development in which there is a progressive integration of emotional response under the control of conceptual and reasoning processes. This might be called an 'ego-development' theory of moral development, and its details are now being worked out (see Kohlberg, 1969).

# CHAPTER 4

# Delinquency

Criminologists, sociologists, psychologists and others have amassed an impressive body of data and theory concerning the conditions that produce delinquency. In the present chapter I can do little more than touch on this. The selection of material for inclusion has been guided by two considerations.

In the first place I shall focus upon delinquency rather than adult crime. The two present rather different problems, for the former is age-linked in a way in which the latter is not. Delinquency rates increase steadily through childhood, reach a peak in late adolescence and decline fairly sharply in the early twenties. Though most adult criminals were delinquent in their youth, the bulk of delinquents merge into the adult, law-abiding population and do not appear before the courts again. This seems to be mainly due to the responsibilities of marriage, family and a job, though it should be added that the many characteristics of temperament and personality which differentiate them from non-delinquents do not change so quickly (see Glueck and Glueck, 1968). Classification as a delinquent does not augur well for future social adjustment but it does not mean that a life of crime will necessarily follow. Adult crime tends to be either a more or less consciously chosen career, or a symptom of serious personality disorder.

Secondly, the delinquent–non-delinquent classification will be used as a way of measuring moral behaviour. Its value in this respect is limited; but the research on delinquency is too valuable to be ignored. And most people see criminal behaviour as the manifestation of a defective conscience and a deformed moral

79

sense. The simple equation of criminal behaviour with a defective conscience is facile and misleading; but that crime is a moral issue can hardly be denied. People who see a decline in the moral health of western societies regularly instance the rising tide of delinquency as proof of the correctness of their diagnosis.

## Delinquency as a Measure of Moral Behaviour

Our first step must therefore be to look more closely at the delinquency classification as a measure of moral behaviour. A convenient way of doing this is to contrast it with the experimental measures discussed in the last chapter.

As in the experimental tests, we can almost always be sure that the individuals have actually committed the offences for which they are being punished. Moreover these offences are judged by society to be morally wrong, and it is probable that the delinquents themselves would acknowledge that they are wrong, at least in general terms if not in their own particular instances. Studies have tended to find little difference between delinquents and non-delinquents in the content of their verbally expressed moral beliefs (Hill, 1935; Stein *et al.*, 1967), though there may be differences in emphasis; for example delinquents judge informing on others to be more seriously wrong than do non-delinquents. There are, of course, differences in the kinds of things which the two groups value, especially if actual behaviour is taken as the index of value. But the differences are fewer than might be expected when values are measured by verbal report. Though delinquents tend to place a high value on toughness, 'kicks', and 'making a fast buck', they have also been found to value highly the same kind of things as non-delinquents. Gordon *et al.* (1963) found that delinquents of all classes rated as highly as non-delinquents such middle-class values as working hard at school, reading good books and saving money.

Though we can be confident that delinquents have done things which they and the rest of society accept as wrong, we can be much less sure that non-delinquents have not also done them.

However, it is plausible to assume that many are relatively guilt-less, and at least one self-report study has shown that delinquents have more often committed serious offences (Elmhorn, 1965). In short, we can take it that the delinquent—non-delinquent classi-fication does correspond to a difference in actual wrong-doing of an illegal kind.

Then, like the experimental tests, the delinquency classifica-tion is to some extent an index of a more general habit of wrong-doing. Typically, delinquents have committed a number of offences of several different kinds, and are more prone to mis-behaviour of the sort that is not illegal. They are more likely to have caused trouble at school and to be sexually experienced, and have a worse record of disobedience and defiance in the home.

But here the similarities between the two measures largely end, and we must turn to the contrasts. A major difference is that most delinquent acts are committed with the full knowledge and support of peers. The actual proportion committed in a group context has been found to vary from place to place and from one kind of offence to another; but it tends to be substantial. In his review of the evidence Sveri (1965) concluded that nearly ninety per cent of delinquents in the five to fourteen age group work with peers. After this age the proportion tends to decline. Among the smallest proportions reported is that by Deacon (1965), who found that in rural England only forty-two per cent of delin-quents operate in groups.

It is also plain that the motives for committing delinquent acts can be considerably more complex than those generated by an immediate incentive. Because experimental tests precipitate an unexpected moral conflict, behaviour in them can be construed as the outcome of the struggle between moral inhibition and the desire for a particular reward. As we saw, motives extrinsic to the situation, such as the need to protest against injustice, can increase cheating on these measures. But in the case of delin-quency these more general motives appear to be frequently, if not always, at work. Stott (1950) studied the process of delin-quent breakdown in 102 delinquents with a view to identifying these motives. Notable among those he found were the need to escape anxiety through excitement, resentment and spite against parents, and the desire to compensate for feelings of inferiority. Others have suggested that the need to feel tough and masculine underlies many delinquent acts. And of course, psychoanalysts are adept at finding more subtle unconscious motives. Whatever these ulterior motives are, their effect is to make the breaking of a moral norm itself a satisfying act.

Finally the delinquency classification is not the outcome of applying the same moral test uniformly to all subjects. Whether or not an individual is a delinquent depends upon whether he has had an opportunity to become one; many non-delinquents are simply not tempted to the extent that delinquents are (see Short, Rivera and Tennyson, 1965).

## The Design of Delinquency Studies

Most of the studies discussed below are based on one of two designs. In the first, samples of delinquents are compared with samples of matched non-delinquents. The matching criteria vary from one study to another, but they usually include most of the following: age, sex, socio-economic level of the home, ethnic origin, area in which the home is situated and educational experience. The idea is to control the effects of subcultural background and thereby allow the influence of psychological factors to emerge more clearly. Unfortunately the necessary controls are seldom applied with sufficient stringency for us to be sure that these subcultural factors have been excluded. In the second design measures of home background and personality are taken when the subjects are very young and before any of them have been officially classified as delinquent. The experimenter then waits to see which children become delinquent and thereby discovers what conditions in early childhood are predictive of later delinquency. Longitudinal studies using this design have obvious advantages, but they are more difficult to conduct, and hence fewer have been made.

Designs like these raise many technical problems of interpretation. This is especially so if we wish to infer the causal influence of an antecedent condition. I cannot go into these problems here (they are discussed at length elsewhere, e.g. Wootten, 1959, and Hirschi and Selvin, 1967). But it must clearly be understood that any causal implications that are drawn in the following pages must be regarded as tentative and speculative.

One problem concerning the first kind of design must be mentioned. Unlike cheaters on the experimental tests, delinquents know they have been found out and socially stigmatized as a result. When delinquents and non-delinquents are compared on personality tests, it remains an open question how much the delinquent's responses have been affected by experiences he has undergone since detection. To be declared a social misfit and an outcast, and to have an official record, is bound to have consequences for the delinquent's image of himself, either by confirming him in his negative feelings about himself, or by giving him status among his friends and thereby enhancing his self-esteem.

## Some Characteristics of Delinquents

### (A) SEX DIFFERENCE

Among young people convicted in the courts, there are about five times as many boys as girls, and those offences committed by girls are characteristically different. They are much more often guilty of sexual misdemeanours or incorrigibility, a class of offence which is primarily centred on the family and includes persistent running away and being out of parental control. When they are guilty of an indictable offence it is usually shoplifting.

There is universal agreement among criminologists that girls and women fall foul of the law much less frequently than men and boys; and that when they do so, by and large their delinquencies do not take on the aggressive and socially destructive qualities of much of the criminal behaviour of the male, and can in fact be regarded in a much less serious light. (Cowie, Cowie and Slater, 1968)

Many of the offences for which girls are sent to correctional institutions would not be the subject of legal sanction if they were older.

The important question is why these sex differences are so consistently found. It is too easy to conclude, as some writers have, that girls have stronger consciences than boys, and this is inconsistent with the evidence from the experimental tests discussed in the last chapter. The answer is more likely to lie in the nature of the social pressures to which the sexes are exposed. Much less research effort has been devoted to the origins of delinquency in girls. Cowie, Cowie and Slater (1968) provide an excellent review of the work that has been done, and offer further evidence from their own study of 318 delinquent girls who constituted the annual intake of an approved school. In the brief discussion that follows I shall lean heavily upon their conclusions.

Disorganization and other pathological features within the family are a more frequent cause of delinquency among girls than among boys. Supporting evidence comes from a number of sources. For example Toby (1957) provided statistical evidence that the differences in the proportions of male and female delinquents were smaller in those segments of the population where family instability was high. Only twenty per cent of the sample studied by Cowie *et al*. came from even superficially normal home backgrounds. In many instances the backgrounds were grossly pathological because of extreme maternal neglect, parental crime, incest and so on. Cockburn and McClay (1965) contrasted the backgrounds of boys and girls in a remand home, and though the girls had not been separated from their mothers more often than the boys, their mothers were significantly more neurotic and unstable, and they had been separated far more often from their fathers. It seems that to a greater extent than in boys, delinquency in girls can be construed as a protest against, or an escape from, intolerable home conditions.

Moreover girls do not form organized gangs among themselves nor are they usually acceptable as members of male gangs. As a result they are less subject to the coercive social pressures towards criminal behaviour that are generated in tightly knit, delinquent peer groups. This does not mean that they are un-influenced by delinquent subcultures, but that this influence is transmitted by individuals rather than groups. Girls may belong to the looser groupings found in cafés and dance halls, where they form friendships with prostitutes and delinquent males who are sometimes much older.

Furthermore it seems that on the one hand there is in general greater adult disapproval of delinquency in girls, and on the other that girls are more dependent upon adult approval than boys. Morris (1965) found that female delinquents were more ashamed of their misdemeanours and less tolerant of delinquent behaviour in others than were male delinquents.

Many attempts have been made to classify male delinquents into types. Much less attention has been paid, however, to dif-ferent types of female delinquent (in any case they may form a more homogeneous group), and those that have been suggested are mostly founded upon psychiatric criteria.* Cowie *et al.* dis-tinguished three groups of delinquent girls on the basis of their psychiatric records. First there were the 'normal' girls (forty-eight per cent of the sample) who, though often emotionally im-mature, appeared not to have suffered obvious psychological damage, and who became delinquent mainly because of their social contacts. They were impulsive, wayward, with little sense of guilt, and tended to be less intelligent than the other groups. Being in rebellion against their parents, they lived mostly on the streets. Then there were the girls with clear psy-chiatric symptoms (twenty per cent of the sample), including strong anxiety and tension, and depression. They were lonely, and starved of affection. Finally there were those with abnormal personalities indicative of serious psychological disorder (thirty-two per cent of the sample).

We can go a long way towards accounting for sex differences in delinquency by pointing to the greater vulnerability in girls to adverse home conditions. These lead to delinquency either through forcing a girl into bad company or through their im-

* For an example of a non-psychiatric typology, see Butler and Adams (1966).

mediate impact upon her mental health. There is also a possibility that sex-linked genetic factors may play a predisposing role in producing these differences. Here all is uncertain, but the hypothesis gains support from the discovery that a proportion of male criminals possess an extra male chromosome, and the evidence that delinquency tends to be associated with an especially masculine physique in boys, and also in girls (Epps and Parnell, 1952).

## (B) INTELLIGENCE

The range of intelligence among delinquents is very wide, but the average is lower than that of the general population. Shuey (1966) concludes from his review of a number of studies that the average I.Q. of white delinquents in the United States is 80·4 and of Negro delinquents 74·4. Other reviewers estimate that the average I.Q. of delinquents is somewhat higher than this but still lower than 100. But such overall averages obscure the fact that intelligence is to some extent related to type of offence. Car theft is more common with brighter delinquents, and physical assault with those of lower intelligence.

In view of the many explanations that can be offered for these differences (such as that the more intelligent delinquent does not get caught, and that intelligent people are better able to get what they want without breaking the law), it is unlikely that they are of much significance for the understanding of delinquency. More interesting is the fact that delinquents tend to do less well on predominantly verbal intelligence tests and better on non-verbal tests.

## (C) PHYSIQUE

Many attempts have been made by psychologists and psychiatrists to classify and measure individual differences in physique (see Eysenck, 1960, for a review). One of the most popular classificatory systems, and the one most often applied to delinquents, is that developed by Sheldon (1940). This scheme postulates three extreme types of body build, with most people falling somewhere in between them. They are the *mesomorphic* (muscular, broad-shouldered, athletic), the *endomorphic* (soft, rounded, fleshy) and the *ectomorphic* (narrow-shouldered, linear, stringy muscled). Glueck and Glueck (1950) compared 500 delinquents with 500 matched non-delinquents and found that the former were considerably more likely to have predominantly mesomorphic physiques. Others have reported similar findings (e.g. Gibbens, 1963). There is also a tendency for those delinquents who are not mesomorphic to be extremely endomorphic or ectomorphic rather than balanced in physique. The connection between mesomorphy and delinquency is usually interpreted along the lines that an aggressive, out-going and adventurous temperament tends to go with this physique, and that this kind of temperament is of all temperaments most likely to react against social and cultural deprivation with antisocial behaviour. Direct evidence for the link between physique and temperament is, however, conflicting, though it has been found in children as young as the nursery-school age (Walker, 1962).

(D) CHURCH MEMBERSHIP

Delinquents are much less likely to be regular attenders at church (Glueck and Glueck, 1950; Ferguson, 1952). Differences in religious attitude and belief, however, are very much smaller, and in some studies have not been found at all (see Middleton and Fay, 1941; Conger and Miller, 1966). This suggests that it is membership of a non-delinquent group that counts rather than any religious character the group may have (see the discussion of self-report data in chapter 3). It should be added that the apparent reform of most delinquents in their early twenties is not accompanied by any conversion to religion; in fact there is an even greater decline in their involvement with religion (Glueck and Glueck, 1968).

## Types of Delinquent

From now on we shall be concerned only with male delinquents. They form a heterogenous group, and in order to understand this heterogeneity and make treatment programmes more effective, a number of attempts have been made to construct a catalogue of different types of delinquent. These typologies have either been derived more or less deductively from a theory (in particular psychoanalytic theory) or they have been allowed to emerge from the analysis of the characteristics exhibited by the delinquents themselves. I shall only discuss this latter, empirical approach here. It should be emphasized that it is not free from the influence of theoretical presuppositions, since these determine the kind of characteristics selected for study. And when we talk of types in this context we are idealizing and simplifying the facts, since there will always be many delinquents who fall in between types.

Many different criteria, criminological, social, psychiatric and psychological, have been used as the basis of classification. Criminological typologies take the nature of the offence as the classifying principle. For our present purposes this is not a very fruitful approach and no more will be said about it. The most relevant social criterion is that which distinguishes solitary delinquents from gang or group members. Wattenberg and Balistrieri (1950) compared boys in these categories and found that solitary delinquents came from a higher socio-economic level of society, and were more likely to have disturbed family relationships. Randolph, Richardson and Johnson (1961) compared the two groups on a number of tests and found higher intelligence and greater evidence of emotional disturbance among the solitary boys. In a study by Brigham, Ricketts and Johnson (1967) solitary delinquents reported greater neglect by their fathers and a more disturbed relationship with their mothers. These findings suggest that solitary delinquents are more likely to be neurotic.

Another approach is to base the classification on psychiatric criteria. It is impossible to assess the extent of psychiatric disorder in the delinquent population accurately, for not only is some sampling bias invariably present in any study, but the psychiatric criteria vary from one study to another. Thus Healy and Bronner (1936) found that ninety-one per cent of their sample of delinquents felt very unhappy, insecure, inadequate and inferior, whereas Gibbens (1963) using more stringent criteria, classified twenty-seven per cent of his sample as neurotic.

Nevertheless the distinction between neurotic delinquents whose behaviour is symptomatic of inner conflict and inhibition and those who act out their emotional tensions in uninhibited conflict with others is perhaps the most fundamental that can be made. Studies comparing matched groups of neurotic and non-neurotic delinquents reveal clear differences in the family contexts of the boys (e.g. Bennett, 1960; and Asumi, 1963). Neurotic boys tend to come from intact families, with parents who are overstrict and themselves often neurotic. The boys tend to show their disturbed behaviour in the family context by pilfering from the home. The less neurotic delinquent boys had weaker ties with their families.

However, in comparisons of this kind the 'non-neurotic' delinquents form a heterogeneous group. An accumulation of studies using more descriptive and psychological criteria support a grouping of delinquents into three main types. Different investigators use different labels, and the types they describe do not always overlap completely; but there is sufficient consistency in the evidence to demonstrate the usefulness of the typology.* The following are brief thumbnail sketches of these types.

The *neurotic* delinquent is timid, overinhibited, sensitive, lonely and anxious and has strong feelings of inferiority. His delinquent acts tend to take such forms as compulsive and solitary stealing, furtive sadism, and sexual abnormality. At other times he is submissive and apathetic, daydreams a lot and feels guilty about his behaviour. He is unlikely to cause trouble at school, and is apt to be seen by his parents as generally truthful and obedient.

The *unsocialized, aggressive* delinquent is defiant of authority, sullen, malicious and generally hostile to others. He tends to be

* The interested reader might consult the following: Hewitt and Jenkins, (1946); Jenkins (1966; 1968); Jenkins, NurEddie and Shapiro, (1966); Tsubouchi and Jenkins (1969); Quay (1964; 1965; 1966); Quay and Blumen (1963); Ferdinand (1966); and Glueck and Glueck (1965a). For other, empirically based, but less closely allied typologies, see Reiss (1952) and Argyle (1961).

unaffected by punishment or praise, is always blaming others and feeling persecuted, and shows little guilt or remorse. Because he is cruel and revengeful, he is seldom liked by his peers; but since he is also feared and respected he quite often becomes the leader of a gang, and one of its core members (see Gerrard, 1964). His dependence on the gang is not based on friendship but upon the fact that his self-esteem rests upon his aggressive domination of others.

The *pseudosocial* delinquent is a loyal gang member. Though defiant, hostile and suspicious towards those in authority, he is not subject to violent uncontrollable impulses, but adapts well to the other members of his peer group and feels some sense of obligation to them. Because the peer group is his main emotional anchor, he conforms wholeheartedly to the group norms. Bryant, Dobbins and Bass (1963) showed experimentally that delinquents conform more to peer group pressure than nondelinquents, and suggest that this is because for many of them the gang has become a substitute family. For this kind of delinquent, delinquency is an adaptive response.

The home backgrounds of these three types of delinquent also vary in predictable ways. The neurotic delinquent tends to come from a small, middle-class and intact family, where attachments to parents are strong, where the mother is over-protective and over-anxious, where there is some emotional instability in either or both of the parents, and where the parents set austere and uncompromising standards for their children. Sanctions against the child are predominantly psychological, in the sense that they threaten rejection or withdrawal of love. These are the conditions which in psychoanalytic theory are said to lead to strong identification with the parents and the development of a harsh, rigid and irrational superego. When they do not result in neurosis or compulsive delinquency, they produce the highly conscientious and tense character, who leads an impeccably respectable life, but whose own instinctual satisfactions are severely curtailed, and who cannot tolerate 'immorality' in others.

The unsocialized, aggressive delinquent more often comes from a lower-class family in which parent-child relationships are marked by mutual hostility, rejection and distrust, and where the parents are punitive, erratic and unjust. In psychoanalytic terms, there would be very little identification with parents, and the aggression they provoke would not be turned inwards. The consequence is a weak and undeveloped superego.

The main feature of the homes of pseudosocial delinquents is not so much parental rejection and punitiveness as parental neglect, distance and coldness; the boys' relationships with their parents are characterized by mutual indifference. This is particularly true of the father–son relationship. For these boys' fathers are not objects of hostility since they are frequently absent. It has been suggested that they are seeking a male substitute for father in the gang (Miller, 1958) and are in flight from the 'female-based' home. Though they have had little opportunity to identify with authority figures and therefore will have weak internalized controls, they do not display many symptoms of a psychopathological kind (Tsubouchi and Jenkins, 1969).

Such a classification manifestly fails to do justice to the variety of personality found among delinquents. But it does represent some of the key landmarks in any preliminary charting of the domain. An exhaustive catalogue of the different types of delinquent would have to recognize varying levels of neurotic disorder and include such groups as the mentally subnormal, those with brain damage, the grossly immature and inadequate and the psychotic. Nothing will be said about these groups here.

There is one other classificatory term, however, that we cannot ignore, namely the *psychopathic*. There is controversy in the use of this term, not over its basic meaning, but over how widely it should be applied. Unsocialized, aggressive delinquents have sometimes been called psychopathic, and this group certainly includes psychopaths. But to equate the two is to dilute the concept of psychopathy unnecessarily. The true psychopath is not so much *anti*social as *a*social. His central characteristic is a near total incapacity for affection and sympathy for others. Life is lived exclusively in the present, and behaviour is in no way directed by long-term purposes. By the same token, though frequently aggressive, he tends not to be guided by long-term resentments and hatreds. For him to want is to take. If others get in the way it is their misfortune if they get hurt, and the psychopath feels no guilt or remorse. His emotional life is barren; he may experience states of intense excitement but not the highly differentiated emotional states which normal people report. He is egocentric, both in the Piagetian sense of being unable to conceive other points of view than his own, and also in the more general sense of being selfish and self-centred.

The delinquent who is driven into continual, aggressive, antisocial behaviour through a deep-seated sense of injustice and frustration may display such psychopathic traits as callous indifference to others but this does not make him a psychopath in the narrower sense. This trait of emotional indifference to the welfare of others has been observed in many men who, far from being at odds with society, are commonly regarded as social successes, men such as scientists and directors of industry (Cleckley, 1964). Such social success depends upon long-term planning and sustained work, things the true psychopath is incapable of. Severe rejection in childhood, and the absence of conditions which foster attachment to others, are common features of the histories of psychopaths. But they have also frequently been found to suffer from neurological abnormalities, and there is evidence that genetic factors play an important role in predisposing individuals to this condition (see McCord and McCord, 1964). Psychopaths are therefore among the most difficult of all criminal groups to cure. Underneath a glib and easy verbal conformity to moral norms, they are profoundly amoral in character.

## Personality Differences between Delinquents and Non-delinquents

In the previous section we looked at some of the ways in which delinquents differ among themselves. They vary in the extent to which they are neurotically inhibited and anxious, the extent to which they can adapt and conform to peer groups, and the extent to which they are driven by resentment and hostility to others, particularly those in authority. However, many non-delinquents are neurotic, though the incidence of emotional disorder may be lower. Other non-delinquents find their primary sense of belonging in the peer group rather than in the family, but since the peer groups do not have particularly anti-social norms, this attachment does not result in serious delinquency. The more extreme forms of unsocialized aggression are almost certain to result in some form of criminal behaviour, but it is obviously possible to contain general resentment and hostility to others within the law. Though parental neglect and rejection are more frequent in the histories of delinquents they also occur in the histories of non-delinquents. In short, the personality types outlined exist in the non-delinquent population though in smaller proportions and in less extreme forms.

We may now ask whether there are any other personality dimensions which tend to discriminate between delinquents and non-delinquents. Here we face a difficulty. Few studies comparing delinquents with matched non-delinquents have taken account of the different types of delinquent. In fact it seems probable that neurotic delinquents are under-represented in these studies; for the delinquent samples are usually drawn from some correctional institution, and there is a tendency for clearly neurotic delinquents to be treated elsewhere, in schools for the maladjusted or in psychiatric clinics.

## (A) EGO-CONTROL

In the last chapter we saw that cheaters on experimental tests scored low on a group of measures which appear to be indices of some general capacity for controlling impulses in situations which do not raise moral issues. Similar findings have been reported when delinquents are compared with non-delinquents.

*Future time perspective*: Barndt and Johnson (1955) gave subjects a story completion test. The stories written by delinquents had significantly shorter time spans. Other studies have required subjects to write down a list of events which may happen to them, or a list of things they may do, in the future. Non-delinquents have been found to look further ahead in time (Siegman, 1961 and 1966a; Stein, Sarbin and Kulik, 1968).

*Motor control in simple tasks*: Some time ago Porteus developed a maze test of intelligence in which subjects have to trace their way through mazes as quickly as possible. This test also yields a qualitative score, itself largely unrelated to intelligence, which is based on the frequency with which subjects cut corners, take their pencils off the page, and break the rules in other ways. A low qualitative score implies concentration and self-control, a high score carelessness and impatience. Repeatedly delinquents have been found to score higher on this qualitative measure than non-delinquents (see Gibbens, 1963, for a summary). Among delinquents themselves those classified as psychopathic gain the highest score of all (Schalling and Rosen, 1968).

*Preference for immediate reward*: Mischel (1961) reported that delinquents were more likely to choose a small candy at once rather than a large one later. Roberts and Erikson (1968) compared delinquents who were relatively conforming to institutional rules with those who rebelled and were antisocial. At the time all boys were forbidden to smoke. Both groups were equally heavy smokers. The antisocial delinquents were much more likely to choose one cigarette at once rather than a packet later. These subjects also made more errors on the Porteus maze test.

The observations of numerous students of delinquency confirm these experimental results. Delinquents do not think ahead much, are not so deterred by the possibly unpleasant consequences of their actions and more often act on impulse.

(B) PERSONALITY TESTS

Studies using standard personality tests have usually found that delinquents emerge as discriminably different (e.g. Glueck and Glueck, 1950; Hathaway and Monachesi, 1953; and Conger and Miller, 1966). They show less restraint and seriousness, less emotional stability and friendliness, are more impulsive, more subject to fluctuations of mood and more excitable, and are more socially assertive and adventurous.

## (C) SELF-CONCEPT

A group of studies * have dealt with the way in which delinquents and non-delinquents think about themselves. All the subjects came from an area where the delinquency rates were very high. They were given a test of their self-concepts at the age of twelve years, before any of them had been officially classified as delinquent, and again four years later after many of them had been. Those who at the later age had not become delinquent, presented a much more favourable picture of themselves at the earlier testing. Among other things they felt fairly sure they would not become delinquent, and thought of themselves as being on the side of law and order, in short, as 'good' boys. The investigators tentatively suggest that a self-image which excludes the 'self as delinquent' may act as an insulator against becoming one.

## (D) EXTROVERSION–INTROVERSION

The application of Eysenck's personality theory to behavioural inhibition was discussed briefly in the last chapter. It does not *necessarily* follow from this theory that delinquents will be extroverts. It is likely that the neurotic delinquents we have described include many who are by nature introverted. It is not surprising therefore that studies comparing delinquents and non-delinquents yield no clear-cut difference between them (see Fitch, 1962; and Little, 1963). But from the description I have given, it is clear that unsocialized, aggressive and psychopathic delinquents will be both extroverted and very neurotic, and there is evidence (quoted by Eysenck, 1964) to support this.

A fundamental aspect of the theory is that punishment is less effective as a means of eradicating wrong behaviour in extroverts. It has been found that in a simple learning task in which wrong responses were punished by electric shock, psychopaths learned little, if at all, compared to normal subjects (Lykken, 1957;

* See Reckless, Dinitz and Murray (1965); Reckless, Dinitz and Kay (1957); Scarpitti, Murray, Dinitz and Reckless (1960); and Lively, Dinitz and Reckless (1962).

Schachter and Latané, 1964). It is not so clear from the theory whether psychopaths are expected to learn less well under positive reinforcement, or reward. Jawanda (1966, reported in Eysenck, 1968) found that among normal subjects those who were relatively neurotic and extroverted learned less well when praised than did those low on these dimensions. Attempts to show that psychopaths learn less well in the same kind of task have yielded equivocal results.*

## Discipline in the Home

There is abundant evidence that the homes of delinquents are less cohesive than those of non-delinquents, more often characterized by mutual rejection or indifference between parent and child, and are more often broken, and that delinquents are more exposed to the social influence of other delinquents both within the family and outside it, so that I need say no more about it here. So far, however, I have not specifically mentioned the question of discipline.

Here is a brief summary of the results of three studies on the home life of delinquents. They are typical of the work done, but have been selected because they are especially thorough, and each used a distinctive design.

First, Glueck and Glueck (1950): the home backgrounds of 500 delinquents and 500 matched non-delinquents were studied by interviewing parents and other relatives. The discipline given to delinquents was predominantly lax and erratic on the part of the mother, and either overstrict or lax and erratic on the part of the father. Both parents used a great deal of physical punishment and little reasoning and praise. The parents of non-delinquents, on the other hand, were firm, kindly and consistent, reasoned much more, and much less frequently used physical punishment.

Secondly, McCord, McCord and Zola (1957): in this study

* See Johns and Quay (1962); Quay and Hunt (1965); Bernard and Eisenman (1967); and Bryan and Kapche (1967).

the home backgrounds of 253 boys aged ten all of whom were expected to become delinquent, were investigated. A follow-up of these boys made it possible to compare the homes of those who subsequently became delinquent with the homes of those who did not. Again lax and erratic discipline which also involved extreme punitiveness and inconsistent demands was strongly associated with criminal behaviour.

Thirdly, Bandura and Walters (1959): these authors intensively studied twenty-six boys with histories of antisocial aggression, most of whom were in the care of probation officers, with a matched control group of normal boys who were neither particularly aggressive nor particularly withdrawn. The mothers of aggressive boys were less effective at socializing their children and their sons were more attached to them than to their fathers. Both parents, but especially the father, tended to encourage aggression outside the home but to repress it with punishment at home. They too made greater use of physical punishment and such verbal assaults as ridicule and nagging, and they reasoned less with their sons. It is interesting to note that the fathers of aggressive boys were much more permissive of heterosexual activity in their sons, that the boys engaged in it more, and that for them sexual behaviour tended to be emotionally uninvolved or fused with aggression, in contrast to the unaggressive boys who associated sex with tender feelings.

Three points deserve comment. The first is the association between delinquency and the high use of physical punishment by parents. There is good evidence that physical punishment by the parents and aggression in boys (especially outside the home) tend to go together (Becker, 1964). Of course it is an open question which is cause, which effect, though probably each is both a cause and an effect of the other; but we can safely conclude that physical punishment, particularly in the context of weak affection, does not reduce a child's general level of aggression. And it is not difficult to see why. Not only does physical assault provoke retaliatory aggression, but also the father is the child's chief model of how adults behave, and when he assaults his son, he is providing an excellent example of the very behaviour he is blaming the child for. The child is bound to become confused as a result. Considered in isolation from its context, there is no evidence that physical punishment is an effective way of bringing about permanent changes for the better in children. For example Palmer (1965) interviewed boys in a secondary school twice, with an interval of two years in between, on their smoking habits. Since boys were caned at the school for smoking, he was able to form two groups of boys, equated for amount of smoking at the earlier age, one of which had been caned for smoking in the intervening two years. At the second interview those who had been caned for smoking reported an increase in the number of cigarettes they smoked daily; those who had not been caned because they had not been found out reported smoking less.*

But it is misleading to consider a single socializing technique outside its context. There are no grounds for thinking that the common practice of occasional smacking,† within the context of a normally cohesive family, does any harm, and it may sometimes be beneficial if only to relieve the parent's feelings.

The second point is that although the mother may be the primary socializing agent, and though it may be meaningless to ask which parent is the more decisive for the child, there are clear signs that the father's role is much more important than was once thought. This comes out in the studies we have described.

---

*It is interesting to note that in a series of studies of reaction to stress, Funkenstein, King and Drolette (1957) found that the physiological pattern of response associated with an anger-out reaction was markedly different from that associated with anxiety or anger-in. It would seem that physical punishment is of all sanctions most likely to provoke the anger-out reaction and this is incompatible with the anxiety which results in behavioural inhibition or self-control. We should therefore expect it to be a less effective sanction. But of course it is not the nature of the punishment alone which determines the nature of the reaction, but also the ongoing parent-child relationship. Funkenstein *et al.* examined the home backgrounds of subjects who habitually responded to stress with anxiety and concluded that 'When authority and affection were perceived in the same parent, the acute emergency reaction was most frequently severe anxiety.'

†Newson and Newson (1968) interviewed a large, representative sample of mothers in an industrial city and found that eighty three per cent 'believe in smacking'.

In addition, Siegman (1966b) found that the absence of a father in childhood was strongly related to antisocial behaviour among university students, and Andry (1960) reported that disturbed relationships between father and son were a more salient feature of delinquent homes than disturbed mother–son relationships. Bacon, Child and Barry (1963) conducted a cross-cultural survey which disclosed that societies where children had least contact with their fathers also had the highest incidence of juvenile theft.

Thirdly, there is the highly inconsistent quality of the discipline in delinquent homes. Not only will the delinquent be confused over what is right and wrong, but he will be angered by injustice and he will learn that whether or not he is rewarded or punished is not predictably related to his own behaviour. This last point is of great importance. In a home where parents are consistent, the child learns that his own behaviour to a large extent determines how others respond to him and this is a crucial element in his general feeling that he can exercise some control over how others behave towards him. If, on the other hand, the child learns to dissociate his own behaviour from the rewards and punishments that come from others, he will feel that bit more powerless to influence his social environment. This in turn will contribute to that general alienation from society which sociologists have noted to be a feature of delinquents (see Taylor, 1968). Many students of delinquency have observed the prevalence of fatalistic attitudes among delinquents. To them it seems that the only way they can elicit a predictable response in others is through provoking their angry indignation by acts of theft and vandalism.

It is time now to consider the bearing of all this upon the nature of moral restraint. Those officially classified as delinquent differ from non-delinquents in the frequency and seriousness of the offences they have committed. This difference is not absolute but a general statistical trend, since some non-delinquents are more guilty than some delinquents. The measure is therefore a crude one. Nevertheless it has some validity as an index of resistance to temptation, and the material reviewed above has this great advantage, that it introduces us to a much greater range of individual difference than we encountered in the previous chapter. Some of the conclusions that emerged in the last chapter receive added confirmation. Antisocial acts of an illegal kind are clearly associated with lack of control in other moral and social contexts and in tasks which have no direct moral or social significance (the ego-control variables). The importance of general motivational conditions, which are not specific to the actual situation in which wrong-doing occurs, is strongly brought out. So likewise is the importance of current group loyalties as determinants of moral behaviour.

But the wider range of individual difference sampled in delinquency studies enables certain other factors associated with moral behaviour to come into view. The importance of attachment to parents is made plain. Those least capable of moral restraint are also those with the weakest attachments. Then we are forced to acknowledge the existence of constitutional and temperamental differences in susceptibility to moral training, and behind these the silent and ubiquitous influence of genetic differences. Whether for temperamental or socio-cultural reasons, the things girls do wrong tend to be different from the offences committed by boys. And the kind of discipline used in the home cannot be ignored. Whether we consider disciplinary techniques on their own, or as symptoms of a particular kind of relationship between parent and child, they make their own specific contribution to the shaping of attitudes and motives in the child.

But perhaps the most striking lesson to be learned from the study of delinquents is that in some cases wrong-doing may result from the child being too inhibited and controlled. Some children become delinquent because they have been subjected to excessively severe parental control and are already especially sensitive to such pressures. The idea that we should make children as moral as possible is a dangerous one; paradoxically, wrong-doing may stem from the effects of too strong a 'conscience'.*

* A full and very readable account of the emotional difficulties underlying behavioural problems in nondelinquent children will be found in Herbert (in press).

CHAPTER 5

# Reactions to Transgression

Temptation conflicts can be resolved by yielding or resisting. Either way the incident is not closed, for both resolutions have their psychological repercussions. The consequences of resisting are not our present concern. But it is worth noting their importance and variety. The immediate feelings may be self-congratulatory or simple relief at a narrow escape. If others know about it, their approval may enhance self-esteem and strengthen the individual's capacity to resist on later occasions. If on the other hand resisting involves the renunciation of some pleasurable satisfaction, it may well be followed by regret and even depression. Despite their great interest, little attention has been paid by psychologists to the personality hazards of virtuous living. But we are all familiar with the self-righteous person whose sympathy and understanding for wrong-doers has largely atrophied, and who finds it intolerable that others should transgress and get away with it. The conditions under which strong temptation can be resisted without leaving a residue of hostility towards, or envy of, those who yield are still unexplored.

In contrast, the psychological effects of infringing a moral injunction have received a great deal of attention, both clinically and experimentally. There are first the cognitive consequences. If I have transgressed I am left with the knowledge that I have done something wrong. If I habitually think of myself as a moral person, this will induce 'cognitive dissonance' or a kind of contradiction in my thinking that must be resolved. It is as if I find myself faced with three propositions: 'I am a good person'; 'It is wrong to do X'; 'I have done X'.* Something must give. I may simply revise my estimate of my own virtue. But if I am reluctant to do this, I may instead argue to myself that through wrong in general the act was excusable in this instance, or that the people who suffered on my account deserved to suffer; or I may even try to forget the fact that I did it.

But merely taking thought may not be enough. Persistent feelings of remorse are not so readily dispelled or glossed over, especially if the offending act is a serious one. I may then punish myself by highly self-critical and self-blaming thoughts, as if dissociating myself from the 'me' who transgressed, or by seeing to it that I suffer in some other way. Various more positive steps are open to me, such as apology, confession, trying to put things right, and making reparation in some form. These moves can be conceived less as attempts at achieving cognitive consistency than as efforts to restore emotional equilibrium.

Defining this emotional disturbance or disequilibrium is not easy. A distinction commonly made is that between guilt, or those unpleasant emotions that are intrinsic to the knowledge of transgression, and fear or anxiety about the social consequences of being found out. Conceptually this is a meaningful distinction; its practical application is more problematic. For though all the responses mentioned above have been taken as expressions of guilt, it is plain that many of them, such as confession and reparation, can be interpreted as techniques of forestalling or ameliorating the disapprobation of others. And this can also be said of self-criticism when this is voiced in the presence of others. However, even if it is difficult to find an unambiguous outward sign of guilt, its reality is seldom disputed; for presumably most people, including most psychologists, have experienced the kinds of feeling to which the term refers.

---

*The point is not whether there is a contradiction in the strictly logical sense, but whether the attitudes and feelings which might be expressed in these propositions are in conflict.

## The Nature of Guilt

The central point about guilt is that it is not an anxiety about some future event, but a disagreeable emotional condition which directly follows transgression, which persists until some kind of equilibrium is restored by reparation or confession and forgiveness, and which is independent of whether others know of the transgression. It is therefore often described as self-hate or self-rejection. Psychiatrists report that pathological guilt, that is, intense guilt that does not appear to be justified by actual transgression and that is not readily alleviated, plays an important role in certain neurotic conditions, especially compulsive-obsessional neurosis.

It is not surprising that there is some divergence of opinion over how guilt should be analysed. According to psychoanalytic theory it is the sign that the ego, by identifying with and acting out an id impulse, has incurred the wrath of the superego and is now itself the victim of these aggressive energies that are channelled inwards through that structure. Since the superego is primarily the inner representative of the parents, this inward drama parallels the experiences the individual underwent when as a child he disobeyed them. Once again the ego endures a sense of rejection and loss of love, and can only appease the superego by suitable evidence of contrition and penitence. If the superego is particularly harsh and relentless, the task of appeasement may be very exacting. Once parental authorities are internalized, they can no longer be escaped. Put more prosaically, transgression disturbs the delicate equilibrium between the ego and superego structures, and the various phenomena of guilt are compensatory processes whose function is to restore equilibrium. It should be added that according to Freud, guilt can be unconscious, though what precisely this means is not clear.

Instead of conceiving guilt as a kind of civil war within the personality, learning theorists take a more simple view. It is just anxiety which, through training procedures in the past, has become conditioned to the thought 'I have done something wrong'.* The various types of post-transgressional behaviour are then seen as learned techniques for reducing this anxiety. This is an obviously plausible interpretation of such responses as confession and reparation. It is less obviously plausible for self-critical and punishment-seeking behaviour, for these mean undergoing yet more anxiety. However, Unger (1964) has presented an analysis of self-punitive behaviour in learning-theory terms, which is consistent with the experimental evidence. The bare outline of his account is as follows. The young child transgresses, and after a short time is punished in some way. As a consequence, the knowledge that he has transgressed becomes a signal evoking the anticipatory anxiety that unpleasant things are to follow. There are then two sources of anxiety at work, the knowledge of wrong-doing and the sanctions themselves. But the latter are *terminal* anxiety stimuli, for their effect is limited and they bring to an end the anticipatory anxiety. That an unpleasant stimulus can serve paradoxically to reduce anxiety has been clearly demonstrated with animals. If an animal has been trained to expect an electric shock a short time after a signal, it displays considerable distress during the interval and clear relief after the shock has come. Anxiety conditioning is remarkably persistent, and if the child's experience has been such that the reduction of this anticipatory anxiety has been consistently

* Davitz (1969) has provided evidence which suggests that this analysis is close to ordinary usage of the terms *guilt* and *anxiety*. He first collected from interview material and written reports thousands of brief statements which described some aspect of an emotional experience. By careful pruning and combining, this collection was reduced to 556 items. Subjects were then given a list of labels for various emotions and asked to choose from the 556 items those that were most appropriate for each emotion. For the emotions of anxiety and fear, the items chosen were closely similar, and the most frequent referred to physical sensations only ('I am wound up inside', 'my whole body is tense'). For the emotions of guilt and shame the emphasis was upon thought rather than physical sensation ('I get mad at myself', 'I keep blaming myself') though basically the same physical sensations were also mentioned. We may tentatively infer from this that in ordinary usage, anxiety and fear are subjectively indistinguishable and are primarily thought of as physical sensations, and that shame and guilt are the same kind of sensation but associated with a specific kind of thought.

associated with punishment of some kind, then it is to be expected that later he will seek punishment to reduce it. If, as presumably often happens, the parents' sanctions consist mainly of strong verbal criticism, then however unpleasant it is in itself, this criticism will become associated with subsequent relief from anxiety. The child can then apply the same verbal evaluations to his own behaviour and thereby gain relief from his anxiety.

In practice these self-punitive responses are apt to be strengthened in another way. For as the child begins to engage in such behaviour, he is likely to discover that it reduces the severity of parental sanctions, or may avert them altogether, which further reinforces the power of self-punitive behaviour to reduce anxiety.

Once again, choosing between these two theoretical alternatives depends largely upon our interests. Those concerned with the clinical and phenomenological aspects of guilt, together with their philosophical and theological implications, have generally been attracted by psychoanalytic formulations (see, for example, Stein, 1969). The learning-theory approach seems too simple and partial an explanation for so complex a human phenomenon. But if our business is the empirical and experimental study of post-transgressional response, then the simplicity of learning theory, together with its experimental backing, is its great asset.

This is a convenient point to discuss a topic intimately linked with guilt but much more neglected by psychologists, namely *blame*. By blaming I mean here a reflex response of aggressive condemnation of others when they infringe the moral code in some way. It is the same kind of intolerance which when directed towards ourselves we call guilt. It is to be distinguished therefore from the simple recognition and disapproval of another's offence, from the reactive anger which follows when we are the victims of another's misdeeds, and from the empathic anger on behalf of other victims. In the sense in which blame is used here, it implies some kind of personal involvement in the fact that someone else has done wrong which is distinct from our reaction to the effects of the transgression. And the most plausible link between ourselves and the offender which brings about this personal involvement is that we too want to commit the offence but restrain ourselves.*

In psychoanalysis blame is the displacement on to others of the aggression which is normally directed towards the self through the superego. It is an alternative to guilt, or a relief from it. But if the aggression can be displaced in this way it is not fully internalized. Anna Freud (1937) argues that blaming is a defence mechanism the use of which implies that the individual's superego is not yet mature. As she says, 'the superego's intolerance of other people is prior to its severity towards itself. ... Vehement indignation at someone else's wrongdoing is the precursor of or substitute for guilty feeling on its own account.' From the moment that aggression is fully internalized 'the severity of the superego is turned inwards instead of outwards and the subject becomes less intolerant of other people'.

Presumably blame, in this limited sense, is evidence of moral immaturity since it implies that the individual's own forbidden desires are strongly aroused by seeing others act theirs out. It is worth recalling in this respect how moralistically intolerant young children can be of their naughty peers, and that at the other extreme the most morally impressive men are markedly disinclined to upbraid and reprove others for their moral lapses.

It would be too much of a digression to pursue these issues further here: We shall return to them again in chapter 8 in a somewhat different context. Our concern now is with the empirical study of guilt. I shall first outline the methods most commonly used in such research, and then review the main findings that have so far emerged.


## The Measurement of Post-Transgressional Response

If people differ in the intensity of their guilt or fear of censure and in the ways in which they cope with these feelings, then it

---

* We are of course using the term 'blame' in a narrow sense. But it is this aspect of blame which is the most psychologically interesting. See Fingarrette (1963) for a stimulating analysis.

should be possible to construct measures of these differences. Several techniques have been used, and each raises its own problems.

## (A) SELF-REPORT

The simplest thing to do is to ask people how much guilt they feel after misbehaviour. Examples of questionnaires and interviews developed for this purpose will be found in Mosher (1966; 1968) and Stephenson (1966). What is measured in this way is a general disposition to feel guilt rather than the guilt provoked by a particular action. Experimental psychologists are sometimes disdainful of measures of this kind; but when the results of using them fit expectations based on other evidence (for example, Stephenson found that psychopaths reported much less guilt than normal subjects), then we can have some confidence in their value.

## (B) PROJECTIVE MEASURES

The basic idea behind projective tests is that the less an individual is constrained by his immediate situation the more his behaviour will express his attitudes and feelings or the kind of person he is. In measuring guilt responses a favoured method has been to give subjects an incomplete story in which the hero, who is in important ways like the subject, has just transgressed. The subject is then asked as an exercise in imagination to complete the story. Normally other incomplete stories without moral implications are given at the same time in order to allay any suspicion in the subject that it is his moral responses that are being measured. The presumption is that the subject will identify with the hero and attribute to him the kind of behaviour that he himself would engage in if placed in a comparable position. The stories are then scored for the presence of post-transgressional responses such as confession or reparation. We can hardly deny that measures of this kind are tapping some aspect of moral attitude and feeling, and it is not unreasonable to suppose that they bear some relationship to actual behaviour. It seems unlikely that a subject habitually free from guilt would tell stories of others who are burdened with it, or that a subject who is burdened with it would make his hero guilt-free. But we do not know how close the relationship to behaviour is. Subjects may make their hero conform to the way they think people ought to behave, or the way they think others would expect him to behave, or the way they observe their friends to behave. We are therefore left with a tantalizing uncertainty in interpreting the measure, and any conclusions drawn from its use must be reckoned highly tentative unless supported by evidence derived from other techniques.

### (C) DIRECT OBSERVATION

Patently the best way of finding out how people react to their own misdeeds is to observe them after they have transgressed. To do this effectively, the conditions under which the misdeed occurs must be controlled. As we shall see a number of studies have done this. Two types of measure have been taken: signs of emotional disturbance and actual behaviour.

### (D) THE JUDGEMENTS OF OTHERS

People closely associated with each other end up by knowing a lot about each other. This is especially true of mothers of young children, for their constant supervision means that little of their child's behaviour escapes their notice. Several investigators have used material from interviews with mothers to assess the child's moral behaviour (e.g. Sears, Maccoby and Levin, 1957). What is usually obtained is a global measure of 'conscience strength'; but since the questions asked emphasize the child's behaviour after transgression they will be treated here as measures of guilt. Once again problems of interpretation arise. On the one hand mothers are bound to be biased, on the other they know more about their children than anyone else.

## The Design of Studies

Two basically different designs have been used in research into post-transgressional response. They will both be briefly outlined.

The first might be called the 'true experimental design'. If we want to demonstrate that transgression has an effect on subsequent behaviour then we must control the occurrence of transgression. To show that it is the transgression itself that affects later behaviour we must be sure that subjects differ only in the fact that some have transgressed and some have not; in short, the experimenter must decide who is to transgress. The usual procedure is to allocate the subjects randomly to at least two groups so that there are only chance differences between them. Then everything else is held constant for the two groups except that in one of them subjects are somehow induced to transgress. A favourite method is to pair each subject with a confederate of the experimenter who persuades him to infringe some rule or do something he disapproves of. The behaviour of the two groups is then compared afterwards in a standard situation to see if the transgressors behave differently. The weakness of this design is that only minor forms of transgression can be used in this way; though for that reason it is perhaps more convincing when effects are demonstrated.

The second design is correlational, and its purpose is to explore the factors associated with individual differences in guilt responses. Subjects are given a measure of guilt and their performance correlated with other variables. These may be parental discipline, or sex difference, or personality difference, or behaviour in a temptation situation. Though studies using this design may suggest a causal influence they cannot demonstrate it.

## The Effects of Transgression

We shall begin by considering the attempts made to demonstrate that transgression has effects on later behaviour. In other words, we shall focus in the main on studies using what I have called the true experimental design and ignore for the moment individual differences.

## (A) COGNITIVE DISSONANCE

It was said earlier that an immediate consequence of infringing a moral injunction may be a cognitive inconsistency which has to be resolved. Mills (1958) examined how yielding to or resisting temptation is related to changes in the way the transgression is evaluated. He first gave all subjects a measure of how wrong they thought cheating to be. Then they were tempted to cheat on a task, either with a strong incentive or a weak one, and a little later again measured for their attitude towards cheating. Subjects who cheated took a more lenient view of the offence on the second occasion, whereas those who resisted, especially when the incentive was high, became more severe in their assessment of cheating. The design of this experiment does not strictly allow us to conclude that the transgression alone produced the change in evaluation, for it could be that those who cheat are less committed to their evaluation of cheating in the first place. But it does provide an example in the moral field of the general tendency for people to reduce inconsistency between belief and behaviour after they have acted.

Several experimenters have used a situation in which, as part of their experimental task, subjects are required to give others electric shocks when they themselves think it wrong to use shocks in experiments. One consequence of inflicting harm on others in this way is that subjects are more ready to do the victim a favour afterwards (Carlsmith and Gross, 1969). If they cannot, they tend to minimize the painfulness of the shocks, especially if they have been offered the opportunity to opt out of the experiment yet have decided to go on, thereby taking more responsibility for their own actions (Brock and Buss, 1962). They also report greater guilt feeling afterwards, particularly if the shock they have administered is relatively severe (Brock and Buss, 1964). Another response that has been found is for subjects to derogate their victim (Lerner and Matthews, 1967). This depreciation of the victim is most likely to occur when the subject cannot compensate him in any way, and when the victim is powerless to retaliate (Berscheid, Boye and Walster, 1968). It seems then that faced with having hurt another, and unable to do anything about it, there is a tendency for people to resolve the conflict by thinking less well of the victim as if in some sense he deserved it. If the victim can retaliate, so that a sort of equity is restored, there is no need to devalue him.

Glass (1964) found that subjects who had been encouraged beforehand to think well of themselves were markedly unfriendly to the victim when they felt themselves in some measure responsible for giving him shocks. Thus the truth of the familiar observation that we tend to dislike the people we have harmed is demonstrated in the laboratory, albeit in an attenuated form.

## (B) REPARATION

One of the consequences of transgression is said to be the desire to make amends. Darlington and Macker (1966) induced a sense of guilt in subjects by making them fail in a task with the result that someone else suffered. They were then requested to donate blood, and were much more likely to comply than control subjects who were not made to feel guilty. Freedman, Wallington and Bless (1967) in a series of experiments induced subjects to lie or to cause others unnecessary trouble, and found them more ready afterwards to do people favours. Interestingly, however, if the favours involved being with the person harmed they were less ready to help.

These experiments suggest that transgression produces both a desire to balance the offence with a good deed, and the desire to avoid the person harmed. That well-known sign of a 'guilty conscience', a refusal to look others in the eye, has been demonstrated by Exline et al. (1961). He found that subjects were much less likely to look the experimenter in the eye after they had been induced to cheat than before.

In a complicated but interesting experiment (Berscheid and Walster, 1967) subjects were given the opportunity of making one act of compensation to the victims they had harmed. The amount of compensation they could give varied, however. Some subjects could give adequate compensation, others could only overcompensate, and others undercompensate. The results indicated that those who could make adequate compensation were much more likely to take advantage of the opportunity and compensate the victim. It seems that if the only resources of compensation available to people are excessive or inadequate, they prefer not to compensate at all.

## (C) SELF-PUNISHMENT

The examples of altruistic behaviour quoted in the last section could be construed as self-punitive since they involved self-sacrifice. But the actions which preceded them were socially visible, and an equally plausible interpretation is that they were forms of social appeasement.

Wallace and Sadalla (1966) tried to separate the true guilt motive from the motive to appease others. Their experiment is worth describing in a little detail. The subjects were divided into three groups at random, one of them a control group. The other two groups were induced by a confederate of the experimenter to play with an expensive piece of machinery that they had been forbidden to touch, and which apparently broke down as a result of their meddling. For one group the experimenter noted the damage but acted as if he assumed that it had nothing to do with the subjects. They could therefore take it that they had escaped detection. The other group were 'found out'. At the end of the experiment, they were all shown a list of other experiments for which subjects were needed, and asked to volunteer. The experimenter particularly drew their attention to one of these, an experiment in which the subjects would have to undergo severe electric shocks. The question was whether the transgressors would volunteer for the painful experiment more often than the control subjects. Hardly any of the control subjects volunteered. Slightly more of the 'undetected' transgressors did, but the difference was not reliably greater than would be expected by chance. However, significantly more of the 'found out' transgressors did. In other words, within this experimental situation, transgression did not lead to self-punishing behaviour unless it had been socially recognized.

In the present state of research we must avoid attaching too much weight to these findings. But none of the experiments mentioned so far has demonstrated unequivocally that a need for self-punishment follows transgression (which does not mean that this motive is not at work). Instead they have shown that transgression generates a need for cognitive readjustment, a desire to balance misdemeanours with positive and constructive behaviour, and a wish to avoid the person harmed. The first two suggest that processes restoring equilibrium or homeostatic processes are at work.* We may presume that the third becomes important when the individual is unable to restore a satisfactory equilibrium with the victim.

## The Generality of Guilt

We turn now to studies concerned with individual differences that have used the correlational design. The first question to be asked is whether people who show guilt responses after one kind of transgression are more likely to do so after others.

Data based upon self-report indices suggest that people differ in their general proneness to guilt. Those who say they feel guilty about one kind of transgression are more likely to say they do about others (Bandura and Walters, 1959; Black and London, 1966; and Mosher, 1966; 1968). But at the same time there is a tendency for guilt over various kinds of aggressive behaviour to be more closely associated with each other than any of them are with, for example, forms of sexual behaviour; and vice versa.

Story-completion tests can be scored in two ways. Either we

---

*Homans (1961) has developed a theory of social exchange which is clearly relevant here. We cannot go into it in detail though it will be mentioned again in chapter 6. But briefly his view is that the continuance of social intercourse depends upon the parties involved feeling that they are getting roughly equal profit from it (the principle of 'distributive justice'.) If the distribution of profit is very one-sided, the relationship will tend to be broken off. Hence if one person feels he is getting too much he will take steps to increase the other's profit in order to preserve the relationship (see also Stephenson and White, 1968).

can treat all responses that might conceivably indicate guilt (such as confession, restitution and self-blame) as equivalent and thereby extract a kind of total guilt score, or we can consider each type of response separately. If we do the former, it seems clear that some people are more generally prone to guilt than others. If we do the latter, there is a high degree of individuality in the kinds of response that people favour. Some confess, others blame themselves and so on. It should be added that self-blaming responses are among the least common (Aronfreed, 1961).

There is very little evidence from direct observation bearing on this question, and what there is is based only on the study of very young children. Sears, Rau and Alpert (1966) derived three different measures of guilt from observing how children behaved after transgression, namely emotional upset, confession (which included elements of self-blame) and what the authors call fixing. This last included such things as trying to put matters right and trying to cover up the damage done. The children were scored in this way after two kinds of transgression. Those who were upset or who confessed on one occasion did not necessarily show the same response on the other, though there was a tendency for those who went in for fixing behaviour on one test to do so on the other. When the three measures of post-transgressional response are related to each other, there is a small tendency for emotional upset and confession to be positively related, and for fixing to be negatively related to both.

While bearing in mind that this last experiment is based on a small sample of young children, it is possible to draw a tentative conclusion. People who show concern about their transgression in one situation will do so in others; but the way this concern is expressed will vary both between people and between situations. This may seem a very cautious conclusion in the light of everyday and clinical experience, but it is all that the data allow.

## Resistance to Temptation and Guilt

We have so far looked at the effects produced by transgression and ignored individual differences in moral restraint, since in the studies mentioned the experimenter decided who would transgress. Now we ask a rather different question, namely whether differences in moral restraint are associated with differences in guilt proneness. Though guilt is defined as a consequence of transgression, anticipated guilt is one of the motives for resisting temptation. We might therefore expect that those who are most prone to guilt would be least likely to transgress. According to psychoanalytic theory, the association between guilt and resistance should be a close one, for both are functions of the same superego. In learning theory the expectations are less clear-cut, for whether moral restraint or guilt is the outcome of moral training depends upon the timing of punishment and the amount and nature of the verbal explanation that goes with it. Nevertheless even with learning theory some association between the two might be expected since the usual disciplinary practices of parents would be likely to produce both.

Moderate confirmation comes from several sources. Those who resist temptation report stronger guilt feeling (MacKinnon, 1938) and exhibit more guilt responses in story completion tests (Unger, 1962a; Grinder and McMichael, 1963). Girls who resist are more likely to make their heroine confess on the story completion measure (Rebelsky, Allinsmith and Grinder, 1963). It has also been found that mothers' reports of their children's guilt at the age of five are related to resistance at the age of twelve. To this we must add the frequent observation that unsocialized, aggressive and pseudosocial delinquents (especially if they are psychopathic) are notably lacking in guilt responses.

Other studies, however, have failed to find any relationship between the two, using similar measures of guilt.* In the Sears

*e.g. Burton, Maccoby and Allinsmith (1961); McMichael and Grinder (1964); Silverman (1967); Johnson, Ackerman and Frank (1968); Graham (1968); and Johnson and Kalafat (1969).

study virtually all the children succumbed to temptation eventually and the measure of resistance was based on the length of time for which they resisted and the extent to which they transgressed. There was a small tendency for boys (but not girls) who resisted longer to show more emotional upset and confession when they finally yielded, but the association was not greater than might be expected by chance. Fixing, on the other hand, was a popular response among those who yielded quickly. The authors interpret this last finding as evidence that when children learn that reparation averts punishment it makes them more ready to risk yielding to temptation.

We can dispute the meaning of the guilt measures used in these studies but we can hardly deny the general drift of the results, namely that there is no *necessary* connection between moral restraint and proneness to guilt. We are as likely to meet people with high guilt and low resistance or low guilt and high resistance as we are to meet people with high guilt and high resistance or low guilt and low resistance. Though this does not strictly compel us to reject the idea that both are functions of the same personality structure (conscience or superego), we do not need to postulate such a structure, and it is more plausible to suppose that the origins of the two are relatively independent.

## Other Correlates of Guilt

### (A) INTELLIGENCE

There is little evidence bearing on the relationship between intelligence and guilt, but what there is suggests that, unlike the results for resistance to temptation, there is no association between them (Allinsmith, 1960; Aronfreed, 1961; Hoffman and Saltzstein, 1967; and Graham, 1968).

### (B) SEX DIFFERENCE

Most of the evidence based on self-report, story completion, mother's report, and observed emotional upset, reveals a greater tendency to guilt in girls, though it is usually slight* and not everyone has found it (e.g. Graham, 1968; Cocking, 1969). A closer examination of the data reveals that this impression of greater guilt in girls is partly due to their greater fondness for confessing after having done something wrong. Confession can be motivated by the desire to punish the self through shame and retribution. But it may also be due to other motives such as the desire to restore relationships and get close to others again, or the wish to forestall punishment and to conform to what others expect. The fact that girls value close personal relationships more than boys (they have been called the 'social-emotional specialists') suggests that it may be social rather than self-punitive motives that result in this difference between the sexes.

(c) AGE

The evidence on age changes in guilt response is very fragmentary, and is based only on story-completion tests. The main findings are that young children complete these stories with accounts of punishment coming from external sources, whereas confession and self-criticism are more typical of older children, particularly adolescents (see Kohlberg, 1964, and Graham, 1968). The hint implicit in this is that as they grow older children take increasing responsibility for how they behave after transgression. It also, in Kohlberg's words, 'poses something of a problem for moral theories which trace guilt to early experiences of punishment'. But since the evidence is slight we must be careful not to place too much weight upon it.

(d) PHYSIQUE AND TEMPERAMENT

If moral inhibition and guilt responses arise from anxiety conditioning, then temperamental differences in the capacity for such conditioning should be related to the latter as much as to the former. There is little direct evidence, but the general picture of the introvert stresses his proneness to guilt. In addition,

*e.g. London, Schulman and Black (1964); McMichael and Grinder (1966); Porteus and Johnson (1965); Kempel and Signori (1964); Rebelsky, Allinsmith and Grinder (1963); Sears, Maccoby and Levin (1957); Sears, Rau and Alpert (1966); Biaggio (1969); and Peretti (1969).

high guilt feeling has been found to be associated with the linear or ectomorphic type of physique (Parnell, 1958).

## The Origins of Guilt

One of the great advantages of learning theory is that it can be directly tested. Several experiments have simulated a typical guilt-producing situation in attenuated form in the laboratory and applied the principles of learning theory to see if they work.* The usual procedure is to introduce the child to a game in which a certain action is defined as wrong. The child is punished in a mild way when he does it. It is then possible to vary the timing of punishment and the amount of verbal evaluation of the 'misdeed' by the adult, and, if need be, introduce a reward for a particular guilt response. And at least within the limitations of the laboratory setting the theory does work. Children can be trained to be self-critical or to put things right when they transgress.

But it has also been shown that the effectiveness of the training procedure is enhanced if the adult first establishes a warm and friendly relationship with the child. This opens the whole question of the context of relationships within which moral training occurs and the bearing this may have upon the development of guilt. Do some kinds of family situation and some kinds of parental sanction produce more guilt than others?

In contrast to the lack of information on the influence of different family backgrounds on resistance to temptation, there is a reasonably substantial body of data on the kind of family which produces children prone to guilt, and in the main the evidence is consistent.† There must be a relatively intense and exclusive

* See Aronfreed (1963; 1964); Aronfreed, Cutick and Fagen (1963); and Grusec (1966).

† See the following: Allinsmith and Greening (1955); Unger (1962b); Sears, Maccoby and Levin (1957); Sears, Rau and Alpert (1966); Stephenson (1966); Hoffman (1963; 1970); Hoffman and Saltzstein (1967); Kohlberg (1963b; 1964); Moulton et al. (1966); Rabin and Goldman (1966); Burton, Maccoby and Allinsmith (1961); Henry (1956); Whiting and Child (1953); and Whiting (1959).

attachment between parent and child. Sanctions must be psychological and signify withdrawal of love and disappointment rather than anger, and must be accompanied by strong disapproval of the child and of the act.

In the last chapter we looked at some of the reasons why physical punishment is not a particularly effective method for training children – it provokes aggression and provides a model of aggression when the response necessary for inhibition is anxiety. For similar reasons physical punishment is not effective in producing guilt. Why then are psychological techniques more effective? There are broadly two kinds of sanction that parents can employ. The first has been called 'power assertion', and includes physical punishment, angry threats, fierce verbal assaults and material deprivations such as the withholding of pocket money. These tend to provoke aggressive responses, especially if coupled with apparent injustice. The second is withdrawal of love. This can be mild or strong. On the one hand the parent can withdraw from the child, ignore him, refuse to speak to him or express dislike of him. On the other hand the parent can be 'hurt', and deeply disappointed and upset, and say things like 'I never thought you would do a thing like that, after all we have done for you.' There seems little doubt that when there's a strong bond of affection between parent and child, the child's realization that he has hurt the person he loves is a most potent cause of guilt.

There are several reasons why. In the first place such a sanction is unlikely to precede the transgression unless the child announces his intention of doing something wrong first; in fact it will probably follow some time after the child has experienced whatever satisfaction his misbehaviour brings. Hence though it may have some influence in preventing the deed in the future, the principal effect will be guilt rather than moral restraint. Then the anxiety it provokes is peculiarly intense and long-lasting. A mother's pained disappointment may continue until the child has 'proved' himself worthy of her love again; and of course he will be strongly motivated to do this. Because his mother is not responding aggressively, and is behaving as if the child's misdeed were a wounding assault on herself, the child's own aggression is not aroused (though of course as he grows older and realizes more clearly what is happening, a groundswell of muted hostility towards his mother may develop). Another element in the situation is the child's empathic response to the mother's emotional upset; through a kind of emotional contagion he will share the mother's disappointment with himself. Finally because of his attachment the child cannot escape from the situation but is held close to his mother until her disappointment subsides. This makes possible prolonged discussion of the incident. It is small wonder that children themselves prefer a sanction that is short and sharp, and which frees them from anxiety quickly and cleanly.

This strong form of love withdrawal, if habitual and associated with strict standards, can have distorting and pathological consequences for the child. He will become generally over-anxious, and will tend to interpret all moral infringements as potentially related to his mother. If his dread of his mother's sanction is not enough to inhibit him from misbehaving, it may well lead him into deceit in order to prevent his mother knowing. As he grows wise and sees injustice and irrationality in his mother's sanction, feelings of conflict and impotence may prompt him to blind and impulsive efforts to escape the trap he feels himself in.

It can be predicted, therefore, that small families, relatively isolated socially so that few attachments are formed outside the family and intense ones within, where parents, and especially the mother, set high standards and react to failure on their child's part to maintain them with strong withdrawal of love, will produce highly guilt-prone children. And especially if the children are girls. For girls are likely to be more sensitive to sanctions involving withdrawal of love and more likely to receive them. Moreover their attachments outside the family will probably be fewer and weaker. There is good evidence that children are less guilt-prone if they are able to form a number of attachments: for example, those reared in Israeli kibbutzim show less guilt than others brought up in small family units, and polygamous societies are less 'guilt-ridden' than monogamous.

The evidence reviewed in the last three chapters offers little support for the psychoanalytic assumption that moral resistance and guilt are functions of the same 'organ' or 'agency' within the personality, and that both are due to aggression turned inwards. It is simpler and more in keeping with the evidence to work with the concept of anxiety and to suppose that resistance and guilt have somewhat independent origins. The differences in origin relate to two things, the timing of punishment and the meaning given to the situation in which it occurs. If sanctions are administered at the same time as an offence, and best of all at the point when it is about to be committed, the most likely outcome will be behavioural inhibition. If the sanction is administered some time after the offence, the likely outcome will be guilt. The talk that accompanies the sanctions can be of two kinds. It can seek to define the nature of the act and the reasons why it is wrong, or it can be more personal and emphasize the wickedness and worthlessness of people who do such things and the hurt it causes the parents. We may guess that the former will be more likely to produce resistance, the latter guilt.

The stress placed by psychoanalysis upon the importance of attachment is amply vindicated, especially in the case of guilt. As we have seen attachment is said to be the normal antecedent of identification with the parents. It was pointed out towards the end of chapter 3 that we can distinguish two senses of the term. The first, the strictly Freudian sense, is that of a *mechanism* whereby aggression is turned inwards and the individual adopts the characteristics of the person to whom he is attached. Since the evidence does not encourage us to persist with the concept of a superego, we can dispense with the mechanism which is supposed to produce it. But the term can have a looser meaning. It can be simply the label for a certain kind of *relationship*. We say a child is identified with his parents when he is attached to them, admires them, and his own self-esteem is dependent upon what they think of him. The term is worth retaining in this sense, for the relationship it refers to is of immense importance in moral development. In the present context its value lies in the fact that it places a sanction of considerable power in the hands of parents, namely the withdrawal of love with its implied devaluing of the child, a sanction which produces little aggression but considerable anxiety.

There is another way in which both moral restraint and guilt may vary among people, which is not brought out by the data but which is clearly implied by cognitive-developmental theory. This is the extent to which they are mediated by the individual's own thinking and therefore in some measure controlled by his will. The progressive elaboration of cognitive structures with age means that there is a steady movement towards autonomy and self-direction. The more closely moral restraint and guilt are integrated with this cognitive development through parental explanation and reasoning the more the individual's moral responses will be conceptually controlled. Temptation situations are then resolved through more or less fully conscious decisions. The individual may decide that in this particular situation it is right to lie or steal because it serves some other, greater good, and can then go ahead and do it without feeling guilt afterwards. He is also able to make his behaviour accord with changes in his moral judgements. If this cognitive integration is minimal (and if moral training has been so severe that transgression is always associated with strong anxiety) moral restraint and guilt will be largely dissociated from the individual's own moral reasoning and take on a compulsive quality. Though his moral judgements may change, his behaviour will still tend to coincide with his parents' demands. Whether he likes it or not, whether it makes sense to him or not, there are things he cannot do, or things he can only do with intense guilt afterwards.

A final source of variability in people's moral inhibitions and guilt responses is their current social attachments and group roles. Moral restraint can be weakened by the contagious example of others, and strengthened by fear of social disapproval. As we have seen, many post-transgressional responses can be interpreted as efforts to restore personal relationships and acceptance by others. We may assume that for those in whose moral development parental influence has been weak and that of the peer group strong, the primary motive behind both behavioural inhibition and post-transgressional response will be the need to maintain acceptance in their social milieu.

The patchy and untidy state of research into the negative and inhibitive aspects of moral behaviour will now be evident to the reader. Much more needs to be done. But one of the consequences of increased knowledge in this field is that parents are faced with new decisions. Normal parents, we may presume, want their children to grow up as moral beings. In seeking this goal they have to rely mostly on their own convictions, intuitions and feelings, and of course on the manner in which they themselves were brought up. As we begin to understand the ways in which parental attitudes and actions determine the moral growth of our children, issues of policy we took for granted become matters for conscious, considered decision.

Perhaps the most fundamental policy decision that parents concerned with their children's morality have to make is whether they wish them to grow into morally autonomous persons or moral replicas of themselves. The natural process of development would seem to be towards such autonomy; but parents have it in their power to further or to retard this development. They further it by making their sanctions such that enough (but not too much) anxiety is generated for behavioural inhibition and for the learning of constructive post-transgressional responses, and by at the same time encouraging self-control through associating this anxiety with reasoning about behaviour that does not stress its personal relationship to themselves. This means explaining to the child that an action is wrong because it is destructive of some good the child himself recognizes rather than implying that the wrongness of the act lies in its affront to themselves. The former encourages the child to stand on his own feet in his moral life. Parents retard moral autonomy and as it were build themselves permanently into the child's personality by limiting and intensifying his attachments to themselves, by using sanctions that evoke severe anxiety, and by rationalizing their use of such sanctions by reference to their own authority and feelings.

The difference between the two policies comes out most clearly in connection with guilt. Guilt serves a useful function as a kind of second line of defence in our moral lives. When an individual does wrong it is obviously desirable that he should be motivated to do something constructive about it. The morally autonomous person feels guilt after transgression; but when he has satisfied himself that he has done all he reasonably could to put things right (which does not mean he has put them right), his guilt is dissipated. This should follow from an upbringing in which parents consistently made the cessation of punishment or the provision of positive rewards conditional upon their child's efforts at restitution and not upon how they themselves happen to feel. This in turn implies parents who care about their child's moral growth and who are to some extent disappointed at his misbehaviour, but who have sufficient understanding not to be shocked or 'hurt' and whose love is not dependent upon his virtue. If on the other hand the parent takes every moral failure personally in the way described, so that each offence is inflated into something serious, then the alleviation of the child's guilt is dependent upon the parent's decision to be nice to the child again, and in the meantime the child is held psychologically captive. The reduction of the child's guilt depends upon the parent's feelings and not upon the child's actions. In this way he remains tied to the parent and the parent can use this control over the child's guilt to get him to conform to his wishes in other ways. In other words he can make the child work hard for the reward of having his anxiety reduced and keep him uncertain as to whether he will get it.

When we control the alleviation of guilt in guilt-prone people we have considerable power over them. The hold that religion has on some people would seem to be based on this. Certainly it is a routine technique among religious evangelists to stimulate guilt in their listeners and then to offer commitment to their brand of religion as the one route to peace of mind. The same technique has been used in political indoctrination.

The choice before the parent is therefore as follows: he can either help the child to develop his own means for reducing his guilt and thereby renounce one source of power over him, or he can take the child's offences as a personal affront so that the child is helplessly dependent on others to reduce his guilt for him. The decision must be made on grounds other than psychological, for of course it depends upon what parents want for their children. All the psychologist can do is point out that the latter course can easily result in the guilt-ridden neurotic, whose creative energies are frustrated and soured, and that any tie to others which is founded upon guilt cannot achieve that polarity and freedom which makes personal encounter vital and alive.

CHAPTER 6

# Altruism

Living in communities demands that people sometimes put the interests of others first; acceptance within any group depends upon the individual acknowledging that he has obligations to the group that may take precedence over his personal wishes. The great religions of the world have urged that a disinterested concern for the welfare of others is one of the highest ideals that men can pursue. Of course such unselfishness does not go unrewarded. Helping others is an insurance premium against the time when we ourselves need help. Societies bestow their recognition and approval upon those who serve them well, and religions promise such benefits as the peace of mind of a clear conscience in this world and rich rewards in the next.

Generosity, sympathy and self-sacrifice are therefore judged good and worthy of cultivation. But people differ widely in the extent to which they possess these traits. At one extreme are the cynical and self-centred who use other people for their personal gain; at the other those whose lives are apparently so devoted to the welfare of their fellows that personal interest always takes second place. These differences are considerable and our problem is to understand why they occur. Altruistic behaviour is complex and serves many different functions for the individual. The first task will be to look at it closely and try to sort out some of the processes involved. Then we shall examine the evidence to find out what other characteristics are associated with generous behaviour. Finally we shall consider the kinds of upbringing and family environment that tend to produce considerate and helpful people.

The study of altruistic behaviour has been more neglected by psychologists than any other aspect of moral behaviour. Yet it is not difficult to measure. True, as with the other aspects of moral behaviour, experimental tests of generosity and helping behaviour have to be confined to a relatively trivial level; but they are not hard to devise.

Broadly two types of measure have been used. First there are the direct experimental tests which involve placing subjects in situations in which they have the opportunity to fulfil another's need by giving or by actively helping, and then recording their behaviour in these situations. Secondly there is the questionnaire. People can be asked to report their own altruistic behaviour; or their reputation for generosity and service can be assessed by asking others who know them, and their attitudes and feelings about helping others can be measured by specially constructed scales. Unfortunately the relation between these two kinds of measure is largely unknown.

## The Nature of Altruism

In general terms we class an action as altruistic when its outcome is primarily beneficial to someone else, and when its performance is dictated by the desire to help another person. Faced with a choice between personal convenience or advantage and furthering someone else's goals, the individual deliberately chooses the latter. The degree of altruism involved might be roughly assessed by the cost of the action to the individual in terms of valued time, energy, material goods, and so forth. It does not follow that altruistic actions have no beneficial consequences for the actor. On the contrary they are bound to have some consequences, and I shall adopt as a working hypothesis the proposition that altruistic tendencies are sustained or diminished according to whether these consequences are satisfying to the person involved or not. But the rewarding consequences for the individual may not be obvious, and the forms they take are often subtle and obscure.

In order to understand its nature better, and at the same time to illustrate the varied approaches that psychologists have adopted, I shall analyse altruistic behaviour by examining some of its elements. These are not necessarily always present but it may be presumed that in any altruistic action a number of them are.

## (A) THE BIOLOGICAL ROOTS OF ALTRUISM

Altruistic behaviour is far from being the prerogative of man. It has been widely and frequently observed in many other species. Male monkeys will feed and defend, sometimes with their lives, females with young; and, less dramatically, monkeys will groom each other, and mothers are devoted in the care and protection they give their offspring (Lawick-Goodall, 1968). Altruistic behaviour has therefore been judged 'innate' or 'instinctive' in other species, and the question this poses is whether the same terms are applicable to human altruism.

We must first look more closely at their meaning. It is now agreed that the antithesis between innate and acquired behaviour patterns is a false one, since all behaviour patterns are conditioned by both genetic structure and environment. But there is reason to think that the strength of these two influences varies between species and between behavioural systems within the same species. It has been suggested, therefore, that it is more profitable to look at behaviour patterns or systems as lying along a continuum with *environmentally stable* patterns at one end and *environmentally labile* at the other.* Environmentally stable patterns are those which, though their component elements may be more or less variable, are relatively unaffected by environmental change in their general shape or pattern. Instinctive patterns of behaviour are therefore those that have a high degree of environmental stability, are universal in a species, and serve the preservation of the population or community and therefore indirectly of the species. Instinctive behaviour is not wholly intel-

* These terms were originally proposed by R. A. Hinde and have been taken up and elaborated by Bowlby (1969).

ligible unless we take account of its social and evolutionary significance.

In man the biological roots of his behaviour are concealed under an elaborate superstructure of culture made possible by his unique capacity to learn, to think intelligently and to communicate. But all we know of evolution points to the existence of such roots. Only the most dogmatic of environmentalists would deny that the universality of the adult's protective response to young children, and even more the mother's response to her own child, indicates the presence of biological influences. Of course these responses cannot always be relied on, but they are so widespread and so environmentally stable in their general outline (however variable in specific content) that they merit the label 'instinctive' as much as comparable behaviour in other species. Campbell (1965) has argued that the readiness with which men are prepared to die in defence of their community or country is not fully understandable unless it is placed in its evolutionary context. The protective behaviour of men towards women has its counterpart in other species too. No account of altruism in man, therefore, can afford to ignore the influence of underlying, biologically primitive predispositions.

## (B) ATTACHMENT AND ALTRUISM

Recognition of its biological roots does not much advance our understanding of altruistic behaviour. It is only in its most general sense that such behaviour can be said to be environmentally stable; its specific form is always conditioned by social forces, individual temperament and the functions it serves for the individual in particular situations.

One condition that influences altruistic behaviour, both in man and other species, is specific attachment to other individuals or to groups. Attachment is not a necessary condition of altruism; most adults would go out of their way to help a young child in distress even if they had never seen the child before, and it is not uncommon in war for soldiers to go to some lengths in looking after wounded prisoners. But of all species man has the greatest facility for forming deep and long-lasting attachments, and it is plain that these greatly intensify and direct his altruistic tendencies. Indeed with the possible exception of the attachment of a very young child to his mother, altruistic behaviour may be taken as one of the defining attributes of all human attachments.

If attachment intensifies altruistic tendencies in one situation, it may weaken them in others; for attachment implies preference. When there is a conflict of interests, altruistic tendencies towards strangers and outgroups may be inhibited in favour of friends and the ingroup. Both Christianity and Buddhism have recognized this biasing effect of specific attachments. They point out that attachment can interfere with both a whole-hearted devotion to the divine and the development of disinterested concern for all people, and they have consequently urged upon their most aspiring adherents a life of discipline in which natural affections are systematically mortified.

It may seem obvious that attachment to someone else should result in altruistic behaviour towards him, but so far psychologists have failed to make the functional link between them fully explicit. There are, however, two strands of thought which throw some light on it. The first, which owes much to psychoanalysis, makes use of the notion of *ego-* or *self-extension*. Attachment is a kind of investment in others which ties their fates to our own, and may even make their problems more important to us than our own. Psychologists sometimes use terms like projection and identification for this process. In more homely language, when we put our eggs in someone else's basket, the fate of that basket becomes very important to us. It is through our relationships to others, our social embeddedness, that we define ourselves. *My* wife, *my* children, *my* friends and *my* country all contribute in varying degrees to my sense of who I am. My self-esteem depends on how those I value value me. In serving the interests of those to whom I am attached, I am therefore strengthening my sense of identity, and, insofar as this increases their attachment to me, enhancing my self-esteem.

This principle of self-extension to others can be used to account for those impulsive and sometimes heroic acts of self-sacrifice which occur in a group setting, such as an army at war.

The processes of increased arousal and loss of self-identity that occur in groups (see chapter 2) make the individual think primarily of the unit to which he belongs rather than of himself; he 'forgets' himself as he merges with the group. Part of what is meant by morale, in the military sense, is that the individual is less aware of his own identity and very much aware of the identity of his unit. Panic and cowardice are more likely to occur when the individual becomes aware again only of himself and his own fate.

A somewhat different approach has been adopted by those social psychologists who explain altruistic behaviour by assuming that we value people and do things for them to the extent that they are in some way positively rewarding to us (see Jones and Gerard, 1967). This approach is well illustrated by the study of friendship.

The experimental study of the conditions under which friendships are formed show that at least three factors are important. We like people whom we see initially as liking, or potentially liking, ourselves. In the long term friendships are sustained when liking is reciprocal and wither or turn into active dislike when it is not. Secondly, we tend to choose as friends people who share our attitudes, values and interests but who at the same time are in some degree complementary to us in skills and psychological needs. The former condition marks out the areas of experience within which profitable interaction can occur; the latter ensures that the interaction will be maximally beneficial to both parties and cause as little conflict or competition as possible.

These conditions suggest the usefulness of conceiving friendship as a social-exchange system in which altruistic action is one of the goods exchanged (see Homans, 1961). A friendship is viable when each party derives profit from it, and when there is an equilibrium in the amount of profit that each receives; help given is matched by help received. Once the exchange becomes one-sided, so that the balance of giving and receiving is disturbed, resentments are generated that threaten to destroy the friendship.

It may seem that altruistic behaviour is somehow debased, and not truly altruistic, when it is treated as part of the currency of a kind of social bartering. But when we remember that the goods in this case include such intangibles as enhanced self-esteem and sense of well-being, it is surprising how far an analysis in these terms will take us. For example it can be applied to maternal behaviour. Under normal conditions a mother's selfless care of her baby is amply repaid by the increased status, importance and attention accorded her, especially when he becomes intensely and exclusively attached to her. Should these rewards not be forthcoming for some reason, her mothering may well be less than devoted.

This approach also contains the idea that altruistic behaviour within an affectionate relationship is regulated by the principle of justice or equity in the distribution of goods. As we shall see in the next chapter, Piaget found a similar principle operating in the moral judgement of children who had attained the level of operational thinking. Everyday experience supports the claim that in most people altruistic tendencies are tempered by a sense of fairness. Many relationships, especially within the family, have been soured by the apparent ingratitude of one member. The springs of altruism tend to dry up when it is not reciprocated but taken for granted.

We have mentioned two ways in which attachment and altruism may be linked. Both imply that altruism is an indirect form of self-seeking. Whether they account adequately for all forms of self-sacrifice within an affectionate relationship the reader must judge for himself.

(C) ALTRUISM AS A HABIT

There are many minor, everyday acts of altruism, such as offering someone a lift or sharing lunch with a hungry companion which some people do 'automatically' and others equally 'automatically' do not. The cost to the individual may be slight; but the gains are often negligible as well, since many such acts occur in chance encounters with people we never see again.

According to learning principles an habitual tendency of this kind stems from a childhood training in which such acts have been positively reinforced. Parents who think their children should share their toys and sweets with other children systematically reward them for doing so. Several experiments attest to the effectiveness of this procedure. Doland and Adelberg (1967) increased the readiness of four-year-old children to share pictures with others by praising them for doing so. Fischer (1963) found that children of a similar age were more likely to give marbles to other children if they had been previously rewarded for doing so by being given bubble gum or praise from an adult. Midlarsky and Bryan (1967) rewarded older children with hugs for giving sweets to needy children and found that this increased their generosity on a subsequent test. Finally, Vogler, Masters and Morrill (1970) were able to make young children much more cooperative towards each other by rewarding them with sweets for cooperative behaviour.

All these experiments have dealt with the *acquisition* of generous habits. According to learning theorists, if such habits are going to be sustained over long periods of time, two things must happen. The child must be weaned from the expectation that he will be rewarded by others every time he acts generously – and this is achieved when the adult progressively moves towards the practice of rewarding the child only occasionally and at irregular intervals; and the child must learn to reward himself by praising himself and by feeling good at having done well (see Bryan and London, 1970, for a discussion of this).

## (D) THE EFFECT OF ALTRUISTIC EXAMPLE

In earlier chapters we examined evidence showing that when a model disobeys a prohibition or violates a social norm, the observer tends to be disinhibited and to follow suit. Similarly, watching someone else being generous and helpful tends to produce similar behaviour in the observer. In a naturalistic experiment Bryan and Test (1967) parked a car with a flat tyre at the side of the road and had a woman standing beside it looking helpless. They were interested in seeing how many drivers would stop to offer help. Under one condition all drivers approaching the car had first to pass another woman driver apparently in the same plight but in this case someone had already stopped and was changing the wheel for her. Under the control condition no altruistic model was provided. The results showed that seeing the example of someone else's altruism significantly increased the number of drivers who stopped.

Hartup and Coates (1967) found that nursery-school children were more likely to give to other children if they had first watched another child being altruistic. In an experiment by Rosenhan and White (1967) ten- and eleven-year-old children watched an adult demonstrate a game in which the prizes were highly valued gift certificates. During the demonstration the adult put half his winnings in a gift box for orphans. The children were then left to play the game on their own after being told that they could please themselves entirely whether they gave to the orphan fund (and the implication was that no one would know whether they did or not). These children gave very much more than others in a control condition who did not witness the model giving. It has also been shown that if the model is obviously pleased with his own altruism, the observer is even more likely to imitate him (Horstein, Fisch and Holmes, 1968).

## (E) EMPATHY AND SYMPATHETIC BEHAVIOUR

One of the commonest forms of altruism is sympathetic behaviour. *Sympathy* can be defined as the total process of perceiving another's distress and taking steps to comfort him or remove the cause.* It involves responding *as if* the other's distress were one's own; and though the ensuing behaviour can be very variable, its goal is the removal of the distress in the other. *Empathy* is one component of sympathy, namely responding to the other person's emotional expression (in this case of distress) with a similar emotional response (again distress). Empathic emotional responses initiate sympathetic behaviour, and this behaviour can be conceived as aiming at the removal of the observer's own emotional upset by removing its immediate cause,

* Children are more generous in their gifts to a peer they see to be friendless than to one who obviously has friends (Liebert, Fernandez and Gill, 1969).

the distress of the sufferer. There is every reason to think that this capacity for empathic response to other people's distress is of fundamental importance in human life and a major factor in much altruistic behaviour. People differ widely in their capacity for empathic response. Psychopaths are noticeably lacking in it whereas others are so sensitive to the suffering of others that they devote their lives to its alleviation. At present far too little is known about its origin and development, but a preliminary analysis can be made.

We cannot ignore the possibility that there is some biological mechanism which predisposes us to respond empathically to distress in others; certainly sympathetic responses occur among other primates. But superimposed upon such a predisposition is the process of conditioning. When baby and mother face a common cause of distress, or when emotional upset in the baby calls forth an empathic response in the mother, then from the baby's point of view, perception of the mother's distress will become conditioned to his own feelings of distress. As a consequence, the later perception of her distress will evoke a similar response in him. We may presume that a good deal of such conditioning goes on in the earlier years (and indeed throughout life). But it is also most likely to occur within a close mother-child attachment, since the devoted mother is constantly mirroring back to her child his own emotional states in an amplified and enriched form. In her efforts to get into tune with him she may well exaggerate her expressions of pleasure or distress in response to his.* In a similar fashion it has been shown that parents stimulate their children's speech by picking up elements of the child's primitive language and playing them back to him in expanded form (Brown and Bellugi, 1964). It is difficult to overestimate the importance of this continual and intimate interaction of mother and child for the development of sensitive empathic responsiveness to others. In a most perceptive study of sympathy in young children, Murphy (1937) reports that empathic responsiveness to others can be clearly seen in the

* I am grateful to Dr John Newson for making me realize just how important this phenomenon is.

second year, and probably develops much earlier, and that up to about the fourth year at least, it is much more intense when stimulated by a familiar figure than by a stranger.

Empathic response is not necessarily followed by sympathetic behaviour. The child has to learn the skills needed for such behaviour, and his mother's example is probably an important factor in this learning. But we can assume that when sympathetic action does occur it will be reinforced by the reduction of empathically induced distress it brings about. Of course, behaviour other than sympathetic (such as running away) can be reinforced in the same way.

As the child grows older, another important factor enters, namely his capacity for conceptual thought. Empathic responses can now be provoked, not only by the visible signs of suffering in others, but also by the realization that they are suffering whether they are showing it or not and even whether they are present or not. A second consequence is that the individual is able to reduce his empathically induced distress without engaging in sympathetic action but by reassessing the situation, for example by seeing the other person as deserving his suffering. Lerner and Simmons (1966) found that adult subjects, when faced with an 'innocent victim's' suffering (he was apparently receiving severe electric shocks), tended to reject and deprecate the victim if they were powerless to help and believed that the victim's suffering would continue. One of the striking features of racially prejudiced people is their failure to respond empathically to the sufferings of the members of the groups they have rejected. This failure in empathy is probably related to their prejudiced belief that the others are not quite human, or that their suffering is merited. Many prejudiced beliefs can be interpreted as ways of rationalizing away, or protecting the self against, empathic emotional response.*

So far we have treated empathy mainly as a response to another's distress. But obviously children can be conditioned in a

* Moral blame can also inhibit sympathy. Piliavin, Rodin and Piliavin (1969) found that people were less ready to help a man who collapsed through drunkenness than one who collapsed through illness.

similar fashion to respond with pleasure to another's joy. Once this connection is established, actions which produce delight in others can be intrinsically pleasing to the person who carries them out. In a rather complicated experiment Aronfreed and Paskal (reported in Aronfreed, 1968) conditioned children to feel pleasure at the experimenter's expressions of joy, and found that they would subsequently engage in more self-sacrificing behaviour in order to produce this joyful response in the experimenter. Everyday experience suggests that this kind of altruism is less stable and more easily suppressed than sympathetic response to distress.

## (F) ALTRUISM AS SOCIAL CONFORMITY

As pointed out in chapter 2, social-group theory maintains that the individual's behaviour is constrained and directed by the norms of both the groups to which he belongs and the roles he occupies in the social structure. When these norms require altruistic action he will be altruistic. Groups vary widely in the extent to which their norms prescribe such action, either towards other members of the group or to outsiders, and some professional roles demand more self-sacrifice from their occupants than others.

The role differentiation inherent in social structure means that relationships between individuals are frequently asymmetrical. At any time one person may be dependent upon another in ways in which the other is not dependent upon him. The continuing stability of social structure requires that behaviour towards dependents should be regulated by a sense of social responsibility. Berkowitz and Daniels (1963) have demonstrated that people feel under a kind of obligation to help those who are dependent upon them. Subjects were given a task to do, and told that someone else's reward was either highly or moderately dependent upon how hard they worked. The other person in each case was a stranger. In this situation the subjects worked harder the greater the dependence of the other person, and this continued to be the case even though there was virtually no chance that the dependent person would ever know how hard the subjects had worked. In other words, the mere fact that someone else was dependent upon their labours elicited more effort from the subjects. The authors interpret these results as evidence that the subjects were obeying a social norm to help dependents. Subsequent experiments* have shown that the strength of this tendency depends upon the individual's social class and background, upon whether he likes the person dependent upon him, and upon whether he has himself been helped recently. Berkovitz and Connor (1966) found that subjects who had been frustrated by failure prior to the experimental test were much less likely to give help. Murphy (1937) noted that sympathetic behaviour in children disappeared when they were frustrated or angry.

The presence of others who decline to help can also inhibit altruism. In a series of experiments † subjects were required to wait in a room before being interviewed in a market-research survey. While waiting, they heard the sounds of someone else in the next room in distress, or they saw smoke coming under the door. Those who were sitting alone were much more likely to go to the help of the unknown person, or to investigate the 'fire', than those who were sitting with a stranger who remained impassive throughout. For instance in one experiment subjects heard a woman in the next room apparently fall and hurt herself. Of those who were alone, seventy per cent went to help compared with seven per cent of those sitting with an unresponsive stranger.

Various possible explanations of this inhibitory influence of a bystander have been offered. For example the presence of others may result in a diffusion of responsibility, it may increase fear about appearing foolish or being criticized, and it may even decrease concern about the emergency by awakening a competing

---

*Daniels and Berkowitz (1963); Berkowitz and Daniels (1964); Goranson and Berkowitz (1966); Berkowitz and Friedman (1967); and Greenglass (1969).

†See Darley and Latané (1968); Latané and Darley (1968); and Latané and Rodin (1969).

need to appear cool and unconcerned in public and not to give way to panic. It is noteworthy that the inhibitory effect is much weaker if the subject and the bystander are friends, though even in this condition the subjects are rather less likely to help than when alone. Subsequent studies have not always found the inhibitory effect. For example, Piliavin, Rodin and Piliavin (1969) attempted to check these findings in a 'real life' experiment. They arranged for a model to fake collapse, either through illness or through drunkenness on a tube train in New York at different times of the day so that the number of other passengers present varied. When the model 'collapsed' through illness, help was immediately forthcoming from someone on sixty-two out of sixty-five trials, and it in no way depended upon the number of other passengers present nor upon the race of the model and the passengers. In the case of the 'drunken collapse', help was offered on eighteen out of thirty-eight trials, and it did to some extent depend upon the race of the participants, people of the same race as the model offering help more often.

Staub (1970) has examined this inhibitory effect from a developmental point of view. Children of different ages were left alone or with another child who was a stranger to them in a room where they could hear realistic sounds of distress coming from a young girl in the next room. Staub found that the overall proportion of children who took steps to bring help to the 'victim' increased sharply from the nursey-school age to the age of eight or nine years, and thereafter declined to a level at the age of twelve and thirteen, which was if anything lower than that for the nursery children. The most interesting result, however, was that the presence of another child increased quite considerably the proportion of the younger children who helped, in direct contradiction to the results of Darley and Latané (1968). The presence of another child seemed to make no difference for the older children who had reached puberty. These older subjects implied clearly in their answers to questions afterwards that what had inhibited them was uncertainty whether their intervention would have been welcomed. Taken together, these experiments do seem to have established the point that self-consciousness can easily inhibit altruism, though the conditions under which it does so are far from clear yet.

### (G) ALTRUISM AS DUTY

We saw in the last chapter that altruistic behaviour may be a means of reducing feelings of guilt after transgression. Guilt may also be a consequence of failing to be altruistic. In the course of bringing up their children parents not only forbid certain actions but also train them to be thoughtful and unselfish by giving them a code of altruistic behaviour and punishing them, at least by verbal disapproval, when they fail to live up to it. Altruistic rules come to impose the same kind of obligatory constraint as prohibitions. It is out of such a sense of duty that some people give to charities.

Obviously a sense of duty may coexist with a more impulsively sympathetic response to others; but it need not. There are those in whom natural warmth and spontaneity are not so much supplemented as replaced by the feeling that they *ought* to love their neighbours and help them. Presumably altruistic behaviour is then sustained by the glow of self-approval it produces.

### (H) ALTRUISM AS A DISGUISE

We started this chapter with the assumption that altruistic action is sustained by its consequences for the actor. It might be argued that this cynically devalues altruism by treating it as disguised self-seeking. This would be unfair. It is no challenge to the worth of altruism to say that this assumption helps us to understand it better. It could still be the case that the altruistic action benefited the recipient much more than the actor.

However, some disguises are so thin that they put the worth of the action in question. The tendency to be sceptical of the do-gooder is partly based upon the suspicion that his gain is greater than that of those he serves. For example altruism may be a form of power-seeking. We decide what is good for others, and make sure they get it. Or we help others in order to create in them an obligation to ourselves which enables us to exercise control over them.* One of the criticisms levelled against the work of some early missionaries is that their aim was to gain docile converts rather than to help people. Murphy (1937) reports that in some young children sympathy is a masked expression of aggression.

Altruism may also be a way of using others in order to resolve inner conflict and tension. Murphy noted that very anxious and obsessive children tended to see others as more anxious than they really were and then to take unnecessary steps to reduce this 'anxiety'. Anna Freud (1937) describes a neurotic form of altruism in a young governess. As a young girl she had had two main wishes in life, to possess beautiful clothes and to have children. These desires she had subsequently renounced, and as an adult was unmarried, shabbily dressed and self-effacing; yet at the same time she was energetically devoted to securing for others the very satisfactions she denied herself.

Instances of this kind are not uncommon. A man who never stands up for his own rights may be insistent upon the rights of others; a father may deny his own desire for leisure and education and devote himself to work in order that his children can enjoy these things. Even though such self-sacrifice may be acclaimed by others, vicarious living is a sign of failure in integrity. Anna Freud calls it defensive:

The defensive process serves two purposes. On the one hand it enables the subject to take a friendly interest in the gratification of other people's instincts and so, indirectly and in spite of the super-ego's prohibition, to gratify his own, while on the other it liberates the inhibited activity and aggression primarily designed to secure the fulfilment of the instinctual wishes in their original relation to himself.

We could extend this analysis of altruistic behaviour further. Indeed we shall later add yet another type, that is the altruism of creativity. But enough has been said for the present to show that there is no single explanation for it. The rest of this chapter will

* C. S. Lewis once quoted the remark: 'She lives for others; you can tell the others by the hunted expressions on their faces.'

be devoted to a review of the very meagre empirical evidence so far accumulated.* Unfortunately these studies make no attempt to distinguish between the different kinds of altruism listed.

## Altruism and Moral Restraint

Since altruism can take so many functionally different forms, it is not very meaningful to ask whether it is a general trait. However, we do need to know whether the measures used are tapping more than just specific responses to a particular situation.

Murphy (1937) found plenty of evidence that sympathetic responses in young children fluctuate with changes in mood and interest. Nevertheless some were generally more sympathetic than others. Hartshorne and May (1929) gave their adolescent subjects a variety of tests of service of others. These included voting money to charities, giving articles to others and making toys for children in hospital. They also obtained ratings from teachers on the general level of helpfulness shown by the children. The outcome was very similar to their findings for resistance to temptation: there was a small but fairly consistent tendency for subjects who were generous and self-sacrificing in one situation to be so in others. Rutherford and Mussen (1968) measured generosity in nursery-school children by seeing how many sweets they would give away to friends. Generous children were independently rated by teachers as more kindly and cooperative and less hostile to others.

We may cautiously infer from this that generosity in one situation is associated with generosity in others. Further support for this correlation comes from studies using questionnaires and ratings: people who express altruistic attitudes in one context are likely to do so in others.†

There is some evidence which suggests that altruistic people are more self-controlled when tempted to misbehave. In the

---

* For other reviews, see Krebs (1970) and Macaulay and Berkowitz (1970).

† See Brown, Morrison and Couch (1947); Turner (1948); Peck and Havighurst (1960); and Friedrichs (1960).

studies just mentioned altruistic attitudes were found to be associated with other forms of good behaviour such as honesty. Moreover in the Hartshorne and May study, total scores for helpfulness were positively related to honesty, though the association was not very strong. On the other hand, helping behaviour has sometimes been found to be quite unrelated to honesty (Schwartz et al., 1969).

Generosity has not been directly tested in delinquents, but all the evidence we have suggests that they are less sympathetic and helpful towards people who are not members of their circle of friends. The values of delinquent groups tend to be self-centred. In neurotic delinquents we would expect either a defensive kind of altruism based on massive self-denial or the obsessive need to follow rules, or its absence due to the fact that inner conflict and preoccupation interferes with spontaneous sympathy for others. Unsocialized, aggressive delinquents, and especially psychopaths, are notably lacking in empathic responsiveness. Pseudosocial delinquents may well be altruistic within their delinquent group, but the norms of the group would inhibit them from altruism towards outsiders.

So there is a slight tendency for altruism and resistance to temptation to go together. This is not surprising. Both involve a degree of self-control and concern for others; helping others and refraining from hurting them are two sides of the same coin. At the same time a rigid and inflexible self-control may inhibit spontaneous sympathy; and altruism is so complex a phenomenon that we would not expect the association to be a close one.

## Some Correlates of Altruism

### (A) AGE

Of the four theoretical perspectives outlined in chapter 2, only the cognitive-developmental implies that altruistic behaviour will be related to age after early childhood is over. And this theory suggests that it will stabilize and generalize rather than increase in strength, since with the attainment of operational thinking seeing other people's points of view will become a relatively automatic feature of the child's thinking.

The evidence is slender. In the Hartshorne and May study there was virtually no relationship between scores for helpfulness and age. Two other studies (Ugural-Semin, 1952; and Handlon and Gross, 1959) which used the technique of presenting children with an odd number of coins or nuts and requiring them to share with another child, found a steady increase in generosity with age, from the nursery school to adolescence. But these two studies deal with generosity at a trivial and habitual level, and there is every reason to think that the value of the objects used in the experiments declines with age. However, when children were asked what three wishes they would make if all of them could come true, altruistic wishes were found to increase steadily with age (Milgram and Riedel, 1969). Midlarsky and Bryan (1967) found that older children were more ready to give sweets to others and Sugarman (1970) found that altruistic attitudes as measured by questionnaires increased with age through adolescence. In their review of the evidence, which included some unpublished data, Bryan and London (1970) concluded that it 'seems quite clear that generosity increases with age, at least through the first decade of life'.

(B) INTELLIGENCE

Again there is little evidence to report. In the Hartshorne and May study there was a very slight tendency for the intelligent child to be more helpful, but the association was nothing like as strong as for honesty. A somewhat stronger relationship was found between intelligence and sympathy by Murphy (1937).

(C) SEX DIFFERENCE

As we have seen in earlier chapters, girls are more socially responsible and more involved in their personal relationships than boys. We should therefore expect them to show stronger altruistic tendencies. Moreover the social pressures at work in our society tend to prepare girls for the more nurturant and self-sacrificing roles in life, such as motherhood and nursing. There is a slight tendency for the evidence to confirm the expectation that girls are more altruistic than boys.

Ugural-Semin (1952) and Handlon and Gross (1959) found no difference between the sexes. In a very thorough review of the data on altruism, Krebs (1970) found that out of a total of seventeen studies, including some unpublished material, no sex differences were found in eleven of them. However, when sex differences are found they tend to favour girls. In the extensive study by Hartshorne and May, there was a very marked tendency for girls to score higher on tests of helpfulness and service. They also had a much higher reputation among their teachers for considerateness for others and for general social responsibility (see also Bronfenbrenner, 1961). Sugarman (1970) reports that girls displayed stronger altruistic attitudes than boys on his questionnaire measures.

Schopler and Bateson (1965) conducted an interesting series of experiments with adults in which they used essentially the same procedure as Berkowitz and his associates in the experiments described earlier (see page 137): subjects were placed in a situation in which someone else was highly or moderately dependent upon them, and they were given the opportunity of helping the other person. The dependent person in each case was a stranger and in one experiment unknown to the subject throughout. A striking difference between the sexes was found. As the degree of dependence of the other person increased, men became less altruistic and women much more so. The authors' explanation of the results is as follows: there is a social norm that requires us to help those dependent upon us; the greater the dependence, the greater the pressure to help; a consequence of this norm is that to be dependent upon others is to have, paradoxically, power over them; for males, to be put in someone else's power is threatening and they therefore build defences against it, which in this case meant disregarding the norm; women on the other hand are not so threatened and are free to respond to the increased dependence.

Personality tests that purport to measure the individual's general awareness of others and the extent to which he takes others' points of view into account have consistently found that women score higher than men (e.g. Gough, 1960). Women also report engaging in more charitable activity (London and Bower, 1968).

## (D) PERSONALITY

Many clinical psychologists and personality theorists have developed a view of the mature personality in which concern for others is a prominent feature.* Certainly emotional disorder disrupts such tendencies. Maslow conducted an informal study of 'self-actualizing' or creative people from all walks of life and found them 'problem-centred' rather than 'ego-centred', and generally committed to the realization of values that took precedence over their personal comfort and gain.

Evidence linking altruism to particular personality traits, however, is scanty in the extreme, and limited to data derived from questionnaires measuring altruistic attitudes. In the study by London and Bowers (1968) extraversion was not related but self-esteem was. Murphy (1937) observed that a child's sympathy for others vanished when his self-esteem was damaged. Gore and Rutter (1963) offer evidence that students who engage in action against racial segregation tend to have a greater confidence in their ability to influence events through their own behaviour than those who, though they share the same evaluation of segregation, are socially inactive.

We said earlier that strong attachment to individuals or groups could lead to a selectivity in the people to whom altruism is directed. A personality trait that has received a great deal of attention from social psychologists is *ethnocentrism*. This is the tendency to sort people into two sharply separated categories, members of ingroups and members of outgroups. Ethnocentric people overvalue ingroups and are submissive towards them, and denigrate outgroups; they have the us–them mentality. Though they may readily devote their energies to the welfare of insiders, they are markedly lacking in concern for outsiders. They have even been found to lack sympathy for the physically disabled (Chesler, 1965).

* For example Maslow (1962; 1970) and Allport (1955; 1961).

## (E) RELIGION

Judging from the accounts in the Gospels, Jesus enjoined upon his followers a high standard of altruism. They were urged to heal the sick, to love their enemies, and to show generosity and compassion to all regardless of nationality and race. We might therefore expect that the more people are exposed to this teaching the more altruistic they would be; religious education is in fact frequently justified on the grounds that it will have this effect.

Hartshorne and May (1929) found a very slight, overall tendency for those who attended Sunday school frequently to score higher on the tests of service: but this tendency was very slight indeed. At the same time they found quite wide differences between denominations that could not be accounted for in terms of class and social background. Protestants were the most altruistic, Catholics the least.

There is no firmer evidence that altruistic attitudes go with reported belief in the Christian religion. Kirkpatrick (1949) found that religious belief was negatively related to a measure of humanitarianism, which in this context meant a tolerant and compassionate attitude towards criminals, Negroes and foreigners. Friedrichs (1960) found a very slight tendency for reported charitable action to go with belief in God but it was unrelated to church attendance. Cline and Richards (1965) could find no evidence at all that what they called the 'good Samaritan' attitude was any stronger in believers than in atheists.

This lack of any clear connection between altruistic attitudes and belief in a religion that advocates altruism may seem puzzling. But of course it all hinges upon what is meant by 'believe'. We can understand the problem better if we consider the relation between religion and racial prejudice. It is now a well documented finding that, in the United States in particular but also in other countries, those who believe in Christianity and go to church are on average more racially prejudiced than atheists and agnostics. However, when the evidence is studied further we find a small minority of believers who are certainly not more prejudiced than atheists and are often less so.

A distinction can therefore be drawn between two kinds of believer. There are those whose tie to religion is primarily based on the fact that religion answers the needs for social status and respectability, for solace and security, and for a sense of being united with others. They could be described as the conventionally religious, and they probably constitute the majority of believers. It is belonging to a church that matters to them rather than commitment to the values of Christianity. They therefore tend to be ethnocentric, prejudiced and lacking in sympathy for outsiders, towards whom they tend to adopt a moralizing attitude. There are also those who do not need these psychological supports from religion but nevertheless are believers, and who attempt to live out the values they are committed to. They serve the ideals within religion rather than making religion serve them.*

This difference in the functions religion can serve is probably related to a paradox inherent in Christianity. On the one hand the ideal of altruism is embedded in the original teachings of Jesus. On the other the elaboration of Christian belief and its social organization has led to the division of people into two categories: believers and unbelievers, the saved and the lost, those in a state of grace and those not, the baptized and the unbaptized, the sheep and the goats, the true believers and the rest, etc. Classifications of this sort tend to foster the us–them mentality and to attract people who already have it. To be one of the chosen or in a state of grace is to be very much an insider. The more psychologically important such classifications are for an individual the more they will militate against compassionate attitudes towards 'them'.


## Influence of the Home

In the light of the analysis of altruism given it is not difficult to infer the family conditions which are most likely to facilitate its

* See Allport (1954; 1966); and Allport and Ross (1967).

growth in children. First, there must be a warm and affectionate relationship between parents and child. This provides the setting in which empathic responsiveness is most effectively learned and gives the first major incentive for altruistic action in the child's life. Secondly, the parents must themselves be sympathetic, both to the child and to others, and set a good example of altruistic action. The child can then learn through imitation a full repertoire of altruistic patterns of behaviour. Thirdly, as the child grows older, his parents need to provide him with a rationale for altruistic behaviour, whether in terms of social exchange or in terms of rational ideals, so that he can learn to extend his altruistic tendencies to people outside his immediate circle of family and friends. One factor of considerable importance is how parents themselves talk about outgroups, particularly the deprived and deviant. If their own defensive inclinations are to reject and moralize over such groups as the unemployed, the sexually abnormal, the racially different, and the delinquent, so that their compassion for such people has dried up, then the child too will learn to discriminate against these groups as not deserving his sympathy. Few things are more corrosive of that sense of belonging to a common humanity from which compassion springs than the tendency to separate other groups sharply off from oneself, whether along social, religious, political, racial, nationalistic, intellectual or moral lines. Ethnocentric parents tend to produce ethnocentric children. Fourthly, parents need to reward their child's generous and helpful actions through their pleasure and approval. They can also, of course, blame or punish him when he fails to live up to their standards. This latter method, however, is likely to be less effective, for it will associate fear of censure with situations requiring altruistic actions, and therefore create in the child the motive to avoid such situations if he can.

As yet there is little direct empirical evidence to substantiate these assertions. In a study of ten-year-old children Brown, Morrison and Couch (1947) obtained ratings of the subjects' friendliness, loyalty and social responsibility from peers and teachers, and gave the children themselves a family-relations questionnaire. There was a marked tendency for those high on these traits to perceive their parents as strongly affectionate towards them. Bronfenbrenner (1961), using similar methods, found that those rated lowest for social responsibility saw their parents as rejecting them. His results also suggested that social responsibility in girls was adversely affected when their relationship with their parents was *too* close and intense.

Hoffman (1963) observed three-year-old children at play and assessed the amount of consideration they showed to other children. He also interviewed the parents. In this sample (which was a small one) consideration for others was not found to be related to parental affection, but it was associated with the extent to which the parents, in their discipline, stressed the consequences of actions for others. Parents of considerate children were also less assertive of their power over the child. In the study of four-year-old boys made by Rutherford and Mussen (1968), generosity was strongest in those whose fathers were warm and affectionate.

As we have seen, altruistic action has many motivational roots: it may follow from being so alienated from ourselves in a group that we are not aware of any other desires than those common to the rest of the group; it may flow from identifying with others and so extending our egos to embrace them so that their good becomes ours; it may be a means of gaining or retaining social acceptance by behaving as others expect us to; it may be part of the currency of social barter, that is, either a payment for past favours or an investment for the future; it may represent that self-conscious conformity to a moral rule which cannot but be followed by the knowledge that we have acted well; and it may be a way of reducing empathic distress or enhancing vicarious pleasure. At the same time there is the moderating influence of the intelligence which, with more or less success, seeks to ensure that the altruistic act is appropriate to the purpose it is serving.

Finally there is an altruism of a more disinterested, problem-centred and creative kind. Some people act altruistically, not for any of the reasons listed, but because the logic of a situation demands it. They dispassionately assess a situation, conclude that the rational and fitting solution to the problem requires from them an action of a certain sort, and then go ahead and do it. The fact that the action is one that others would label unselfish does not enter into their considerations. Their attention is wholly focused upon the realization of a general value (that is, not a self-orientated one) such as the increase of health or justice in a community, the efficient and humane running of an institution, or the creation of knowledge. This kind of altruism has been almost entirely neglected by psychologists – indeed certain of the theories they have adopted seem to imply that it could not exist; but though in daily life it is frequently unobtrusive and taken for granted, it does exist, and we cannot ignore it.

The individual's characteristic type of altruism will be largely conditioned by parental example and precept. It is the parents who to a considerable extent determine whether their child's altruistic tendencies will be biased and directed by powerful needs for status and personal advancement and by anxiety to please others, or whether they will be stultified by the prejudices of an us-them categorizing of people. It is up to them whether the values they communicate to their child are egocentric in the sense that for him the desirable goal is 'me achieving' or 'me being good', or whether the emphasis is put on bringing about a desirable state of affairs regardless of the identity of the people who do it. Theorists like Maslow argue that problem-centred, value-orientated altruism is not achieved through the frustration of the individual's basic needs; on the contrary, it becomes possible precisely when these basic needs (for food, security, love, etc) are satisfied. But such altruism also depends upon the nature of the individual's moral reasoning and values, and it is to the study of these that we must now turn.

# CHAPTER 7

# Moral Insight

Although in many ways related, resistance to temptation, guilt responses and altruism are also to a large extent independent of each other. Extreme altruism, for instance, does not *necesssarily* go with strong self-control in the face of temptation or intense anxiety after transgression. Different individuals may exhibit a variety of patterns on these three aspects of moral response. This is why we have treated them separately.

On the face of it there is much less justification for dealing with the cognitive aspects of moral behaviour separately. The term 'cognitive' is used here as a convenient label for referring either to the structures or to the processes involved in perceiving, conceiving, remembering, deciding and thinking. Taken together these processes constitute our understanding of our environment and the meaning we discover in it. As such, cognition is an inescapable element in all behaviour above the primitive reflexes. Whether or not an individual resists temptation, feels guilt or helps others is partly determined by how he construes the particular situation. Conversely, his actual responses in any situation can be taken as indices of the meaning it has for him.

But people do not think about moral issues only when directly faced with them. On the contrary, they engage in a great deal of reflection on their moral experience, they commit themselves to moral beliefs, they argue with others about moral problems, and they pass judgement on the behaviour of others and attempt to justify their own judgements. In order to understand an individual's morality we must examine what he says as well as what he does. Talk about morality is itself morally relevant behaviour.

When verbal behaviour and action are consistently in accord with each other, we say that an individual has integrity. But such integrity is sufficiently uncommon for us all to be aware that the profession of a moral belief is not always a reliable guide to how a person will behave when forced to act. Of course, the absence of any connection at all between the two would be taken as a sign of serious abnormality. One reason for inconsistency is that situations in which we engage in talk about morality are usually very different from those in which we are faced with an actual moral challenge. Different outside pressures are at work. Another reason is that the cognitive structures which underly and direct both verbal behaviour and action may themselves lack coherence and stability. What he has learned in the past may lead an individual to discriminate between talking and acting in such a way that he feels no particular need to make them consistent with each other.

We are justified, therefore, in taking moral thinking as a separate topic and in asking for evidence of how it is related to behaviour. In the next chapter we shall look at people's moral ideologies, that is the nature of their moral beliefs and the functions these beliefs appear to serve. Here I shall concentrate on moral concepts and reasoning. The approach will be developmental.

## The Work of Piaget

Research into the development of children's moral thinking began around the turn of the century, but Piaget's brilliant and seminal monograph, *The Moral Judgment of the Child* (1932) has provided the major stimulus for research in this field. Since much of the earlier work can be interpreted as being in agreement with Piaget (see Johnson, 1962a), I shall begin with an account of his monograph and then discuss the main lines of research that have followed from it.

The monograph falls into four sections. The first three contain pilot empirical investigations of the moral thinking of Swiss children between the ages of about four and twelve. The fourth is a general résumé of his theoretical position. In the following account I shall endeavour to present the empirical conclusions first and then describe the explanatory theory. This is less easy than it might seem for Piaget characteristically inserts a great deal of theoretical speculation and interpretation into his factual reporting.

The first section is taken up with an examination of the child's conception of the nature and functioning of the rules of a game – the game of marbles. Piaget chose to take rules in the context of a game because this meant that he could by-pass the influence of adult teaching, and study the child's spontaneous thought directly, and also because it enabled him to observe how the child's conception of rules was related to his conformity to them. In addition he thought that the results would throw light on how the child conceived moral rules.

Piaget's method was to play the game with a child but to feign ignorance of the rules and to ask to have them explained to him. Then in the course of playing he probed the child's understanding of the rules by asking such questions as 'Where do the rules come from?', 'Who made them?', and 'Can we change them?'. The idea was to pose the child with problems he had never had to face before and thus throw him back on his own resources. Piaget, needless to say, was acutely aware of the difficulties in interpreting the responses of young children to adults' questioning and he took steps to ensure that he really was tapping the child's genuine thinking.

The results reveal a clear shift in the child's conception of rules over the age range sampled. The young child, from around five to seven, regarded rules as deriving from the semi-mystical authority of older children, adults and even God. Rules were therefore sacred and inviolable. They had always been as they were and could not be altered or added to. Paradoxically, in his actual play the child unashamedly bent the rules to suit himself and was not disconcerted by the idea of both players winning.

The older child of about ten or more had a very different conception of rules. He was quite clear that they were invented by children themselves. He had now internalized the rules. He felt they were *his* and therefore that he could change or modify them. But since at the same time he recognized that the purpose of the rules was to make a game possible and to avoid quarrelling and unfairness, he also accepted that the rules could only be changed if all players agreed. Hence though he felt free to change the rules he also felt under an obligation to persuade others first. As Piaget puts it: 'The collective rule is at first something external to the individual and consequently sacred to him; then as he gradually makes it his own, it comes to that extent to be felt as a free product of mutual agreement and an autonomous conscience.' At the same time the child keeps meticulously to the rules and develops a keen interest in them.

In the second section Piaget turns to an examination of the criteria the child adopts in making his moral judgements. He presented children with hypothetical situations embodied in brief stories and asked them to assess how wrong the action was and to explain why it was wrong. The situations usually concern children who either tell lies or steal something.

Several developmental trends emerge. Though the young child can discriminate between intentional and unintentional actions he takes little or no account of intention in his moral evaluations. From the point of view of morality intention does not count. The child's judgements are centred on the sheer amount of damage done by the action. Thus the accidental breaking of a number of cups was 'naughtier' than the breaking of one in the course of deliberate stealing, and an unintentional falsehood which had serious consequences was worse than an intentional lie that did not. The child's judgements are *objective* in the sense that he tends to measure the gravity of a lie by the degree of its literal departure from the truth: a wild and totally unconvincing fantasy was judged worse than a realistic and successful deceit. Lies are bad because you are punished for them, and lying to adults is worse than lying to peers.

The older child may still take some account of the material

consequences of an act, but he now gives precedence to intention in his judgements. A falsehood intended to deceive is 'obviously' worse than one due to ignorance or a mistake. Lying to people in authority is not necessarily worse than lying to equals, and the reason why lying is wrong is that it betrays the trust without which fruitful and worthwhile social interaction is impossible.

The third section deals with the child's ideas about punishment and justice. Piaget used essentially the same technique as in the second section: children were presented with hypothetical situations and invited to comment on them. Again certain trends emerge. The young child feels a need for misdeeds to be balanced by punishment of some kind, but the form the punishment takes can be quite arbitrary (the *expiatory* conception of punishment). What matters is that the individual should pay for his offence with suffering of some kind, and there is a tendency to think that the greater the suffering the better. These children 'are almost unanimous in defending severe punishment both as legitimate and as educationally useful'. Obedience tends to be equated with virtue, and punishment decreed by authority is accepted as just because of its source. It is acceptable for a class of children to be punished for the offences of one member if that member does not own up and the others refuse to reveal his identity. Finally the young child tends to construe a misfortune as a punishment when it follows closely upon some misdeed. This is the principle of *immanent justice*. The basic assumption is that natural forces are somehow in league with people in authority and ensure that the disobedient suffer.

The older child sees punishment differently. Its purpose is not so much to balance a misdeed as to bring home to the offender the nature of his offence and to deter him on future occasions. Hence the punishment should as far as possible fit the crime: if a child takes someone else's dinner he should be deprived of his own. This is punishment by *reciprocity*, and Piaget lists a number of forms it can take. Some children went further and said that punishment should take account of the offender's circumstances and needs, recognizing that what is a mild punishment for one person may be severe for another. And some were prepared to accept that there was no need for punishment at all if the offender could be reformed without it. Justice is no longer tied to authority, for 'justice has no meaning except as something above authority'. There is 'a gradual diminution in the preoccupation with authority and a correlative increase in the desire for equality'. Punishing innocent people for the offences of others is always wrong, and there is much less recourse to the notion of immanent justice.

Piaget groups together the characteristic features of the moral thinking of the young child under the label *moral realism*. They all share the assumption that moral rules are external and rooted in authority with the consequence that their application tends to be literal and socially insensitive. Moral realism is 'the tendency which the child has to regard duty and the value attaching to it as self-subsistent and independent of the mind, as imposing itself regardless of the circumstances in which the individual may find himself'. The older child's morality Piaget calls the *morality of cooperation* or *reciprocity*. He clearly thought it a more rational and desirable kind of morality. The basic elements are the child's awareness of other people's points of view, his realization that moral rules grow out of human relationships, and his incipient moral autonomy. As Piaget says, 'One must have felt a real desire to exchange thoughts with others in order to discover all that a lie can involve.' Consciousness of the 'need for reciprocal affection' among equals brings with it a dawning realization that morality is not a matter of obeying authorities but of evolving guiding principles for achieving mutually agreed and valued ends.

In terms of their psychological functioning these two moralities are, in Piaget's view, quite different. It does not follow, however, that a child will exhibit either one or the other. Quite the contrary. Though they can be conceived as distinct, the moral thinking of any child is always a mixture of the two. Indeed many elements of moral realism can be detected in the thinking of adults, such as the notions of immanent justice or expiatory punishment. As Piaget says:

There exist in the child certain attitudes and beliefs which intellectual development will more and more tend to eliminate; there are others which will acquire more and more importance. ... The two sets of phenomena are to be met both in the child and in the adult, but one set predominates in the one, the other in the other.

What are the conditions which tend to eliminate one set and encourage the other? In Piaget's view there are two major factors at work. The first is the transformation from egocentric thinking to operational thinking in the development of the child's intelligence; the second is a progressive change in his social relationships. The two interact closely with each other.

Egocentrism in the child was defined in chapter 2 as his incapacity to see that points of view other than his own exist, and therefore as his lack of awareness that he has a point of view of his own. Coupled with this, the child has not yet clearly learned to differentiate thinking from events, what is mental from what goes on outside him (thus he thinks that objects feel and know, and that the name of a thing is somehow part of it rather than assigned to it by people). At the same time his social relationships are primarily centred on his parents, and they take the form of *unilateral respect*. His parents constrain, control and direct him. Thus 'every command coming from a respected person is the starting point of an obligatory rule'. The child encounters rules from adults. The source confers a semi-mystical authority upon them; his inability to conceive of other points of view means that once he has accepted the rule into his own thought it cannot be changed or modified; since *he* now sees things that way, that is the way they must be; his inability to differentiate what is thought from what is external reality means that the rules he has accepted are part of the external reality to which he must adjust.

From the age of about seven onwards the child is increasingly capable of operational thinking. But according to Piaget, the full extension of this capacity into the sphere of social relationships, so that the child is able to take account of other people's points of view, is not automatic but depends on the quality of those relationships. It is through the clash of wills in the context of *mutual respect* within the peer group, and through the need to resolve conflicts between equals, that the child is forced to apply this capacity to his social relationships. The outcome is the morality of cooperation. Finally, though Piaget does not enlarge on the point, the attainment of formal operations enables the child to generalize into universal moral principles his experiences of give and take in the peer-group setting.

Because the child always begins life egocentric, and because his first relationships are always unilateral, moral realism must precede the morality of cooperation. But the appearance of the latter can be delayed or thwarted either by slow intellectual development or by social experience in which unilateral respect for authority heavily predominates. Piaget's theory is therefore both developmental and social. It follows from it that even though the adult is capable of operational thinking, when his relationships have been and still are mainly unilateral, he will exhibit marked traces of moral realism in his thinking.

Social constraint – and by this we mean any social relation into which there enters an element of authority and which is not, like cooperation, the result of interchange between equals – has on the individual results analogous to those exercised by adult constraint on the mind of the child ... the adult who is under the dominion of unilateral respect for the 'Elders' and for tradition is really behaving like a child.

A theory as speculative and general as Piaget's is bound to be vulnerable to criticism on many counts (see Bloom, 1959). Perhaps the two principal weaknesses are that he fails to specify in any detail exactly what he means by unilateral and mutual respect, and he largely ignores the impact upon the child of explicit and rational teaching about morality. This last point raises some interesting issues. In order to understand them, we must return to Piaget's theory of development and repair an omission in the outline given so far.

This chapter began with a distinction between *practical* and *theoretical* moral thinking (as I shall henceforth label them). Practical moral thinking is the way an individual conceives those situations in which he is actively involved and which demand a moral response from him. It is therefore inseparable from the moral response it conditions, and can be inferred from that response. Theoretical moral thinking is the way an individual thinks and talks about moral problems, real and hypothetical, his own and others', when he is not immediately involved in making moral decisions. Now Piaget's theory is really intended to explain the way practical moral thinking develops. But the evidence he has to rely upon is samples of the child's theoretical thinking. He therefore has to suggest how practical and theoretical moral thinking are related. He links the two through the notion of *conscious realization*. In theoretical moral thinking the individual makes consciously explicit by reflection, the moral principles upon which he actually functions. Theory is the conscious realization of practice. In claiming this Piaget is applying to the moral sphere a general principle which he has derived from the study of intelligence. As he says: 'the child's verbal thinking consists of a progressive coming into consciousness, or conscious realization of schemas that have been built up by action'. It follows that there will always be a time-lag between practical and theoretical morality, a delay before a developmental change at the practical level is registered at the theoretical level.

Though Piaget does not say so, this time-lag must limit the nature and extent of the influence that adult moral teaching can have upon children. Since theoretical thought limps behind practical and is its conscious realization, it follows that practical morality may shape theoretical but that theoretical does not shape practical. Moral theorizing is the adult's theoretical morality, and any influence it has is on the child's theoretical morality. The conclusion must be that adult theorizing will not affect the child's practical morality, and that its influence upon his theoretical morality can only be either to retard it, or to help it catch up with his practical morality.

A further implication of this hypothetical time-lag needs to be made clear. According to the theory, an adult whose present and past relationships have been dominated by unilateral respect will show moral realism in his practical morality and therefore also in his theoretical morality. But the converse does not follow. Because he exhibits moral realism in his theoretical morality it does not at all follow that he will display it in his practical morality. An adult who has largely outgrown relationships of unilateral respect, and who is thoroughly mature in his practical morality, may still display moral realism in his theoretical morality either because he does not go in for moral reflection much or because he has accepted from others a certain perspective upon morality which prevents his theory catching up with his practice.

On Piaget's theory the two main signs of moral realism, in adults and children, are that the individual submits to an authority as the source of moral prescription and fails to see the relativity and fallibility of his own point of view. Now Piaget claims that these two are both logically and psychologically inseparable. And it is important to try to see why. The person who claims that a given moral rule is 'absolute' because it emanates from an infallible authority has failed to see that he himself is the source of the judgement that the authority is infallible – no one else can make it for him. Now to treat the utterances of an authority as infallible necessarily entails the assumption that the judgement that the authority is infallible is itself infallible. If on the other hand an individual sees that his judgements about the infallibility of an authority are themselves fallible and may be mistaken, this uncertainty necessarily extends to the utterances of the authority. Psychologically speaking, the young child accepts parental decree as absolute because he has no view of his own and knows of no other conflicting authority. Submission to authority is in reality identification with it. In the adult the same kind of identification with authority is likely to be motivated in many ways, but among them is sure to be an intolerance of that uncertainty which must come if we try to evolve a point of view of our own.

## Subsequent Studies Based on Piaget

So much for Piaget's monograph. How well have his ideas and conclusions fared in the light of later research?

### (A) AGE CHANGES

Though Piaget did not expect that children would ever be entirely consistent in their moral thinking, he certainly believed that moral realism declines with age. It is clear from the evidence that certain details of Piaget's theory require modification, particularly in connection with the development of concepts of justice. But the existence of a general age trend of the kind he described has been overwhelmingly substantiated by later studies, and these studies have included Chinese, Lebanese, Israeli and English and American children.*

### (B) INTELLIGENCE

There is reasonably consistent evidence to show that, independent of age, the more intelligent a child is the more mature his moral judgement tends to be. The main exception is to be found in his conception of justice, where the evidence is equivocal. In these studies, however, intelligence was gauged by standard tests, and it is very doubtful whether these measure what Piaget understood by intellectual development. More interesting therefore is a study by Stuart (1967) in which subjects were given a test of *decentring*, the process that heralds the end of egocentrism and is thus intrinsic to operational thinking. Stuart was measuring more directly what Piaget meant by intellectual development, and his results showed that those subjects who decentred most readily were the more mature in their moral judgements.

* See Lerner (1937); MacRae (1954); Medinnus (1959; 1962); Johnson (1962b); Durkin (1959a and b); Loughran (1966); Najarian-Svajian (1966); Breznitz and Kugelmass (1967); Kugelmass, Breznitz and Breznitz (1965); and Bull (1969a).

## (C) SOCIAL RELATIONSHIPS

According to Piaget's theory we would expect children of strict and controlling parents to be retarded in their moral development and children who had a full and happy relationship with their contemporaries to be advanced in their moral development. So far the evidence is inconclusive.

MacRae (1954) did not find that children whose parents were authoritarian were retarded in moral insight. He did find, on the other hand, that such children were less likely to agree that friendship could take precedence over obedience to a rule. The results of a similar study by Johnson (1962b) are equally discouraging. Abel (1941) found that institutionalized, mentally defective girls were less mature than a control group of similarly retarded girls who were brought up in their homes. If we can assume that institutions are more authoritarian than homes this might be taken as providing indirect support for Piaget's theory.

Other studies have failed to show that reduced dependence on adults and close integration into peer groups are related to moral insight (Boehm and Nass, 1962; Porteus and Johnson, 1965). An ideal situation for testing Piaget's theory is the Israeli kibbutz. Children brought up in a kibbutz are far more subject to the socializing influence of peer groups than children reared in ordinary families. In a study involving nearly 1,500 adolescents, Kugelmass and Breznitz (1967) compared subjects from kibbutzim with those from ordinary family backgrounds and found no differences in the extent to which they made use of intention in their moral evaluations.

So far then the evidence does not support Piaget's theory. This does not mean that we must abandon it, for it would be surprising if people's moral reasoning were not affected by their personal relationships. Moreover in Piaget's view the crucial factor in retarding moral development is a relationship of fear, dependence and respect towards authority. It does not follow that because a child has dominating parents he has an attitude of this kind towards them, for he might well be in rebellion against them. Studies which measure the child's situation rather than his attitudes do not really test the theory. It is quite possible that membership of certain kinds of peer group could strengthen attitudes of respect towards authority. Evidence of the relationships between attitudes and moral judgement does tend to support Piaget.

A great deal of attention has been paid by social psychologists to the *authoritarian personality* (see Adorno *et al.*, 1950). Briefly, an authoritarian person is one who only feels really secure when he has his niche within a social hierarchy, who is submissive to those above him and dictatorial to those below him, who conceives human relationships in terms of power rather than love, and who therefore has little taste for democratic, egalitarian relationships with others. He thrives on a network of relationships of unilateral respect. So far no one has tested the moral thinking of such people along Piagetian lines; but there is a fairly solid accumulation of evidence from studies of their attitudes to suggest that they do exhibit a good deal of moral realism in their thinking. For instance they see moral rules in terms of authoritative decree, they demand arbitrary and severe punishments for social deviants, and they often show the kind of superstition that sees the hand of fate in chance events.

(D) MORAL INSIGHT AND THE OTHER MORAL VARIABLES

Piaget observed that children who had internalized the rules of a game kept to them better. We might infer from this that mature moral insight would be associated with greater self-control in the face of temptation. Grinder (1964) and Medinnus (1966b) found no relationship between insight and resistance to temptation. The more rules are internalized, the more we might expect guilt to follow their violation. Porteus and Johnson (1965) found a clear, positive association between guilt as measured by the story-completion technique and maturity of moral judgement. It is not clear what we should expect the relationship between moral insight and altruism to be; but in any case there appears to be no evidence relating the two yet.

## (E) SEX DIFFERENCES

It is possible to argue that either sex will be more morally advanced than the other. On the one hand it could be said that girls are more subject to adult constraint and enjoy less freedom with children of their own age and therefore would tend to be less morally mature; on the other hand their intellectual maturation tends to be more rapid and they more readily apply their intelligence to social relationships and so should be *more* morally mature. In fact, with very few exceptions, studies have failed to find any significant differences between boys and girls.

## (F) RELIGIOUS TEACHING

It will not have escaped the reader that there are aspects of Christian morality, at least as popularly understood, which parallel the moral thinking of the immature child. Moral rules find their justification in the authority of the Bible or the Church, and they are therefore 'absolute' and eternal. The notion of expiatory punishment is discernible in the doctrine that, through his death on the cross, Jesus 'paid' for the sins of all men. The notion of immanent justice is contained within the conception of a God who controls all events and whose central purpose is to train man for the kingdom of heaven. Above all, Christians place emphasis upon obedience to the moral law which derives from God.

However, it does not necessarily follow that Christians are psychologically immature in their moral thinking, as some people have claimed.* The important distinction must be drawn between having rational grounds for holding a moral opinion and being psychologically compelled to hold it. To see the relevance of this we must once again return to Piaget's developmental theory. The very young child is unable to think about morality in other terms than moral realism, for his intellectual egocentrism effectively prevents him from doing so. The somewhat older child is intellectually capable of the morality of coopera-

---

*e.g. Nowell-Smith (1961). Piaget also seems to subscribe to this view.

tion, but if he has had little or no experience of relationships of mutual respect, it will not be meaningful to him. The great majority of adults, we must presume, have had enough experience of unilateral and mutual respect for both moralities to be meaningful, but, depending upon the quality of their relationships, they will find one more congenial, more 'obvious' and 'natural' than the other. Personal bias of this kind is shown by the religious person who assumes it self-evident that a moral rule loses its compelling force when its divine origin is denied. To others, both religious and non-religious, the divine origin of rules is equally plainly irrelevant to their sense of moral obligation, since this is an obligation to people not to God. But personal bias may not be decisive in determining the position an individual adopts. Perhaps because he has to relate his morality to his religion or his atheism, or because he is studying moral philosophy, he may well be persuaded to accept a position which is not really congenial to him.

As far as the early development of moral judgement is concerned, there are two reasons why we should expect instruction in Christianity to retard development. The first is the content of the doctrines on morality which Christianity has (at least in the past) put forward. The second is the fact that the child is expected to develop attitudes of unilateral respect to a great many authorities in addition to his parents, such as priests, saints, the Bible, theologians of the Church and, of course, God. He is at the bottom of a very awe-inspiring hierarchy.

As yet, however, the evidence is inconclusive. MacRae (1954) found more moral realism among children attending church schools. On the other hand, in Boehm's study (1962) children from Catholic schools were more advanced in their readiness to apply the criterion of intention in their moral evaluations. She attributed this to the fact that Catholic moral teaching stresses the importance of intention. Other studies have failed to find any effect that might be attributed to religious teaching (e.g. Whiteman and Kosier, 1964; Tidmarsh, 1964), though Wright and Cox (1967b) examined the reasons given by over 2,000 adolescents for their moral judgements and found that although only a very small proportion appealed to authority, those that did were invariably devout.

## (G) SOCIAL LEARNING AND MORAL INSIGHT

Piaget's cognitive-developmental theory entails the presumption that age changes are always in the same direction and that in some sense they are irreversible. Social-learning theory is non-developmental and specifies how behavioural patterns are acquired and lost at any age. According to this view a child's moral reasoning will be determined by modelling and social reinforcement processes. It should therefore be possible to change the child's types of reasoning at any time through suitable training.

Two experiments (Bandura and McDonald, 1963; and Cowan *et al.*, 1969) have clearly demonstrated that, between the ages of five and twelve, mature children can be made immature and immature mature through exposure to an adult model who consistently expresses one or other types of moral thinking; and Crowley (1968) has shown that training can make a child more mature. These results have been hailed as damaging to the cognitive-developmental viewpoint (Bandura and Walters, 1963; Bandura, 1969b). They certainly raise difficulties for it. But the problem is complicated. What these experiments have shown is that a child's way of talking about moral issues can be changed over a period of a few days. It is not clear, however, how relevant this is to a theory which postulates a slow and progressive change over a period of years in the cognitive structures underlying behaviour. The social-learning approach is moreover faced with the problem of accounting for the predominance of immature thinking in the very young child when presumably the only models to which he is exposed, namely his parents, are predominantly mature in their reasoning.

## The Work of Kohlberg

The major contribution to our understanding of moral judgement since Piaget's monograph has come from Lawrence Kohlberg.* Taking his stand firmly in the cognitive-developmental theory of Piaget he has systematically extended it to all aspects of socialization and in the process modified it and recast it in his own terms. His main interest so far has been in moral development. Here he has rejected Piaget's insistence upon the importance of social relationships. This rejection is based partly upon the lack of supporting evidence and partly on the fact that, as we have seen, this part of Piaget's theory is not really developmental. The only aspects of moral judgement that change with age have also been found to be related to intelligence.

Kohlberg has studied the moral reasoning of children over a wide age range and has arrived at a sequence of developmental stages which differs in important ways from that of Piaget. His approach was to present children with hypothetical moral dilemmas and then to probe in depth their thinking about them. The situations he used were ones in which obedience to moral law or authoritative decree was set against concern for the needs and welfare of individual people. For example in one of his situations a man's wife is dying from cancer and urgently needs a drug; the man tries all possible legal means to obtain it but fails; he eventually steals it. Kohlberg was less interested in the subject's opinion on whether the husband was right to steal it or not, than on how he set about justifying his opinion.

Exhaustive analysis of the child's responses to such problems yielded at least thirty different aspects of moral thought, each of which was found to develop through at least six stages. We have not the space to go into all these aspects of morality here; they included such dimensions as 'motive for moral action', 'concept of rights', and 'basis for respect for authority'. Suffice it to say that Kohlberg's analysis is very complex and thorough. However, the six developmental stages must be briefly described. They fall into three fundamentally different *levels* of moral thought, each with two stages.

The first two stages are said to be at the *premoral* level. Stage one is a morality founded on punishment and its avoidance. There is no true moral obligation, no concept of the rights of

*See Kohlberg (1963a; 1963b; 1964; 1969).

others, and no true respect for authority, only conforming deference to those who have the power to punish. Stage two is a hedonistic morality, centred on the notion that actions that satisfy needs are justified for that reason. Conformity to the rules is for the purpose of gaining favours and rewards from others. This conception of morality is based on the idea of social exchange in which each party is bent on maximizing his profits regardless of the profits to the other, that is, a profit-seeking uncontrolled by any sense of distributive justice. These two stages are premoral because they are in a sense prepersonal. A person's behaviour is seen as justified in terms of its gain or loss to himself, regardless of how it affects others.

The third and fourth stages are said to be at the level of *conventional role-conformity*. Moral value resides in conformity to the expectations of others, and therefore, unlike the premoral level, involves understanding and adjusting to other people's points of view. The purpose of right behaviour is to please others – Kohlberg calls it the 'good-boy' orientation. The right action is defined by the general consensus of others, and the motive behind right action is the desire to remain accepted by others. Morality in the fourth stage is based on respect for authority. Moral obligation is equated with duty to social and religious authority and the motive behind moral action is the desire to avoid letting authority down and incurring its censure.

The third level of moral maturity, comprising the fifth and sixth stages, is called the *morality of self-accepted moral principles*. Morality is now internalized and autonomous, and it is judged right that an individual should go against the expectations of others and the decree of authority if his conscience dictates that he should. The fifth stage is the morality of contract, of individual rights, and of democratically accepted law. Fundamental to this stage is the recognition that all individuals have rights which are independent of their status, role, or social importance. Finally the most mature morality, that of stage six, is the *morality of individual principles of conscience*. The morality of the previous stage is now lifted to the level of universal principles for guiding conduct.

This developmental scheme has close affinities with Piaget's, but it is also a major advance both in conceptual refinement and in empirical anchorage. Kohlberg has not only shown that these stages follow the same sequence in widely differing cultures, he has also demonstrated that a child who is at a given stage in one aspect of morality will also tend to be at the same, or neighbouring stages in other aspects.

Since Kohlberg's theory relies even more than Piaget's on the influence of maturation in bringing about age changes, it is incumbent upon him to show that the child's moral level is not wholly a function of social influence. Turiel (1966) examined the effect of adult example upon the moral thinking of children. In his experiment adults consistently displayed a type of moral thought which was either one stage above, two stages above, or one stage below that of the subjects. The results showed that it is easier to lift children one stage than either to lower them a stage or raise them two stages. This does indicate that level of intellectual maturation is an important determinant of the child's moral thinking. Another experiment by Rest, Turiel and Kohlberg (1969) gave similar results. In a study of thirteen-year-old boys and girls LeFurgy and Waloshin (1969) placed each subject in a group situation where everyone else present displayed a level of moral thinking either above or below his own. A high proportion of the subjects adjusted their moral thinking to fit those they were with, and this was true whether the effect was upward or downward. Moreover the effect of this social influence could be detected 100 days later. But the long-term effect of the upward influence was much stronger than that of the downward influence. In other words, though it may be relatively easy to induce temporary changes in either direction, long-term changes are more easily effected in an upward than in a downward direction.

Research into Kohlberg's moral stages has only just begun. But already there is a suggestion that they may be more closely related to other aspects of moral behaviour than Piaget's stages were found to be. Kohlberg himself and Schwartz et al. (1969) report that yielding to temptation in experimental tests and conviction for delinquency both tend to go with immature moral insight. Ruma and Mosher (1967) found a strong association between maturity of insight and three different measures of guilt.

Haan, Smith and Block (1968) gave Kohlberg's moral-judgement scale to a large number of college students and Peace Corps volunteers. The subjects also provided biographical data and completed various personality tests. The relatively few subjects who came out at the level of self-accepted moral principles were independent of their parents, very active in social-political protest movements, thought of themselves as rebellious, and were agnostic, atheist or areligious. Most of the subjects tested were at the conventionally moral level. They tended to be politically conservative, relatively inactive in social-political organizations, religious, and conforming to parents and other authority figures. Those at the premoral level were in some respects similar to those at the most mature end of the scale. They were rebellious, radical and non-conformist. But their protest behaviour was a symptom of underlying personal conflict rather than a function of moral ideals. Finally, Nelson, Grinder and Biaggio (1969) found clear signs that children who resisted temptation on experimental tests tended to be more mature in moral judgement than those who yielded.

It must be emphasized again that throughout this chapter we have been dealing with people's moral *theories,* that is, the way they discuss moral problems that are not for the moment theirs. The study of what people say about hypothetical problems discloses a number of distinct moralities, each more or less consistently organized around a few general principles. The number of such moralities is still an open question. Piaget discovered two, loosely centred on the ideas of submission to authority and reciprocal respect for equals; Kohlberg in his more subtle and painstaking analysis detected six, each with its key idea or ideas; and there may be more.

The research quoted above points firmly to one general conclusion: that these moralities are linked to age. They are not linked in the sense that each is a phase through which all people pass on the way to adulthood; no one has yet described a childhood morality which could not be found in some adults. They are related to age in the sense that some demand a higher level of intellectual maturity, and, we must presume, a wider and more varied range of social experience for their understanding and adoption than others. It is solely in this sense that they have been called 'mature'.

It does not follow that because a morality demands more intellectual maturity for its adoption that it is therefore more rational and coherent than others that are less demanding. Most of the moralities classed here as immature have been defended, in their more sophisticated forms of course, by reputable moral philosophers. McCord and Clemes (1964) classify moral philosophers into four types according to the nature of the theories they espouse. And it is not difficult to see the parallel with Kohlberg's types, though of course we are talking about general similarities in perspective – a child's version of a morality will be very different from an adult's version of the same one, and this in turn will be different from a moral philosopher's version. Our interest is not in the logical status of these moralities but in their psychological significance. The presumption is that each is symptomatic of a set of attitudes and feelings, and that these attitudes and feelings are the fruit of past experience, teaching and reflection. The study of the attitudes that lie behind the different moralities and which make them intrinsically plausible to different people has barely begun.*

We need to know how people's theoretical moralities relate to the rest of their moral lives. There are two aspects to this problem. The first is the link between theoretical morality and the way an individual thinks of the situations in which he is actually being called upon to make moral decisions. For example, a man may consistently interpret moral obligation in theory as obedience to an authority. Does this mean that when he feels a moral obligation this is experienced as a need to obey an authority, and if so, is he any different in this respect from some-

* See McCord and Clemes (1964) and Haan, Smith and Block (1968).

one who does not interpret moral obligation in this way? Or, to take another example, does the individual who in theory interprets accidents as punishments construe the actual accidents, at the time they occur, that follow his own transgression any differently from someone who rejects the notion of immanent justice? In short, does adherence to different theoretical moralities imply different ways of conceiving actual moral situations? Most students of theoretical morality have assumed that it does. But the truth is that we do not know, and it is not obvious that it should.

The second aspect is the relationship between an individual's theoretical morality and the way he actually behaves in morally challenging situations. If he interprets moral obligation as obedience to authority is he more or less likely to resist temptation or act altruistically? I quoted earlier some evidence of an association between insight and behaviour;* but it is slender, and much more research is needed if we are to understand how the two are related. Kohlberg, among others, has put forward what has been called the 'ego-development hypothesis', which holds that, under favourable conditions, there is a growing integration with age of all kinds of moral behaviour under the control of thought and reason. This is a useful idea that helps to organize much of the evidence. But it cannot yet be said to be established. It might be argued that one of the features of the greater sophistication that comes with adulthood is precisely a dissociation between moral theory and actual moral response. Whichever way it is, the value of studying people's reasoning about hypothetical moral dilemmas remains problematic until we know how this reasoning fits into the general texture of their moral lives. After all, it is not unreasonable to suppose that *why* a person thinks an action wrong is much less important than *that* he thinks it wrong. Which brings us to the topic of moral ideology.

* In addition, those who have studied criminal psychopaths frequently report that the way they talk about moral issues is markedly different from normal people. See Stephenson (1966).

# CHAPTER 8

# Moral Ideology

We frequently draw a distinction between what a person says he believes and what he 'really' believes. For example, if someone says that it is wrong to exceed the speed limit in towns, yet frequently does so and without any sign of regret, shame or remorse, then we might be tempted to conclude that he does not 'really' believe that it is wrong. A 'real' belief is one we attribute to another in order to render his behaviour intelligible, whether or not he admits it, and sometimes even though he repudiates it – we 'know better' what he believes.

In this chapter we shall be concerned exclusively with verbally expressed or avowed beliefs and not at all with 'real' or inferred ones. More accurately we are interested in what an individual sincerely thinks himself to believe, and his verbal report is taken as an index of this. The qualification is important. What people say they believe is influenced, to greater or lesser degree, by the company they happen to be in at the time. We sometimes realize that what we are saying does not correspond completely with what we would say if we were being entirely honest. Virtually all the evidence to be reviewed consists of expressions of moral belief made in response to questionnaires and interviews under conditions in which the subjects know that their replies are to be used for research purposes and that their anonymity will be preserved. It would be naive to suppose that social pressures to distort responses are thereby totally excluded; but it is plausible to claim that they will be reduced as much as they can be.

By moral ideology we shall mean the total complex of beliefs about what is right and what is wrong that an individual acknowledges as his. This complex is called an ideology in order to draw attention to the fact that moral beliefs can command as much proselytizing zeal and vociferous defence as can religious and political beliefs. The emphasis here will be upon the negative components of moral ideology, that is the beliefs that define wrong action, for more work has been done on them; but the chapter will conclude with a discussion of the more positive values which guide behaviour. Moral beliefs, like other kinds, can be considered from the point of view of their content and from the point of view of their function in the individual's emotional economy. We will deal with the former first.

## The Content of Moral Belief

Though the same basic moral principles can be found in all the great ethical systems, opinions will always vary within a society as to the emphasis that should be given to different principles and the way they should be applied. In a traditional and static society this divergence of judgement will be relatively small; but in a society which is undergoing rapid social change, like contemporary England, there are bound to be whole areas of moral belief where we cannot count with any confidence upon the agreement of others. In this situation surveys of what others believe can be interesting and informative. It is impossible to give an authoritative account of the moral beliefs of English people today; the evidence simply does not exist. But we can in a more modest way illustrate how the degree of consensus can vary from one moral issue to another by looking at the results of two surveys.

In 1963, ABC Television Ltd commissioned a survey of people's attitudes towards religious programmes in the course of which a number of questions were asked about moral belief (Social Surveys, Gallup Poll Ltd, 1964). A representative sample of 2,211 adults over the age of sixteen was studied. They were given a short list of fairly common, everyday actions and asked to indicate whether they approved, disapproved, or were unconcerned about them. Table 1 gives the percentages of those who disapproved of the actions. The significance of the sex differences shown will be taken up later.

Table 1

| | Percentages of subjects disapproving of certain actions | | |
| --- | --- | --- | --- |
| | Total | Men | Women |
| Exceeding speed limits | 75 | 71 | 80 |
| Drinking and driving | 90 | 88 | 91 |
| Leaving litter | 86 | 82 | 90 |
| Taking too much change when a shop assistant makes a mistake | 84 | 82 | 86 |
| Failing to declare all income for tax purposes | 34 | 30 | 38 |
| Taking small quantities of stationery or material from place of work for own use | 61 | 57 | 65 |
| Not paying all the fare on bus or train | 76 | 74 | 79 |

From Social Surveys, Gallup Poll, Ltd. 1964

Certain other findings are worth mentioning. Of the total sample, 26 per cent thought that homosexuals should be punished by law, 27 per cent that they should be condemned by society but not punished, and 36 per cent that society should tolerate them. Again 39 per cent thought prostitutes should be punished by law, 24 per cent that they should be condemned but not punished, and 31 per cent that society should tolerate them. Finally 85 per cent said that if they were in the United States they would support the campaign for equal rights for Negroes. Plainly there is quite a high degree of consensus over litter dropping and driving under the influence of alcohol. The morality of petty theft from large institutions, and of deviation from the sexual norms, is however, much less clearly agreed.

In the second survey (see Wright & Cox, 1967a and b, and Cox, 1967), a narrow section of the population was selected for study. A total of 2,278 boys and girls, mostly aged between seventeen and eighteen, from the second year of the sixth forms of a random sample of 100 maintained grammar schools in England, completed a long questionnaire which included a section on moral belief. The subjects were given a list of eight kinds of behaviour and asked to indicate whether each was 'always wrong', 'usually wrong but sometimes excusable', 'usually excusable but sometimes wrong', or 'never wrong', or whether they had not yet made their minds up. The results are given in Table 2. Again, discussion of the sex differences will be deferred till later. The survey was carried out in 1963.

These boys and girls are plainly united in their respect for

## Table 2

*The percentages of the total sample endorsing the different rating categories—1963 data*

| Moral issue | Sex | Always wrong | Usually wrong | Sometimes wrong | Never wrong | Undecided |
|---|---|---|---|---|---|---|
| Gambling | Boys | 10·7 | 16·9 | 57·0 | 8·3 | 7·1 |
| | Girls | 19·4 | 27·1 | 37·9 | 3·5 | 12·1 |
| Drunkenness | Boys | 30·6 | 46·5 | 17·9 | 2·0 | 3·0 |
| | Girls | 44·9 | 44·4 | 7·8 | 1·1 | 1·8 |
| Smoking | Boys | 14·9 | 10·2 | 32·4 | 31·6 | 10·9 |
| | Girls | 12·3 | 8·9 | 36·2 | 24·4 | 18·2 |
| Lying | Boys | 19·1 | 73·9 | 5·2 | 0·5 | 1·3 |
| | Girls | 23·8 | 72·8 | 2·2 | 0·3 | 0·9 |
| Stealing | Boys | 70·8 | 27·5 | 0·6 | 0·3 | 0·8 |
| | Girls | 71·2 | 27·8 | 0·5 | 0·1 | 0·4 |
| Premarital sexual intercourse | Boys | 28·6 | 27·6 | 20·5 | 10·2 | 13·1 |
| | Girls | 55·8 | 25·2 | 6·6 | 2·4 | 10·0 |
| Suicide | Boys | 32·0 | 28·7 | 13·0 | 15·2 | 11·1 |
| | Girls | 33·4 | 32·7 | 10·1 | 8·7 | 15·1 |
| Colour bar | Boys | 74·0 | 16·8 | 3·2 | 2·4 | 3·6 |
| | Girls | 85·3 | 8·9 | 1·6 | 1·5 | 2·7 |

From Wright and Cox, 1967b

property and the rights of others; but issues like gambling, smoking and premarital sexual intercourse are highly controversial. The results suggest a tentative generalization, that the morality of antisocial acts commands more general agreement than the morality of anti-ascetic acts. Further supporting evidence can be found in a survey of students at Oxford (Thornton, Webb and Weir, 1964) and at an American University (Middleton and Putney, 1962). Antisocial acts against impersonal institutions probably fall into a category of their own.

It is easy to attach too much importance to the actual values of the percentages we have quoted. The results of surveys are notoriously sensitive both to the way questions are worded and to current events in the political and social scene. Careful interpretation is needed in the light of the precise nature of the questions asked.

Differences between societies are issues too peripheral to the main themes of this book for detailed comment, but it can be said in passing, that comparative studies of the moral beliefs and values of students from countries as diverse as Burma, Japan, Korea and the United States have been made. In general very little difference has been found in the kinds of action judged wrong, or in the positive values held. The differences that do exist are ones of emphasis and severity of judgement.* On present evidence there is no justification for saying that one country has higher or lower standards than another in any overall sense.

One of the most confident assumptions made about English society today is that moral standards are declining. In order to demonstrate that a change of this kind is taking place it would be necessary to conduct the same survey twice, with identical sampling procedures and questions, and with a reasonable interval of time between the two occasions. Furthermore all aspects of moral belief would need to be sampled in the questions so that changes on any one issue can be set in their proper context. Satisfactory evidence of this kind does not exist. Because of this dearth of reliable information Wright and Cox decided to repeat

* See, for example, Berrien (1965); Glicksman and Wohl (1965); Tomeh (1968); Rettig and Pasamanick (1959; 1962); and Rettig and Lee (1963).

their survey in 1970, seven years after the first occasion. The same schools took part and the same questions were asked, though an additional moral issue, that of drugs, was included. The population sampled is of course limited to a small segment of society, but within this limitation the data provide fairly reliable evidence of changes that have been occurring. The material has not yet been published and analysis is still incomplete. But the main outlines of the results are clear. The percentages of boys and girls falling into the various rating categories for the moral issues are

## Table 3

*The percentages of the total sample endorsing the different rating categories – 1970 data*

| Moral issue | Sex | Always wrong | Usually wrong | Sometimes wrong | Never wrong | Undecided |
|---|---|---|---|---|---|---|
| Gambling | Boys | 8·8 | 16·4 | 55·7 | 11·5 | 7·5 |
| | Girls | 13·2 | 24·9 | 46·5 | 2·9 | 12·5 |
| Drunkenness | Boys | 17·7 | 35·7 | 34·5 | 8·3 | 3.8 |
| | Girls | 22·4 | 47·4 | 24·0 | 2·0 | 4·2 |
| Smoking | Boys | 20·9 | 11·4 | 21·7 | 34·5 | 11·6 |
| | Girls | 18·2 | 11·5 | 26·3 | 30·2 | 13·7 |
| Lying | Boys | 18·4 | 70·2 | 6·9 | 1·7 | 2·9 |
| | Girls | 17·3 | 74·5 | 6·2 | 0·1 | 1·8 |
| Stealing | Boys | 65·0 | 30·5 | 1·6 | 1·6 | 1·3 |
| | Girls | 64·7 | 32·8 | 0·7 | 0·2 | 1·5 |
| Premarital sexual intercourse | Boys | 10·3 | 12·8 | 30·4 | 33·7 | 12·8 |
| | Girls | 14·6 | 19·5 | 30·0 | 17·7 | 18·2 |
| Suicide | Boys | 28·5 | 23·6 | 10·6 | 19·3 | 18·0 |
| | Girls | 29·4 | 26·1 | 10·2 | 17·2 | 17·1 |
| Colour bar | Boys | 65·6 | 18·1 | 3·7 | 4·9 | 7·7 |
| | Girls | 76·4 | 14·7 | 1·7 | 1·5 | 5·7 |
| Non-addictive drugs | Boys | 29·3 | 17·8 | 18·9 | 19·8 | 14·1 |
| | Girls | 41·6 | 19·6 | 17·3 | 7·8 | 13·6 |
| Addictive drugs | Boys | 65·9 | 14·0 | 4·1 | 7·8 | 8·2 |
| | Girls | 73·2 | 14·2 | 2·6 | 2·7 | 7·3 |

From Wright and Cox, unpublished data

given in Table 3. A comparison with Table 2 will indicate the nature and extent of the changes.

With the exception of smoking, there has been in every instance a shift away from the unqualified condemnation of a form of behaviour. In the case of smoking there has been an increase at both extremes. During the intervening seven years the campaign to stop school children from smoking has been intensified, and the consequence appears to be an increased polarization of attitude. In the cases of lying and stealing, and perhaps gambling, the change is slight and in the direction of greater recognition of extenuating circumstances. Of more interest are the results for colour bar, since the first survey was conducted before colour emerged as a publically discussed problem in England. It is plain that there has been some erosion of moral condemnation of racial discrimination. But in the light of the degree of hostility towards coloured immigrants expressed in public by reputable politicians and newspapers, what is perhaps surprising is the resistance of these moral attitudes to change. The number who are prepared, on an anonymous questionnaire, to condone racial discrimination remains very small. This is in agreement with the evidence reported by Rose (1969).

Far and away the most dramatic change has been in regard to premarital sexual intercourse, and particularly among girls. The results need interpretation however. In addition to giving their ratings of moral issues, subjects were also asked to give reasons for their views. Analysis of these reasons from the 1970 survey is not yet completed. But the preliminary indications are that there has been little or no increase in the condoning of promiscuity. The change has been rather in the direction of an increase in the number who adopt what Reiss (1967) has called the 'permissiveness with affection' standard. It seems that as the link between sexual intercourse and marriage is weakened in the minds of these subjects, so there is a strengthening of the link between sexual intercourse and love. It is questionable whether this represents a 'decline' in moral standards.

We may sum up these changes by saying that condemnation of antisocial actions has declined very little, and then only in the direction of a more qualified condemnation. As far as anti-ascetic actions are concerned there has been a considerable change in the direction of a position which holds that provided no one else is hurt, and in the case of sexual intercourse provided the couple love each other and are responsible, it is no one's business to pass moral judgements on them.

## Some Correlates of Moral Belief

### (A) SEX DIFFERENCES

Women are more likely to disapprove of an action, and to be more uncompromising in their condemnation, than men. The two surveys quoted earlier illustrate this tendency very clearly; and it has been found with some consistency, and in several different countries.* Closer examination of these studies reveals a trend for the sex difference to be at its greatest in relation to anti-ascetic actions. This is especially so for 'immoral' sexual acts; in their professed beliefs women are a good deal less permissive of premarital and extramarital intercourse than men (though they are if anything more permissive of homosexual acts between consenting male adults). It has sometimes been said that because of their biological roles, women tend to be conservers rather than innovators; and this certainly seems to be reflected in their attitude towards morality. However, the evidence of Wright and Cox reported above suggests that this difference between the sexes may be getting smaller.

These conclusions are all based upon evidence from studies in which subjects expressed their commitment to general moral rules or issued blanket condemnations of classes of wrong-doer. When we turn to studies in which their readiness to blame particular individuals for particular offences is measured, these sex differences largely disappear. Klinger *et al.* (1964) reported that neither sex was more lenient than the other over all when judging

* See the studies cited in the previous section and those mentioned under (c) below; also Hartshorne and Shuttleworth (1930); Eisenman (1967); Kempel and Signori (1964); Knupfer, Clark and Room (1966); and Reiss (1967).

dishonest behaviour but that members of each sex tended to be more lenient when the offender was of the same sex. Richey and Fichter (1969) also failed to find any general sex difference in a similar study.

## (B) AGE

As we saw in the last chapter there is a developmental progression in moral reasoning throughout childhood and adolescence. There is little sign that the content of moral belief changes much, though there are shifts in the emphasis given to different kinds of belief.

A favourite technique has been to ask children to list the most wicked deeds they can think of. Gooch and Pringle (1966) review previous studies using this method and report data of their own. They draw certain tentative generalizations. There is considerable variability in the kind of item mentioned at all ages, though murder and stealing are mentioned most frequently by those between eight to eighteen years. Younger children tend to confuse trivial and serious acts, they are less able to generalize and report highly specific deeds, like stealing a particular object. Older subjects not only generalize but take account of mitigating circumstances. They also tend to stress much more the sins of the 'spirit', like disloyalty and betrayal of others. Pressey and Kuhlen (1957) report evidence that from the age of twelve onwards there is a steady decline in the numbers who think smoking, divorce and playing cards wrong, and a steady increase in the numbers who condemn bribery and conceit. Before puberty responses often appear conventional and 'second-hand'; in adolescence they are more likely to bear the stamp of the individual's own reflection.

From the middle twenties onwards, the trend is for moral beliefs to become progressively less flexible, and for people to grow less permissive in their judgements (see Pressey and Kuhlen, 1957: Social Surveys Ltd, 1964). It seems likely that the tendency for older people to think that moral standards have declined reflects this developmental trend towards greater conservatism in themselves as much as it does a genuine social change.

## (C) RELIGION

People who express strong commitment to Christian belief and who attend church fairly frequently have more stringent and exacting moral beliefs than non-believers; they judge more actions wrong, judge them more wrong, and are less ready to recognize extenuating circumstances.* This is as true for litter dropping as for stealing. But there is a clear tendency for the divergence between devout and non-religious to be at its greatest for anti-ascetic actions, and among these for all 'immoral' sexual acts. Of course this is not surprising; but it underlines the fact that the Church is the main institution within society concerned with propagating an ascetic morality.

However, though religious and moral beliefs are usually associated with each other, there is evidence which clearly indicates that the influence of Christianity in no way halts or impedes social changes in moral belief in the direction of greater permissiveness. Wright and Cox were able to check whether changes in belief between 1963 and 1970 were any less among committed and active Christians as defined by professed belief and regularity of church attendance. In fact the results showed plainly that the changes were as great, and in some cases greater, among the devout as among the non-religious, and this was as true of anti-ascetic issues as of antisocial. Linner (1968) quotes evidence to show that Church influence also fails to slow up changes in actual sexual behaviour. In Sweden a survey of premarital sexual activity among young people was carried out in 1960 and again in 1965. There was a marked increase in the incidence of reported premarital intercourse, and this was as great or greater for those in church affiliated schools as for those in entirely secular institutions. Finally Reiss (1967) was able to show that when culture and tradition favoured permissive sexual standards, as among American Negroes, strong commitment to the Christian religion made little or no difference.

*For example: Chesser (1956); Dedman (1959); Gorer (1955); Klinger, Albaum and Hetherington (1964); Middleton and Putney (1962); Thornton, Webb and Weir (1964); Wright and Cox (1967b); and Ruoppila (1967).

## (D) OTHER MEASURES OF MORAL BEHAVIOUR

First of all it is clear that the tendency to adopt a high moral tone is a general trait in the sense that people who have strict moral beliefs in one area of behaviour tend to have strict moral beliefs in other areas of behaviour. Then it might seem obvious that people will resist temptation and experience guilt only with regard to those actions they judge wrong, and that the greater the emotional commitment to a moral belief the greater the congruence between belief and action. On theoretical grounds we might expect people to strive after consistency between belief and action, either by shaping behaviour to fit belief or by modifying belief to accord with behaviour (see Festinger and Freedman, 1964; and Abelson *et al.*, 1968). Either way, expressed commitment to moral belief would be positively associated with resistance to temptation and guilt.

In fact psychologists have signally failed to demonstrate this. Pittel and Mendlesohn (1966) conclude a fairly exhaustive review of the evidence with the assertion that 'no studies have demonstrated that strength of moral values, resistance to temptation and proneness to projective guilt all covary'. In other words, differences in moral belief within the same society are not reliably predictive of differences on these other measures. However, people's reports of their own conduct tend to coincide with their moral beliefs, especially when they are strongly committed to these beliefs (see Middleton and Putney, 1962; and Campbell, 1964). And the values of delinquents do differ from those of non-delinquents, even though the differences are much smaller than might be expected.

Pittel and Mendlesohn attribute the generally inconclusive outcome of research so far to deficiencies in the way moral attitudes and beliefs have been measured; and many of their strictures are well deserved. But even if there is more consistency between belief and action than has so far been revealed, there are factors which are bound to limit its extent. It is not uncommon for people to decide later in life that a given action is no longer wrong but because of early conditioning still be unable to commit it, or at least commit it without guilt. In psycho-analytic language, the superego is to a large extent unconscious and therefore outside the influence of changes in conscious moral belief. More fundamentally the situations in which people express their moral beliefs are radically different from those in which they have to act upon them. Though the main function of moral belief is to guide action it obviously has many other functions. Declarations of moral belief identify to others the kind of person we are and thereby determine how they will act towards us. More important we define ourselves to ourselves through the beliefs we hold. If I think of myself as an individual-ist it becomes important to me that my beliefs should never wholly coincide with those of others; on the other hand if I derive pleasure from thinking of myself as an upright and res-pectable citizen then I shall take care that my beliefs are iden-tical with those of other respectable citizens. Not only, then, will the *expression* of my moral belief have immediate social consequences, but the conscious *holding* of the belief may also serve an important function in my personality. It is to these personality functions of moral belief that we must now turn.

## Moral Belief and Personality

In the study by Wright and Cox mentioned earlier, examina-tion of the reasons given by subjects for their moral judgements revealed three fairly distinctive styles of moral thought. They showed up most clearly on the anti-ascetic items, and particu-larly on premarital intercourse.

The first is represented by those who apparently thought very few actions were ever wrong, and whose attitude was cynical (e.g. lying is 'OK as long as you do it well') or summarized in the formula 'what other people do is their business and no one else's'. The prevailing tone was one of minimal concern – it does not matter what you do as long as you do not interfere with others. Only a small minority of the sample fell into this group.

At the other extreme were those who thought most of the

actions were always wrong, and whose 'reasons' were highly charged with feeling. For example one subject wrote 'I think of sexual intercourse before marriage as disgusting and think that people should treat intercourse after marriage with respect instead of wasting their whole lives by one cheap act'; and another 'for people to indulge in sexual intercourse before marriage shows complete lack of control and I find such people despicable'. Some subjects appeared to assume that for a girl to have sexual intercourse before marriage was equivalent to 'being used', and of course no one wants 'second-hand goods'. Typically the justifications given for condemning an action as always wrong were that it involved loss of self-control and therefore of self-esteem, or that it violated the edict of an authority like the Church or the Bible.

Subjects in the third group were certainly not lacking in moral concern, but they were more discriminating, less emotionally coloured in their remarks, and more tentative and ready to acknowledge extenuating circumstances. For example one subject wrote of premarital intercourse 'This depends entirely on the people concerned. I can see nothing wrong if the people concerned take a responsible view of their actions and love each other'; and another, 'If two people are in love, a truly genuine love, there is nothing against their sharing that love physically if it does not involve a third party. But if it is a mere matter of sex at its crudest then I feel it is wrong.' Actions were judged wrong when they had unpleasant consequences for others or when they would have a destructive effect on the personality of the actor if he persisted in them.

It is difficult to read through these comments without a strong impression that these styles of moral believing correspond to more general personality differences. Unfortunately the survey itself affords no evidence as to what these personality differences might be. All that can be said is that these styles of believing are related to religious commitment. Subjects in the first group are usually atheist and male. Those in the second group report a high degree of certainty of belief in various aspects of Christian doctrine and say that they attend church fairly frequently; and girls tend to predominate over boys. The third group comprises all shades of religious opinion and belief, the common factor being an open and questioning attitude. But even if we have no evidence relating these forms of moral belief to personality, there is a striking parallel between them and the three ways of resolving the adolescent crisis as described by the psychoanalysts, in particular Anna Freud (1937).

In Anna Freud's view adolescence resembles infancy in that once again 'a relatively strong id confronts a relatively weak ego'. As a result of sexual maturation, the 'relation established between the forces of the ego and the id is destroyed, the painfully achieved psychic balance upset, with the result that inner conflicts between the two institutions blaze up afresh'. Two extreme solutions to this conflict are possible.

Either the id, now grown strong, may overcome the ego, in which case no trace will be left of the previous character of the individual and the entrance into adult life will be marked by a riot of uninhibited gratification of instinct. Or the ego may be victorious, in which case the character of the individual during the latency period will declare itself for good and all.

In this latter case the id impulses 'are confined within the narrow limits prescribed for the instinctual life of the child'. From the point of view of many parents, such an adolescent is likely to be regarded as 'good', for he identifies with the values of authority, is a model of that obedient and respectful behaviour they like, and he remains much more closely attached to his parents than to his peers. But a heavy price is paid for such 'virtue'. Not only does the individual miss out on a whole developmental phase, with a consequent crippling of his instinctual life, but 'ego-institutions which have resisted the onslaught of puberty without yielding generally remain throughout life inflexible, unassailable and insusceptible of the rectification which a changing reality demands'. Just as we should expect the former type of adolescent to show little moral concern in his expressed beliefs, so we would expect the latter to be rigid and uncompromising in his moral beliefs, to be intolerant of self-indulgence in others, and to be very preoccupied with self-control and obedience.

The third way of resolving the adolescent crisis is the middle course between these extremes. The ego gives ground but is not swept away, and its integrity is not lost. The strengthened impulses of the id are allowed controlled expression and in the process the ego itself is changed. Values are modified, not lost. We should expect such adolescents to manifest a real moral concern and involvement, but also to be discriminating, flexible and individual in their judgements, and more able to tolerate diversity of opinion in others.

In the last chapter I mentioned in passing the phenomenon of the authoritarian personality as revealed by the researches of Adorno *et al.* (1950). Anna Freud's second kind of adolescent seems destined to become an authoritarian person. For in addition to his tendency to be racially prejudiced and ethnocentric, the authoritarian person is described as respectful and subservient towards authority, brusque and rather contemptuous towards his subordinates, repressive of his own instincts, conservative and convention-bound in his beliefs, generally opposed to licence and self-indulgence and in favour of discipline, and punitive and unsympathetic towards 'sinners', particularly if they are judged 'inferior' in some way.

Adorno and his associates were only peripherally interested in moral belief; they sought to define authoritarianism as a general personality trait. But characteristic differences in moral judgement between authoritarian and non-authoritarian people exist, and they are well brought out in an experiment by Alper, Levin and Klein (1964). These investigators selected two groups of subjects, one high on authoritarianism, the other low on it, using the same measuring devices as Adorno and his associates. All subjects were then asked to read a story the essence of which was as follows: A (the only woman in the story) loves B who does not love her; C, however, does love A; with the knowledge of E and the connivance of D, A spends a night with B; the next morning B throws A out; she then goes to C who, knowing that she has spent the night with B, throws her out also. All subjects were then asked to rank the five characters in the story from 'who acted best' to 'who acted worst', stating reasons for the rank-order chosen.

There were a number of significant differences between the two groups, the most striking being that authoritarians were markedly more critical of A and approving of C. C's rejection of A was judged especially praiseworthy because 'he doesn't let his emotions rule over his morals (B might have V.D.)', and he 'doesn't want a used woman'. Subjects low on authoritarianism were much more indulgent towards A, whose behaviour was entirely natural and understandable, but condemned C with some asperity, since his behaviour was clearly incompatible with a real love for A.

Since the pioneer work on the authoritarian personality was published, a massive amount of research has been carried out to check the original findings and, although a number of damaging criticisms have been levelled against the methodology used, many of the original contentions have survived surprisingly well, at least in modified form. I cannot discuss all criticisms here (see Brown, 1965) but one must be mentioned. The authoritarian personality, as defined by Adorno *et al.*, tends to be politically right-wing. As has been pointed out many times, dogmatic inflexibility is by no means the prerogative of the right. This emphasis in the original research stems from the fact that the authors were primarily interested in ethnic and racial prejudice, and it appears to be the case that people who are politically left-wing are less likely to be prejudiced in this way. But the general criticism has served as the point of departure for Rokeach (1960; 1968), whose theory of the open and closed mind is an attempt to understand the nature of dogmatic believing whatever the content of the belief may be. Rokeach also was not directly concerned with moral belief; but his work is so clearly relevant to an understanding of moral belief that I must give a brief outline of it.

Everyone has a total belief-disbelief system. It includes not only the beliefs and disbeliefs that he can verbalize but also all those implicit in his behaviour – though in fact Rokeach's research has mostly concerned expressed beliefs. This total system divides into a belief subsystem and a disbelief subsystem. Disbeliefs are not just the mirror opposites of beliefs, for to assert one belief is often to imply a number of disbeliefs (for example, belief in Christianity may mean the rejection of Marxism, Buddhism, atheism, humanism, etc.). It is not clear how Rokeach would apply this distinction to moral belief, but we shall assume, provisionally, that statements defining wrong actions correspond to disbeliefs, and definitions of good actions to beliefs.

Rokeach then proceeds to describe the ways in which belief-disbelief systems can vary. First there is the degree of *isolation* they exhibit. A belief system has a high degree of isolation when the component beliefs are prevented from coming into relationship with each other. Thus a man may keep his religious beliefs separated off from those he acts upon in his business life. It is only possible to assert that lying, stealing, and other actions are *always* wrong, and that kindness and concern for others are *always* right, by keeping these beliefs relatively isolated from each other; for reflection would show that there could be occasions when they conflict sharply with each other.

A consequence of isolation is the holding of contradictory beliefs. On one occasion a man may affirm a faith in the intelligence of the common man and on another inveigh against the stupidity of the masses; or he may claim that lying and stealing are always wrong but that it is permissible for his country to deceive a foreign country, and to appropriate and retain its territory. A further consequence of isolation is the *accentuation of differences* between beliefs and disbeliefs. For example a man may assert that Christianity is wholly true and that it has absolutely nothing in common with Marxism which is wholly false. Or he may regard sexual intercourse within marriage as always good, even obligatory, whereas outside marriage it is always very wicked.

The opposite condition to isolation is one in which the continuing juxtaposition of previously unrelated beliefs leads to the ready perception of contradiction and the consequent modification of beliefs in the interests of greater consistency. The constant formation of new relationships within the system means that the boundaries between beliefs and disbeliefs are never fixed and final. There will be areas of uncertainty, and a tendency to qualify judgements. Instead of issuing a blanket condemnation of stealing, for instance, the individual will distinguish a whole range of conditions under which stealing varies from being permissible and even obligatory to being wholly reprehensible.

Belief-disbelief systems can also vary in their degree of *differentiation*. A differentiated system is one in which beliefs and disbeliefs are articulated in great detail; it implies that the individual knows a great deal about things he believes and disbelieves in. Lack of differentiation is typified by the Christian who has never really studied Christianity but is certain it is true and who knows nothing of Marxism but is sure it is false. In the moral sphere such lack of differentiation might be exemplified by an individual who totally condemns stealing or homosexuality without pausing to inquire why people do such things and whether these actions might not have positive value on some occasions.

A *closed* mind is one which has a relatively high degree of isolation, contradiction and accentuation of belief-disbelief difference, and which is poorly differentiated, especially in its disbelief subsystem. The system tends to be frozen, static, resistant to change and intolerant of ambiguity and uncertainty; the individual *knows* what is true and what is false, what is right and what is wrong, and has no intention of altering his views. People with closed minds tend to interpret experience as always confirming what they already believe. The *open* mind is by contrast a growing and developing system; it is so to speak perpetually unfinished. Not only is there a continuing and spontaneous tendency for the elements within it to be brought into new relationships with each other and thereby modified, but the system as a whole is sensitively responsive to the tuition of a changing reality. 'Belief systems,' says Rokeach,

serve two opposing sets of functions. On the one hand they represent Everyman's theory for understanding the world he lives in. On the other hand they represent Everyman's defence network through which information is filtered in order to render harmless that which threatens the ego. (Rokeach, 1960)

The former function predominates in the open mind, the latter in the closed mind.

The defensive functions that moral belief may serve are doubtless as many and varied as there are people. But we can point to some of the more obvious possibilities. To begin with, strong and emotional condemnation of an action could be a defence against a rather persistent inclination to perform it. By emphasizing the wrongness of an action the desire to perform it is drowned out. Then people may have special vested interests which bias their moral beliefs. This could be true in a literal sense: those who live on the private income from investments are inclined to defend stoutly the morality of a system which enables them to do this. It has been suggested that the tendency for the middle and upper classes in Victorian England to propagate a morality of thrift, hard work and respect for one's betters was nourished by their desire to retain their comfortable position of superiority in the social system. Certain social institutions, such as the Church, specialize in the task of defining the moral standards of society, and occupants of roles within these institutions are under particular pressure to maintain an impeccably high moral tone in their utterances. At a more individual level, emotional commitment to lofty moral standards is one relatively easy way of bolstering a sense of moral ascendancy over others.

Whatever the nature of the ulterior motives at work in the closed mind, their presence is betrayed by a variety of signs. Since the degree of certainty felt usually goes well beyond what is justifiable in terms of evidence and reasoning alone, it has to be defended in other ways. The most simple and characteristic of these is the appeal to authority. If the moral rule can be derived from an authority which is regarded as absolute and infallible then at one stroke the problem is solved. Not only is the subjective certainty justified but there is the additional security generated by the knowledge that other problems can be solved in a similar way.

Since beliefs function as a kind of defensive carapace holding the personality together, the existence of other people who think differently is threatening to personal stability. The closed-minded individual therefore tends to avoid encountering conflicting points of view and to stay close to others holding similar views. If he cannot help meeting opponents, then he is apt to resort to a number of defensive techniques. These include efforts to suppress the expression of alternative viewpoints by law, by social ostracism, or by other indirect means, urgent attempts to convert the wayward non-conformer, and such devices as sarcasm, derision and 'shouting down'. The most subtle and effective defence is to give a psychological explanation of differing viewpoints, for instance by attributing them to ignorance or some disreputable motive. The classic example is the way some psychoanalysts effectively encapsulate themselves against criticism by construing it as evidence of an emotional resistance to the truth, symptomatic of repression. The easiest way of disposing of advocates of a more permissive morality than one's own is to interpret it as a rationalization of moral turpitude. What these and other defensive moves have in common is that they divert the individual from actually listening sympathetically to what his opponent has to say, considering it on its own merits, and learning from it.

The more inflexible the individual's belief-disbelief system the more he is handicapped in the solution of problems which require creative innovation. Rokeach (1960) gave his subjects a problem the solution to which demanded the suspension of certain basic beliefs about the nature of the universe and playing along with new and unfamiliar beliefs. Highly dogmatic subjects with closed minds were less successful at it. It has been said that the reason why many missionaries in the past failed to have much influence upon the peoples they visited was because they were unable to enter sympathetically into a cultural frame of reference that was alien to their own. There is a clear parallel here between this inability to see other points of view and the egocentrism of the young child described by Piaget. In two experiments Feather (1964; 1967) has shown that strong commitment to beliefs can distort the individual's capacity to reason logically. He found that subjects who were fervently committed to religious beliefs were more likely to judge false, pro-religious arguments as valid, and valid anti-religious arguments as false, than other subjects who did not have strong beliefs on the matter.

Since people with closed minds tend to react with anger to those who disagree with them, it is plausible to conjecture that they will be more prone to moral indignation against others who actually break the moral rules than the open minded. Moral indignation is such a complex and important human response that something must be said about it. Unfortunately psychologists have almost completely neglected it, and therefore what follows is entirely speculative. The brief discussion of blame in chapter 5 is also relevant (p. 105f).

Any analysis of moral indignation must take account of the following elements that may be present in various combinations. There is first simple *reactive anger* which is the individual's response when he himself is the victim of the wrong-doing. Secondly there is *empathic distress* at seeing or hearing about the victim's suffering. This is the response which leads people to comfort, recompense and help the victim, and to take steps to ensure that the offence is not committed again. Thirdly there is *vicarious reactive anger* on behalf of the victim. Identification with the victim leads us to feel the anger we would feel were we the victim. But judging by the intensity of the anger shown by people at offences as diverse as vandalism and relatively mild sexual assault on children it seems plain that these sources of anger are supplemented by another factor which I shall call *moral anger*. It is as if the mere knowledge that the act has been committed incenses people so that they cannot rest until they see the offender punished. If the letters written to newspapers are any guide, moral anger can sometimes unleash punishment fantasies of a quite barbaric kind. Yet even when this is not the case it is felt to be intolerable that people can do these things and escape punishment. Now though it would be difficult to establish the point it certainly seems that moral anger is often the strongest element present in people's reactions. Of course it is usually justified in terms of the victim's suffering. But it is frequently obvious that real concern for the victim has receded into the background. It is notorious, for instance, that in our society more energy is spent in advocating severer punishments for offenders than in urging compensation for victims. It certainly seems that moral anger can be an alternative to or escape from empathic distress at the victim's plight, a way of drowning it out.

The presence of moral anger is most clearly seen when there is no victim of the offence or when the offender is also the victim, or at least the one who suffers by far the most from the offence. The best illustrations are anti-ascetic actions like taking soft drugs, refusing to work, and various sexual 'offences' like masturbation, homosexuality and premarital sexual intercourse. There are people who feel compelled to declare their disgust and disapproval of such things and who want to see the offenders suffer in some way, if not through legal means then through shame or social ostracism. The treatment of unmarried mothers still affords classic examples of 'sinners' who are already suffering being made to suffer more by the 'righteous'.

The nature of moral anger remains puzzling. However, if we look more closely at it two things become apparent. First of all, if we leave aside those serious offences that provoke horror in nearly everyone, then it seems that people specialize in the kinds of behaviour that spark off their fiercest indignation. For example it may be anti-ascetic actions, or social and economic injustice, or disrespect for, and disobedience of, established authorities. Secondly this intensity and selectivity implies a deep personal involvement in the offences. It is as if the person's security has been put at risk and he can only feel safe again when the offender has been punished. Certain moral beliefs serve special functions for him in containing and stabilizing his own desires and fears and when he sees others disregard them he feels personally threatened.

Psychoanalysis is the only theory which has so far taken seriously the phenomenon of moral indignation. The usual interpretation is along the lines that perceiving cruelty or sexual self-indulgence in others provokes the strong but unconscious desire to do the same, and thereby alerts the repressive aggression of the superego. The resulting tension and conflict are resolved by displacing this aggression away from the self on to the offender. The presence of the unconscious desire to do the same thing can sometimes be detected in the punishment fantasies which accompany efforts to see that the offender pays for his offence. From a learning-theory point of view the basic assumption would be that through generalization the perception of someone else committing an offence of a kind for which the individual has in the past himself been punished arouses anxiety. If previous learning has established the pattern that seeing the offenders punished reduces this anxiety, then he will be strongly motivated to ensure that this happens again. The social psychologist would point out that the morally indignant stance is apt to be socially approved and respected and it declares our solidarity with particular groups of people who share our values – our membership and reference groups.

It should be stressed that of course there may well be entirely respectable and rational grounds for seeking the punishment of those who break important moral rules. Our concern has been with the primitive, irrational and more or less compulsive *need* to see them punished, and this, as I have said, is only one strand in the emotional reaction to the wrong-doing of others. But whatever the explanation of moral anger it seems likely that we shall find it most often in those people who have high emotional investment in specific and inflexible moral beliefs, whose belief system is, in Rokeach's sense, a closed one. For them, moral indignation will effectively inhibit any sympathetic understanding of the offender's predicament and it will make the recognition of extenuating circumstances very difficult.

## Values

Values have been defined as 'meanings perceived as related to self' (Allport, 1968). To value something means to prefer it, to invest energy in it and to work for it. The thing valued can be an object like an old car, an action such as the offer of help from others, a state of body or mind such as health, knowledge, virginity or salvation, or a social abstraction like status or democracy.

The concept of value is therefore closely related to the concept of motivation. This is especially true for *operative* values, or the values we infer from the way an individual actually behaves. Our concern here is with *conceived* or *expressed* values, however, and the relation between these and motives is more complex. Nevertheless we can assume that expressed values are not unrelated to operative ones, particularly if these expressed values are measured under conditions in which the subject has every reason to be sincere and truthful.

The interests and values that guide men's behaviour are myriad. It would obviously be a step forward if it could be shown that these values reduce to a limited number of types of value. Many attempts have been made to do this (see Eysenck, 1960, for a review), among which two are of special interest here. Both started with theoretical presuppositions rather than any extensive examination of the values actually held by people, and consequently neither is fully comprehensive.

The first value typology owes its origin to the speculative theories of Spranger (1928). The starting point of Spranger's theory was the assumption that the infinitely varied attitudes people express can be reduced to six basic ones which are in fact implicit in every action – 'the totality of mind is present in every mental act'. In 1931 Allport and Vernon took up this classification and constructed a test on the assumption that people vary in the extent to which these values predominate in their thinking and action and that it is possible to classify people in this way (see Allport, Vernon and Lindzey, 1960). The test provides a measure of the relative importance of each value for the individual. The values are as follows. The *theoretical* value stresses truth, the importance of knowledge, reasoning and critical thought. The *economic* value emphasizes what is useful and practical – the 'pay-off' of any action. The *aesthetic* value bases judgement on the form or elegance of an act, its fitness and appropriateness for the occasion. The *social* value places the primacy upon love of others, and sympathetic and unselfish service. The *political* value is concerned with power and control in human affairs. Finally the *religious* value implies the importance of a contemplative and mystical attitude in which individual acts are placed within the context of the unity of creation and derive their meaning from this context.

The Allport-Vernon scale has been used in a great deal of research. It is clear, for example, that value patterns are related to occupational choice, and that on average females tend to score higher than males on aesthetic, social and religious values, and lower on theoretical, economic and political values. In both sexes there is a tendency for certain values to go together. Thus people high on the economic value tend to be high on the political one as well; and the religious and social values tend to go together. Whereas upbringing is doubtless of great importance in shaping an individual's value pattern, it is likely too that basic differences in personality such as those between extroverts and introverts also play their part (see Eysenck, 1960).

The second approach to the classification of values is that of Morris (1956). From his study of the major ethico-religious systems of the world, Morris postulated seven basic 'paths of life', each representing a different way of ordering values. Ordering of values was held to follow from the differential emphasis of three 'components of personality' labelled *dionysian* (tendencies to release and indulge existing desires), *promethean* (the tendency to change and remake the world), and *buddhistic* (the tendency to regulate the self by holding desires in check). However, when Morris set out to construct a test to measure the extent to which people felt drawn towards the various paths he was obliged to add to them until eventually he ended up with thirteen 'ways of life'. In the final form of the scale the subject is presented with thirteen paragraphs, each describing a way of life, and is required to rate the extent to which he favours each.* Armed with

---

* I cannot reproduce all thirteen ways. These two are given as illustrations

*Way 3:* This way of life makes central the sympathetic concern for other persons. Affection should be the main thing in life, affection that is free from all traces of the imposition of oneself upon others or of using others for one's own purposes. Greed in possessions, emphasis on sexual passion, the search for power over persons and things, excessive emphasis upon intellect, and undue concern for oneself are to be avoided. For these things hinder the sympathetic

this measuring instrument, Morris proceeded to conduct a number of empirical studies. It is clear that preference for certain ways of life goes with preference for certain others. Analysis of the patterns of preference revealed five underlying primary values rather than the three components of personality with which Morris started. These five primary values emphasize:

(a) 'responsible, conscientious and intelligent participation in human affairs', and appreciating and conserving what has been achieved rather than initiating change;

(b) 'vigorous action for the overcoming of obstacles' and the initiation of change rather than preserving what has been achieved;

(c) 'a rich inner life of heightened self-awareness', insight, a deep sympathy with all living things and the repudiation of control over persons and things;

(d) receptivity and sympathetic responsiveness to others, service to them and submission to their needs;

(e) sensuous enjoyments of all kinds.

Cross-cultural comparisons of students from the United States, India, China, Japan and Norway all yield the same five underlying primary values, though the ways of life most favoured vary among these different cultures. In all countries there was a tendency for women to value more highly than men those ways of

---

love among persons which alone gives significance to life. If we are aggressive we block our receptivity to the personal forces upon which we are dependent for genuine personal growth. One should accordingly purify oneself, restrain one's self-assertiveness, and become receptive, appreciative, and helpful with respect to other persons.

*Way 10:* Self-control should be the keynote of life. Not the easy self-control which retreats from the world, but the vigilant, stern, manly control of a self which lives in the world, and knows the strength of the world and the limits of human power. The good life is rationally directed and holds firm to high ideals. It is not bent by the seductive voices of comfort and desire. It does not expect social utopias. It is distrustful of final victories. Too much cannot be expected. Yet one can with vigilance hold firm the reins to his self, control his unruly impulses, understand his place in the world, guide his actions by reason, maintain his self-reliant independence. And in this way, though he finally perish, man can keep his human dignity and respect, and die with cosmic good manners. (See Morris, 1956.)

life expressive of (d) above, and to favour less highly those associated with (b). The study of age differences shows that over thirty-five 'there is a marked decline in the appeal of activistic and energetic conceptions of the good life and some increase in the appeal of the more conservative, receptive, meditative and socially responsible conceptions'. Within the sample drawn from the United States, physique was found related to preference for particular primary values. Primary value (b) was favoured by those with muscular, athletic or mesomorphic physiques, (c) by those who were linear, stringy muscled or ectomorphic, and (e) by those with a soft, rounded or endomorphic physique. The other two primary values were not related to physique. Morris also reports some evidence of an association between preference-on-the-ways-of-life test and temperament (see also Butt and Signori, 1965). This research, like that done on the Allport-Vernon study of values, leaves little doubt about the intimate link between the individual's personality and his dominant values.

In this chapter I have dealt with the two aspects of moral ideology, beliefs about what is wrong and the values that define the positive goals in life. The former correspond to the conscience part of the superego, and are acquired initially from parents in a context of punishment and anxiety; the positive values, which make up the ego-ideal, are said to stem from anaclitic identification with the parents, that is from love and admiration for them. There is every reason to think that most people who have been closely attached to their parents in youth remain marked by their values for life. Certainly, research constantly finds a strong connection between the values and beliefs of young adults and those of their parents in societies where the small nuclear family is the norm. And in adolescence it is common for parents to be idealized in the sense that the adolescent sees his parents as closer to his ideal for himself than he sees himself (Wright, 1962). Studies of the development of the ego-ideal reveal two trends. The first is for the range and variety of people who influence the child's ego-ideal to widen steadily. And the second is for the ideal, which in childhood is rather literally embodied in actual persons, to become increasingly abstract during adolescence, and dissociated from the images of particular people (see Van den Daele, 1968).

This second trend brings up again the point discussed at the end of the chapter on altruism, namely the extent to which the ego-ideal remains an *ego*-ideal. We can speculate that the wider the range of people who influence the adolescent and the less he is dominated by admiration for any one, the more readily his ego-ideal will be transformed from the image of the person he wants to become into a scheme of values he wants to see realized among people generally.

Finally the relative importance of the two components of the superego, the conscience and the ego-ideal, can vary. We have all met, on the one hand, people so preoccupied with meticulously avoiding doing wrong that their creative energies suffer, and on the other hand those who pour their energies into the realizing of positive values and are careless whether they depart from the rules a little in the process. Presumably this also reflects the emphasis that parents put on the two aspects. But it leaves us with the possibility that too great an emphasis upon the conscience can frustrate the development of the more positive and creative aspects of morality.

# CHAPTER 9

# Character

The five main facets of moral behaviour, resistance to temptation, guilt, altruism, and moral insight and belief, have now been examined in some detail. Each has been considered more or less on its own. The questions that remain concern the manner in which they are related to each other, and how they are organized and integrated within the individual.

As we saw in chapter 2 in discussing the concept of conscience, there is a way of talking about moral behaviour which seems to carry with it the inference that its different aspects are all due to the functioning of a specific part or 'organ' of the personality, or to some unitary moral force. People's consciences are strong or weak. If strong, they resist temptation, feel strong guilt when they do succumb, act unselfishly, and are severe in their moral judgements and beliefs; if weak, they lack self-control and are self-centred, pursue their own ends irrespective of the consequences to others, and are without guilt or remorse.* It is sometimes suggested that the origins of a weak conscience are lack of religion and a permissive upbringing – and even the genetic inferiority of belonging to another race, class or nationality.

This view is manifestly too simple. As the evidence reported in previous chapters makes clear, individual differences in one aspect of morality are only weakly and uncertainly associated with individual differences in others. People who resist temptation well are not necessarily likely to feel more guilt when they

*There are obvious parallels with the notion of 'general intelligence', which people have either more or less of, and which shows itself in a number of different ways.

transgress, or to be more altruistic. Improved measuring techniques and more extensive sampling may reveal stronger associations than have yet been discovered. But it is unlikely that the various dimensions will ever be found to be closely related, for each is very complex and influenced by a great many different kinds of learning experience.

It is more realistic to assume that individuals will display a wide variety of profiles on these five dimensions, and that the problem is not one of accounting for different strengths of conscience but of defining and explaining characteristic overall patterns or styles of moral response. In other words, are there distinctive character types, and if so what are they like and how do they develop?

It is not our business to explore the various nuances of meaning attached to the notion of character (see Rosenhan and London, 1968). But in saying that a person has a certain kind of character we mean more than that he exhibits a given profile on the five aspects of moral behaviour. Character is defined not so much through an inventory of actions performed, as by a description of the principles that give coherence and meaning to an individual's behaviour, and of the relatively enduring dispositions and motivations that underly it. It is perhaps for this reason that most of the existing character typologies had their point of inception not in empirical data but in some theoretical perspective on personality as a whole. Indeed there is no further evidence to report. The question I shall ask is this: given the evidence we already have, what at present looks like the most useful 'character-map' for finding our way about among the myriad differences that people display?

Broadly speaking, the typologies advanced by psychologists and sociologists fall into three groups. First there are those that relate character to social structure. Different social structures are analysed, or different features within the same structure, and then inferences are drawn about the nature of the people who most naturally 'fit' these structures. (Two influential examples are the theories of Fromm, 1947, and Riesman, 1950.) These theories are of great interest, but the authors nowhere make explicit how their different types might be expected to behave in terms of the five dimensions we have been concerned with. At the other extreme are those typologies that derive immediately from empirical study but which are based on only one facet of moral behaviour. Examples have been given earlier in the book, particularly in the chapters on delinquency, moral insight and moral ideology. Some of them have implications for behaviour on other moral dimensions, but these implications have not usually been worked out. Lastly there are typologies that have sought to describe character in terms of all aspects of moral behaviour.* Most of them have roots in experimental data though they go well beyond it.

Since these typologies are speculative and sometimes arbitrary, there is little point in attempting to review them in detail. Fortunately they overlap a good deal, and there are many common themes. So instead I propose to devote the rest of this chapter to outlining a typology which coincides with none of them but which is a kind of composite of them all. At the same time, in order to summarize and integrate many of the themes of earlier chapters, it will go beyond them. But it must be clearly understood what a typology of this kind means. It does not imply that everyone will fall into one or other of the types described. On the contrary, few people will exactly fit any one of them. For as the term is used here, a 'type' is not a category or pigeon-hole into which people can be placed. It is more like a landmark represented on a map, or a convenient reference point in a complex matrix of interrelated variables. Each point is defined, at least in principle, by a certain set of positions on the various dimensions of moral behaviour. The criteria adopted for selecting these reference points were that they should be reasonably representative of all the possibilities and that they should be related to an intelligible if primitive underlying rationale.

At this point we must digress for a moment. So far no mention has been made in this book of the possible influence of the

* For example: Havighurst and Taba (1949); Sullivan, Grant and Grant (1957); Peck and Havighurst (1960); McCord and McCord (1960); Bronfenbrenner (1962a; 1962b; 1970a); and Loevinger (1966).

psychologist's own moral values on his study of moral behaviour, for the normal consequence of adopting the empirical approach is to exclude such influence. In deciding whether a given form of behaviour is to be classified as morally relevant, for instance, the psychologist can take his cue from the norms of the society to which his subjects belong. In principle it should be possible to study character without the intrusion of the investigator's evaluative stance, but in practice it is not easy. The proponents of character typologies are apt to leave the reader with the suspicion that the author's values are not so much excluded as hidden and disguised.

Character is usually conceived within a developmental perspective, so that certain character structures are held to be more *mature* than others. It is the use of the term *mature* which betrays the psychologist's evaluative bias. With regard to many characteristics that change with age, such as height and intelligence, it is possible to define as mature that form which is exhibited by older people, and the psychologist is not necessarily committed to the view that the mature form is more desirable. But though it is possible to link different character types to different stages of development, the relationship is tenuous and uncertain, and all types can be found among adults. In designating one of them the most mature, the psychologist cannot appeal to the unequivocal and objective criterion of age, and is therefore necessarily giving expression to his view of which is the most desirable.

The developmental perspective will not be much in evidence in the account that follows, but its influence is nonetheless present. To protect the reader, the evaluative bias should therefore be made explicit. It lies in the assumption that the more mature the character is, the more it can be justly described as autonomous, flexible, rational, and sympathetically altruistic. The most desirable character type is that which combines independence and individuality with moral sensitivity and concern for others – the type here labelled autonomous-altruistic. The presumption is that optimal psychological development throughout life involves a progression in the direction of just such an autonomy. But obviously this is a personal view and not shared by everyone (the educational programmes proposed by some people seem designed precisely to frustrate such a development).

The character typology to be described is represented schematically in figure 1. It allows for six main types of character, and they are arranged along two dimensions. The baseline represents the relative importance during upbringing of the major socializing influences, parents and other adults in authority on the one hand and the peer group and friends on the other. The mid-point is intended to indicate a hypothetical point of equilibrium between the two influences, so that moving to the left means an increasing preponderance of adult influence and moving to the right a lack of balance favouring peer influence. There is, however, further meaning carried by the mid-point of this dimension. It implies an upbringing rich in democratic moments with adults and relationships of mutual respect within individual friendships with peers. The vertical dimension has three related meanings. It indicates the extent to which the socializing influence, from whatever source, has been taken in, internalized and made his own by the individual. It therefore also represents the degree of intensity and effectiveness of the socializing influence. Finally it indicates the extent to which the individual is *still dependent* upon these sources of influence. In this last sense the relationship is curvilinear. Both the *amoral* and the *autonomous-altruistic* characters are independent of the influence of both authorities and social groups, the former because they have never been effectively brought under such influence, and the latter because they have to a large extent grown through and free of such influence. Because the actions and beliefs of the *autonomous-altruistic* character sometimes run counter to those of both authority and the rest of society, he is apt to be accused of being amoral. Yet the difference between them could not be greater.

It must be stressed that this is a typology based upon environmental influences. There are also, of course, inherited differences between people in the way their nervous systems function, in their physiques, in their general activity levels, and so on, and

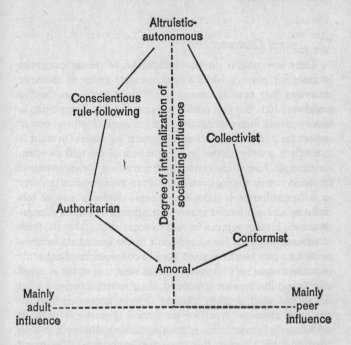

*Fig. 1. The character typology*

these are of great importance for moral development. They help us to understand why some children are more susceptible to moral training than others; and to some extent they help to explain why the training the child receives takes the form it does, for the child's temperament partly determines the way his parents treat him (see Bell, 1968). Nevertheless though the importance of these constitutional differences must never be forgotten, their role in producing the various character types will not be discussed here. Such a discussion would be too speculative in the present state of knowledge.

## The Amoral Character

In many ways this is the least satisfactory of the six categories of character, since it labels a heterogeneous group of character structures that have in common only their profile on the five moral variables. But that profile is simple enough. Temptation is never resisted, either alone or in the presence of others, out of respect for a moral rule or out of concern for others (to want is to take); it is only resisted in the interests of the self, as when, for example, fear of the certain and immediate consequences of an action swamp the motive to do it. Post-transgressional anxiety or self-punishment is unknown, though misdeeds may be followed by action intended to avert punishment by others. Altruistic action, insofar as it can be said to occur at all, takes the form of advance payment for some benefit in the immediate future – never for a past benefit received nor as a consequence of empathic response to another's distress. It might seem that as far as moral insight and ideology are concerned, the distinction between what is said and what is 'really thought' is more important than for any other character type; for the amoral character is likely to say whatever is most in his interest at the time. However, it is an open question whether this character 'really thinks' in moral categories at all. Kohlberg defines his reasoning as premoral. That is to say action, or refraining from action, is justified in terms of whether or not it leads to pleasure or the avoidance of pain. People who refrain from doing what they want, just because they think it wrong, are to the amoral character simply stupid. In Piaget's sense he is egocentric; other people only really exist for him insofar as they are functionally relevant to his own desires, fears and needs.

Any list of the kinds of people who meet this general description would have to include the following. First there is the *premoral infant* – we all start life amoral. In fact the premoral infant is the purest example of the amoral character, for in his case socializing influences have not yet had time to take effect. For all other character types socializing influences have been at work; it is just that in the case of amoral characters these influences have been grossly inadequate, distorted or morally corrupt. It may therefore be questioned whether anyone is as wholly amoral as the premoral infant. Then there is the *psychopathic* character (sometimes called the 'grown-up infant'). It is probable that this character is constitutionally less able than others to benefit from socializing influences, though it is also the case that in the personal histories of most psychopaths these influences have anyway been insufficient and defective. Thirdly there is the *unsocialized, aggressive* delinquent in whom early and frequent experience of bitter conflict with parents has led to the angry rejection of all humanizing influences, adult and peer. His own hostility towards and suspicion of all others insulates him against them.

The psychopath and the unsocialized, aggressive delinquent have been intensively studied and their amorality amply documented. There are others, however, among them the most intelligent and sophisticated, who have not been known to have broken the law and who are often successful in the eyes of society, but who at times betray such a callous lack of concern for others as to suggest that underneath their façade of social adjustment they are as amoral as the psychopath. For convenience they will be called the *normally amoral*. They are the people who have learned the art of simulating moral sentiment for their own purposes, and of exploiting the moral self-restraint of others without themselves feeling any moral compunctions. They utilize the loyalty and honesty of others without feeling any need to be honest and loyal themselves. Because they are aware of the importance of appearing moral, only close relatives and those powerless to harm see the full extent of their amorality.

Just how common such people are there is no way of telling. Some psychologists who have written about them describe them as psychopaths who have learned to wear the 'mask of sanity' (e.g. Cleckley, 1964). But in fact they differ radically from what is ordinarily understood as the psychopath. They are often realistic, have insight into the motivation of others, are able to plan ahead shrewdly, and can discipline themselves quite ruthlessly in order to achieve what they want. Above all they are not distractable and aimless; on the contrary it is precisely their single-minded pursuit of such things as power or fame or wealth or pleasure (or scientific truth?) which leaves no room for moral considerations.

If we are to understand the origins of the amoral character, three factors must be given prominence. The first is inborn temperament. I mentioned in earlier chapters the evidence amassed by Eysenck which points to the fact that extremely extroverted and emotionally labile people learn moral controls less well. We can now add that there is a possibility (it is no more) that the emotional detachment from others that characterizes the normally amoral may stem from a temperament which by nature finds close and warm human relationships difficult (the so-called schizoid temperament). All the evidence we have indicates the prevalence of a childhood in which close affectionate ties with parents or peers were absent. And such deprivation can occur in homes which remain intact and which may be superficially judged 'good'. The phenomenon of 'masked deprivation' of maternal love is well known. Beneath the over-anxious or sentimental fuss she makes over the child, the mother remains basically indifferent or hostile towards him. Then there is the importance of example. Parents may not only set an example of disregard for others (from which the child himself suffers) but even preach it. But what is perhaps most likely to disrupt normal moral development is the preaching of morality by parents whose relationships to their children are full of insincerity and deceit.

Any full account of the amoral character would have to take note of many other complicating factors. For instance some people whose upbringing has been more or less normal may become progressively more amoral later in life, either as part of the conscious decision to follow a certain kind of philosophy, or because moral sensitivity and concern have quietly atrophied in a life devoted to power or wealth or been corroded by poverty and frustration. Presumably too it is possible to be brought up to internalize an amoral point of view. What remains an open question is whether it is possible to be *wholly* amoral given a normal start in life. However opportunist the individual's life style and however governed by expediency, an experience in early life of close attachment to devoted parents must surely set some limits to his amorality.

## The Conformist Character

The distinguishing features of the conformist character are held to stem from the fact that during upbringing attachment to the peer group has taken precedence over attachment to parents. It is virtually impossible for children to be brought up without adult caretakers, or older children who function as adults. But it can easily happen that because of parental neglect or indifference, or for other reasons, the child is from an early age thrown into the company of other young children and develops his main attachment to the peer group and receives most of his social training through it.

When the peer group serves some of the functions of the parent the child's relationship to it will be somewhat abnormal. In their study of infant monkeys reared without mothers but in the company of other infants, Harlow and Harlow (1969) found that the normal pattern of the development of play with age-mates was totally disrupted. Infants used each other as objects to cling to rather than to play with. As adults, however, they appeared to achieve a social adjustment which was not obviously very different from that of monkeys reared normally. Comparable observations of children can be found in a report by Freud and Dann (1951). During the war six children were born in a concentration camp at about the same time. Though the adult caretakers were constantly changing, the children stayed together. After the war they were taken to Anna Freud's nursery in England where they were closely observed for a year or so. Their relationships to each other were, by the usual standards, plainly abnormal. For instance there was virtually no trace of rivalry, jealousy or competition among them; and though they were closely attached to each other they seemed unable to form even the most shallow bond with adults or other peers. But perhaps most interesting was the absence of differentiated friendships among the group; each child was attached to the group as a whole rather than to others as individuals, and no single child had emerged as the leader.

This last point brings up a distinction that social psychologists have tended to ignore. The existential philosopher Martin Buber calls it the difference between the *social* and the *interhuman* (see Buber, 1965). The social exists where a number of people are bound together in a group by shared experiences and reactions, and where loyalty to the collective takes precedence over loyalty to any individual. The interhuman is what goes on within a two-person friendship. The tendency is, says Buber, for the group 'to suppress the personal relation in favour of the purely collective'; for when friendships start to differentiate out of collectives, then the unity and cohesion of the collective is threatened. People become more individual through their friendships, that is, through the interhuman, and are therefore less ready to be submerged in collectives.

When the individual has been primarily socialized through the peer group, so that it is from this group that he derives his sense of identity, security and belonging, then it is to be expected that he will have few, if any, individual friendships but be intensely loyal and devoted to the group as a whole. His relationships to other members are likely to take the form of symbiotic merging when things are going well and aggressive rejection if others let the group down. Such a person is not egocentric but group-centric.

As the result of this kind of upbringing, the conformist character needs always to have his allegiance anchored in a collective. Since he tends to give himself totally to the group, he cannot easily divide his loyalties among several groups. Moral control is not a function of any specifically moral dispositions, but follows indirectly from his need to conform to the expectations of other group members. His morality is the morality of the group, and if he changes his group allegiance, his morality changes with it. He is good at resisting the temptation to violate a group norm, especially if there is any possibility that other members would know if he did violate it. If the group norms prescribe delinquent acts then of course he will be delinquent (the pseudosocial delinquent). The worst possible sanction for him is rejection from the group and he will strive hard to avoid this. He experiences shame rather than guilt. Whereas the nearest thing to blame of which the amoral character is capable is a reactive anger against those who frustrate him, the conformist character feels reactive anger on behalf of the group, either against outsiders or against non-conforming and individualistic members. In one sense the conformist is very unselfish, for he will sacrifice a great deal for the group and be courageous in its defence. Moreover if the group norms prescribe certain kinds of altruistic action towards outsiders, then he will conform. But sympathy for individuals is not well developed in his personality.

His moral reasoning corresponds to Kohlberg's third level, in which the justification for morality is found in the consensus of others. This does not mean that he will display Piaget's morality of cooperation or reciprocity. For there is a weakness in Piaget's theory. According to Piaget the child experiences mutual respect and reciprocity within the peer group, and this helps to liberate him from the unilateral respect for adult authority he has laboured under hitherto by deepening his insight into the nature of moral rules. But the reciprocity Piaget talks of is really an aspect of the interhuman. For the conformist character the group takes over the functions of parents, and hence is the object of unilateral respect just as the parents are for others. Group law carries the same absolute authority as does parental. What these considerations suggest is that Piaget underestimated the extent to which relations of unilateral respect with authorities are a necessary antecedent of the liberating effect that peer experience can have, and that without it the experience of the group cannot lead to the morality of cooperation.

## The Authoritarian Character

Both the conformist's and the authoritarian character's morality is a function of contemporary social relationships rather than of individual reasoning and decision. Both have imperfectly internalized moralities, and are controlled by the expectations of others. But though they are both bewildered and disorientated without social support, the nature of their social dependence is different. The conformist seeks to merge with the collective and become as it were a unit among others. The desire of the authoritarian, on the other hand, is to feel different from others by occupying an important niche in a hierarchical social structure. His preoccupation is with status and power; he needs to feel that there are those he can look up to uncritically and those he can look down on as inferior. Again, like the conformist but for different reasons, he finds democratic relationships among equals difficult, though there is a ready merging with others of like mind who occupy the same social niche.

The authoritarian person is identified with the established hierarchical structure in society, and bent upon preserving it. His sense of identity, security and worth depends upon his social position and upon the power he has over others. He is conventional and conservative, and his moral beliefs echo those of the people whose status and power he sees as greater than his own and with whom he therefore wants to be associated. His system of beliefs is relatively closed and static. Hence it is often inconsistent and permeated by a tendency towards rigid categorizing and stereotyping. Since he is intolerant of ambiguity, things are seen in black and white terms: people are good or bad, strong or weak, the right sort or 'one of them'. He is frequently hostile towards and suspicious of 'intellectuals', whom he accuses of being too clever to see the 'plain facts'.

Morality is a matter of obeying rules that have been sanctioned by authority and tradition. Since self-esteem is founded upon social position, the authoritarian person is strongly motivated to conform. But internal controls are weak. Most descriptions of the authoritarian personality agree in stressing the existence of much inner conflict stemming from frustrated sexual and aggressive impulses. It is to be expected that when status and position are at stake, the individual will behave with careful propriety. But when tempted to transgress in private, or under conditions in which only unimportant and uninfluential people will ever know, his resistance is decidedly weak.

Moral beliefs tend to be absolute and unquestioned – if something is wrong it is always and completely wrong. At the same time, since the authoritarian's moral beliefs originate from others and are accepted without criticism or insight, he will tend to obey the letter rather than the spirit of a moral rule; and since the basic need to maintain social position takes precedence over all moral sentiments, his judgements on the morality of other people's actions will be much affected by their status in his eyes. He tends, at least on the surface, to idealize those in authority – an attitude which of course makes his own submission less disturbing to self-esteem; but if the authority for some reason loses status and power, his revenge at being betrayed can be ferocious. In general, however, the authoritarian finds it difficult to believe that those in authority are other than the best people. Hence upper class offences like the successful deceiving of the Inland Revenue or the illegitimate stretching of an expense account are treated indulgently, while shoplifting and even student demonstrations arouse indignant fury.

The two main sources of personal threat to the authoritarian personality are actions by others which endanger the stability of the social order thereby putting his own position in jeopardy, and the blatant, pleasurable self-indulgence of others (as in sex and drug-taking) which through contagious example undermines his own precarious self-control, so that he risks betraying himself. Towards offenders of these kinds, the authoritarian character can display an indignation which borders on ruthless hate. To the observer anyway, this selective blaming of others implies that moral categories of thought are being used to clothe and justify a more primitive reaction of confused aggression.

The authoritarian's concern with morality stems from his need to maintain personal stability through status and power.

The upbringing of the authoritarian character is unbalanced in the opposite direction to that of the conformist character. There is close parental supervision, and peer influence is not allowed to conflict with it. The children are attached to their parents, but especially in the case of the father the relationship is not warm and affectionate.

Discipline in the families of the more authoritarian men and women was characterized in their accounts by relatively harsh application of rules, in accordance with conventional values; and this discipline was commonly experienced as threatening or traumatic or even overwhelming ... [and] the high authoritarians came, for the most part, from homes in which a rather stern and distant father dominated a submissive and long-suffering but morally restrictive mother, and in which discipline was an attempt to apply conventionally approved rules rather than an effort to further general values in accordance with the perceived needs of the child. (Sanford, 1956)

Hierarchy dominates the family, democratic moments are rare, and the children are expected to obey father at all times. The consequence of such a regime is bound to be an attitude towards parents which is compounded of fear, respect, covert hostility, and dependence, with only the most modest admixture of affection.

Spontaneous sympathy and generosity towards others is not a prominent feature of the authoritarian. Insofar as he is altruistic it will be to the extent and in the manner appropriate to his position, though of course to those of higher status he will be cooperative and helpful to the point of being obsequious. Nor is he likely to go in for much self-blaming when he does wrong. His immediate response to transgression is twofold: to avoid being found out and to deny responsibility. Of all character types the authoritarian is most likely to adopt a strategy for reducing post-transgressional dissonance which leaves his evaluation of himself unimpaired (see chapter 5). His stock reaction to the accusations of others is indignant repudiation. It is interesting to note that in the original study by Adorno *et al.*

(1950) authoritarians presented a surface picture of people confident of their own righteousness and worth (the real self and the ideal self seemed identical), but at other times they betrayed unmistakable signs of an underlying self-contempt.

Finally it should be added that this sketchy outline of the authoritarian character type is really a description of one of a cluster of related types. But for a full account the reader must turn to the original research.

## The Collectivist Character

Very little attention has been given to the collectivist character by psychologists and this is probably because it is comparatively rare in western democracies. It was Bronfenbrenner (1962a and b, 1967, and 1970a and b) who drew attention to its importance, following his study of Soviet social psychology and educational theory and practice. But it is well known that the ideology at the foundation of Chinese communist society holds up the collectivist character as a national ideal. And in non-communist societies the Israeli kibbutz comes close to an environment designed to produce it (see Spiro, 1958).

It must not be thought that Russian, Chinese and Israeli societies are being equated. The differences between all three are massive. However, what they have in common is that the peer group is made the dominating socializing influence in childrearing, not because parents have abdicated their responsibility but because of the educational policies deliberately adopted by the society. By comparison with countries like England and the United States, looking after children is to a large extent taken out of the hands of parents and assigned to professional workers of various kinds who are trained to endorse, shape and exploit peer-group influences in the interests of the community.

In their different ways these three countries are founded upon ideologies which stress the value of devoted and heroic self-sacrifice in the service of the collective. Individuality, the seeking of personal glory, the desire to stand out as different from and better than others, all this is deprecated. What matters is the greatness of the nation, and the individual should be prepared, willingly and gladly, to offer his life in its service, if necessary in total anonymity, and in whatever way he is needed. When people are selected for special recognition it is in order that an example can be held up for others to imitate.

Clearly this ideology is in sharp contrast to the emphasis placed, in western democracies, on individualism and the value of the single-minded pursuit of personal advancement. The interesting point here is that this ideology has led to certain distinctive emphases in child-rearing. Individual competition is avoided, but competition between subgroups to see which can be most productive and useful to the group as a whole is sedulously encouraged. Sanctions for misconduct are, as far as possible, administered by the group, which, at that moment, is held to represent the whole society. Misdeeds are by definition acts which are injurious to the collective. The function of adults is to expose the offender to the rest of the group. His punishment is the shame of knowing that others know he has let them down, together with any reparation the group may think fit to exact from him. Planned and systematic use is made of shaming, and great stress placed on the value of confession as a means of being accepted back into the group. An important aspect of upbringing is that the young come to see, quite early on, that parents, teachers and other adults are also answerable to the collective. In Russia and China it appears to be generally accepted that the authority exercised by parents over their children is delegated to them by the state, and can be taken away if they are not doing their job properly.

The collectivist character might be expected to develop from these child-rearing practices. The only evidence we have, however, comes from the study of children brought up in a kibbutz, and though it offers support for saying that the character really does follow from this upbringing, the situation in Israel is complicated by the fact that the influence of western individualism is much stronger than in Russia or China, and it cannot therefore be taken as an ideal instance of a society designed to produce the collectivist character. So what follows is mainly inference and speculation.

The collectivist character has a more internalized morality than the conformist. Though deeply immersed in the group, he is not uncritical of it. His devotion to the collective is a conscious, ideological devotion. It is the ideology which determines what is judged good for the group, not what the group itself may think. The individual identifies less with his immediate group or with the authority structure of his society than with the common ideology and national myth. This identification gives him a small measure of independence of both the group and authority, for both can be measured against the ideology, which everyone is supposed to serve. The ideology itself is regarded as absolute, though, as is frequently seen in religion, individuals can introduce new ideas so long as they can show that they are in fact more faithfully interpreting the original beliefs.

The moral beliefs of the collectivist are determined by the prevailing ideology rather than by group norms. An ideology can extend much further into an individual's life than can group norms. Those ideologies which favour the collectivist character have usually extended their control over virtually the whole of an individual's life, so that his physical and mental health, his work, his family life, his sexual habits, his reading and leisure, all become the business of the collective. Whether the collectivist character is 'better behaved' than other types is debatable, though there are signs that people reared under the conditions we have described lead disciplined and hard-working lives. But the price paid for the collectivist character is almost certainly the devaluation of the interhuman. It is usually crucial to collectivist ideologies that personal relationships should be secondary to the individual's duty to the collective. Heroic altruism on behalf of the collective can easily go with indifference to the fate of individuals.

## *The Conscientious Rule-Following Character*

As we move from the conformist character through the authoritarian to the collectivist, moral behaviour is progressively loosened from the control of current social relationships; the individual is increasingly able to act morally on his own, without others knowing, and even in the face of their opposition. His moral beliefs also become increasingly stable; the conformist's beliefs fluctuate with changes in his group membership, whereas the collectivist's commitment to his ideology ensures that his moral beliefs will be resistant to change – indeed they are often as closed as those of the authoritarian. With the conscientious, rule-following character moral rules are so effectively internalized that the individual obeys them irrespective of what others expect and do. Behaviour is inner-directed; but, unlike the altruistic-autonomous character, this inner moral programming is fixed and rigid. The individual's moral responses have a compulsive quality and are largely inaccessible to reasoning – there are things he just has to do and others he just cannot do no matter what anyone says.

He is the classic example of the man with a strong conscience, who always meticulously observes the rules. He resists temptation not only in private, but also when it is reinforced by the efforts of friends to persuade him to yield. If he does something wrong, the result is intense and lasting guilt. Altruism is primarily motivated by guilt or by the compulsion to conform to rules that enjoin sympathetic and charitable action. In his moral reasoning he appeals to fundamental and unalterable moral principles. He may rationalize these principles in terms of divine authority but he has no psychological need for such authority – if it were taken away his morality would remain more or less the same. In his moral judgements of others he applies his principles with scrupulous impartiality and regardless of their status or power.

There is not, of course, a single conscientious character, any more than there is a single conformist or authoritarian character – we are all the time dealing with clusters of character structures that merge imperceptibly into each other. If the conscientious type tends to be authoritarian, his tight self-control will probably go with a relatively closed system of moral belief and an intolerance of the fact that others can transgress without feeling guilt, together with a desire to see offenders punished unless they show they are sincerely repentant. The itch to meddle in the moral life of others is controlled, however, by a desire to be fair and a lively awareness of his own frailty. If the conscientious character inclines towards the altruistic-autonomous, he will probably be more open minded in his moral beliefs and he will not feel the need to impose his way of life on others. He will accept that though he has no choice but to live by a narrow and restrictive code, other people have different standards and it is not for him to set himself up as their yardstick. He may well be more sympathetic and indulgent towards the failings of others than he is towards his own – indeed, like some Christian saints he may even go to the extreme of taking responsibility for the misdeeds of others and punishing himself in their stead.

There are other variants. But the central reference point for this character is the person who has been so oversocialized that his life is overshadowed by the need to avoid 'sin'. He may of course be neurotic, and even end up compulsively breaking some of the moral rules to his own acute distress. But if not, he is likely to attract to himself such labels as over-anxious, inhibited, guilt-ridden, scrupulous, and so on. Affection, sympathy, generosity, and even healthy, spontaneous anger are hedged round with anxiety and the desire to do the right thing at all costs. He finds it difficult to enjoy anything easily, naturally, and for its own sake, without first having to assess its moral worth.

The child-rearing conditions we should expect to find associated with the conscientious character are not hard to list. They include the following: a heavy predominance of adult over peer influence; a close, warm and affectionate relationship to parents who impose a restrictive and uncompromising moral code upon the child; sanctions which evoke anxiety rather than aggression in the child, and which therefore are expressive of parental distress rather than parental anger; a great deal of explanatory talk which stresses the importance of moral principles, their nature and how they should be applied. The parents themselves set an example of controlled, conscientious and non-violent living. Unlike the parents of the authoritarian character, they do not assert their power over the child and demand his instant obedience. Their child is tied to them through affection and guilt rather than through fear and respect. The authoritarian child grows free from the domination of his parents as he too acquires power and status; the route to emotional freedom for the conscientious child is through making his parents happy, and this in turn means accepting their values and becoming what they want him to be. When the strain of following this route is too great, he may develop neurotic symptoms, or run away, or react violently against all his parents stand for. He is something of a greenhouse plant. Close parental supervision ensures that he does not get into bad company. He tends to be socially isolated, having a few intense friendships with kindred spirits, but being only marginally a member of peer groups. Finally we must add that for the full development of the conscientious rule-following character it is probably necessary that in addition to this rather suffocating upbringing the individual should have an inherited predisposition which makes him especially susceptible to these influences.

## The Altruistic-Autonomous Character

The conscientious character is autonomous in the sense of being relatively independent of current social pressures. But like the other characters described so far, the content of his moral code is decided by others. The particular interpretation of basic moral principles favoured by his parents is so ingrained that he is unable to modify it; or, more accurately, he may change his theoretical beliefs, but the values he actually lives by have been so thoroughly built in through years of intensive conditioning that they are very resistant to change. The autonomous character has an additional freedom: he chooses the rules he lives by, and feels free to modify them with increased experience. But the modifications he makes are not theoretical – they are followed by changes in his behaviour. This means, of course, that the abandonment of all moral controls is for him a live option in a way in which it is not for the conscientious character. The reason why he does not do this is that his experience of personal relationships has convinced him of the validity of basic moral principles. Although committed to these principles he is flexible, even original and creative, in applying them to particular situations. Of all characters he is least bound by the letter of a moral rule and therefore most likely to devote energy to sorting out moral problems.

It is assumed here that the autonomous character is the most developmentally mature of all types because the natural process of development is towards such autonomy. The other characters are thought to result from the distorting and arresting of this optimal development at certain points. Obviously this developmental perspective is questionable; the characters could just as well be regarded as equally mature alternatives. Its advantage is that it provides a rationale for saying that each of the other characters could develop into moral autonomy. If for example an authoritarian person is to grow into moral autonomy, he must critically review his moral beliefs, reflect on them at length, work them out again for himself, and seek to gain awareness of his own previous conditioning. Each of the characters faces special handicaps in this task. But in general terms there are three main difficulties. There are first the motivational biases which give the individual a vested interest in accepting one set of moral beliefs rather than another. Then the main stimulus for critical reflection upon one's own moral views is encounter with others who think differently. Some characters, however, like the authoritarian and collectivist, encapsulate themselves against such encounters by habitually regarding those who disagree with them as unworthy of serious consideration. Lastly, if someone has been deprived in early life of the relationships of trust and affection which teach us the importance of moral principles, it is not easy for him to make up for this deprivation later on.

But if the other characters face handicaps, there are certain conditions in upbringing which facilitate the achievement of autonomy. In the end they reduce to two: an optimal balance between adult and peer influence and a rich and varied experience of the interhuman, that is, of personal relationships that are neither symbiotic merging into collectives nor affected by differences of power and status. These conditions are interrelated.

During childhood and adolescence relationships with parents and peers complement each other. Children become separate people from their parents by having an area of privacy which they do not share with them. Friends of the same age normally supply this. At the same time the child's relationship with his parents provides him with an area of privacy which he does not share with his friends, and this serves to protect him from becoming submerged in the peer group. Similarly by encountering different values in his friends he learns the relativity of his parents' point of view; and his parents' values give him a vantage point for assessing those of his friends. It is through being identified with the points of view of both parents and peers at the same time that he is stimulated to work out his own – a point of view that will coincide with neither but owe something to both.*
The fact that the child is not wholly identified with either parents or peers makes possible a polarity in his relationships to each. Because his point of view is different from that of both, his relationships are not one-sided and unilateral, at least for much of the time. As Piaget made clear, the young child egocentrically accepts his parents' beliefs, or those of the peer group if this is the main socializing agent, as his own because at the time he himself has no point of view with which they can clash. The development of operational thinking in the sphere of human relationships seems to depend upon the extent to which the child experiences conflict between his own point of view and that of someone else within a context of affection and trust so that in some sense he shares both points of view. As experiences of this

---

*Reiss (1967), in his study of the premarital sexual standards of students, found that a substantial number of them thought their own standards were similar to those of both their parents and their friends, but that their friends' standards were rather more permissive than their own and their parents' standards less permissive.

kind become more frequent, and the child matures intellectually, these differing points of view are progressively dissociated from actual people and are represented in the individual's mind as abstract principles that he has somehow to reconcile – and thus he reaches the stage of formal operations in his social thinking.

As far as the conformist and authoritarian characters are concerned, the asymmetry of their *current* social relationships keeps them effectively egocentric in their moral thinking. The collectivist has been too long protected against encountering opposition, or too effectively insulated against it by his beliefs (that is, the other man thinks as he does *because* he is a capitalist, Marxist, etc.), to benefit from it. The conscientious character may be more intellectually open, but the intense emotional conditioning he has undergone tends to dissociate his reasoning from the way he is compelled to act. Only the autonomous character has been stimulated to take a hand in his own moral development, by trying to reason things out for himself and by trying to understand why people differ. One of the conditions that makes moral creativity possible is a clear awareness of the relativity and bias of one's own point of view.

In the family of the autonomous character parents and child are of course firmly attached; but the relationship lacks the rather suffocating intensity found in the homes of the conscientious, and is more easygoing. Though firmly committed to their child's welfare, the parents do not fuss and they approach the moral training of their child with altogether a lighter touch. Their own values are manifested in example rather than precept, and these values stress the importance of affection for others and productive work; preaching does not come easily to them. The parents of the conscientious character could be called believers in original sin, those of the autonomous believers in original virtue; the former act on the assumption that unless children are trained from the beginning with vigilance and strictness, no good will come from them, whereas the latter have a much greater trust in the developmental process, and are disinclined to meddle unless they have to. Their authority is unselfconscious and unassuming, and springs naturally from the fact that they are adults and care for their child. The assertion of their authority is liberally interspersed by moments of familial democracy. They see no reason to indoctrinate their children with the idea that parents are special people to whom unlimited gratitude and respect are due. On the contrary, they display a continuing respect for their child's point of view and when they have to overrule it feel obliged to explain why as fully as they can. Offences are not unnecessarily stressed as personal affronts. Sanctions are the minimal necessary, and consist mostly of a firm declaration that the act (as distinct from the child) is disapproved of. The accompanying explanation emphasizes the consequence of the act for others and the spirit rather than the letter of the rule that has been broken. The aim is to get children to see that their wrong acts are destructive of something they themselves recognize as valuable.

In the character that results from such an upbringing, moral restraint is very much under the control of conscious reasoning and decision processes. In psychoanalytic language, it is a function of ego rather than superego control. But much more attention is given to the realization of positive values in human affairs than to resisting temptation. Post-transgressional anxiety is always a stimulus to constructive and reparative action. Altruism has its roots in the individual's system of values, and in such things as generosity and sympathy. Moral reasoning is at Kohlberg's sixth level, that of individual principles of conscience, and the individual's moral belief system is open and developing.

I must stress again that this typology is informal and speculative. The types are landmarks, or vantage points intended to help us make sense of the great variety of character displayed by real people; the differences between them are relative not absolute. Most people, it may be assumed, fall somewhere in between them. There have been very few attempts to test directly and empirically the usefulness of this scheme (though see Peck and Havighurst, 1960, Bronfenbrenner et al., 1965, Bronfenbrenner 1970b, and Hoffman, 1970); most of the evidence is indirect, and it has been recounted in earlier chapters so that the reader can judge the plausibility of the typology for himself.

It remains to consider briefly the bearing of the four theoretical perspectives described in chapter 2 on this typology. Obviously each theory is relevant to all types of character; but equally obviously each has greater relevance to some characters than to others. Social-group theory comes into its own with the conformist character, for he is closest to being only a function of the groups he belongs to, and his moral behaviour is largely predictable from a knowledge of the norms of these groups. The authoritarian character is also inexplicable without a knowledge of the norms associated with the roles he occupies in the social structure. Though group pressures are important in the development of the collectivist character, commitment to the collectivist ideology to some extent frees him from them; instead he deliberately uses them to further the ideological aims.

Psychoanalysis is particularly relevant to the authoritarian and conscientious characters. The former is someone with an insecurely internalized superego, which is yet powerfully aggressive and readily turned outwards in punitive hostility to others; the latter is someone with a strong and well-internalized superego that has become something of an inner tyrant. Learning theory is in many respects an alternative to psychoanalysis with the advantage that it does not postulate any special psychological structures. But since it specifies the processes of learning wherever they occur, there is no character for whom the theory has special relevance. Finally the relevance of the cognitive-developmental theory is most unambiguously confirmed by the autonomous character. Of all the theories, this one minimizes the distinction between thought and action, for thought is defined as more or less adaptive, internalized action. The theory postulates a developmental progression in the direction of increased integration of behaviour under cognitive control, and this is the hallmark of the autonomous character. In this sense it corresponds to psychoanalytic ego theory. But cognitive-developmental theory does much to right the imbalance created by both psychoanalysis and learning theory by restoring intelligence to its central role, without which the autonomous character would not be understandable. Yet it should be noted that in its rationale for the practice of personal analysis, psychoanalytic theory offers a prescription for how growth into moral autonomy might be achieved for those who lack it. We need not accept the theory, however, to agree that understanding our own motivational biases and social dependences will to some extent liberate us from them.

# CHAPTER 10

# Religion, Education and Morality

In most western democratic societies there are four major social groupings or institutions which shape the individual's moral development, the family, the peer group, the Church and the school. The influence of all four of them may have wilted under the onslaught of the mass media; but whether or not the world of advertising and pop culture has affected morality, it is likely that its influence would only result in behaviour when it is supported by the immediate peer group – and in any case, it would take us too far afield to discuss this question here. Of the four influences listed, by far the most important is the family, with the peer group coming a clear second. Both these have been recurrent themes in previous chapters and I shall say no more about them. Instead I shall directly examine the other two. In doing so, the discussion will become parochial, for throughout I shall have in mind mainly English and American society and the Christian religion.

## Religion

It is frequently said that religion is a declining influence in England today, since only a small minority still attend church. But it is far from dead, and the issues raised by religion are very much alive. Many of those who do not go to church apparently look upon it as important for the nation's moral health (Wright, 1965).* Nearly all children receive some religious education, and

* In the I.T.A. survey (1970) eighty-nine per cent of the population agreed that 'religion helps to maintain the standards and morals of society'.

the great majority of the population admit a measure of religious belief which, however rudimentary it may be, indicates a reluctance to abandon religion completely. But the real justification for discussing religion here is the frequent claim that unless morality is founded in religion it will slowly collapse. It is indisputable that historically one of the major functions of organized Christianity has been the propagation of a moral code, and today it is probably the only institution which advocates a firm ascetic morality. In the past, too, religion was a major sanctioning institution, or agent of social control, a power which it now exercises only over its believing adherents. The claim seems to be that because religion was intimately related to morality in the past, if you take religion away, morality cannot survive. The implication is that there is some kind of psychological link between the two, though people who make the claim are notoriously coy over saying explicitly what the link is.

Unfortunately there are so many facets to both religion and morality, and so many ways in which they might be related, that I shall not be able to do justice to the topic in the space available. All I can do is to discuss briefly some of the more obvious ways in which the two are connected.

First, it has been argued that the authority of the deity is *logically* necessary if people are to provide a rational justification for their moral code. The fact that the God who made the universe also instituted the moral laws is held to be the only cogent reason for obeying them. But this claim is highly controversial if not fallacious. For as has been pointed out many times, the premiss 'God wants me to do this' does not lead to the conclusion 'therefore I ought to do it' unless a second premiss is added, namely 'I ought to do what God tells me to do.' This second premiss cannot be deduced from the first; we cannot invoke the authority of God to support our assertion that we must submit to that authority. In other words the individual's morality must, logically, be founded upon an assertion of obligation which is not itself derived from any statement about God. Of course, this need be the only moral assertion he makes – the rest can be left to the theologians – but this one he must make on his own* However, most people are not troubled by such logical niceties, and the logical claim can be translated into its psychological counterpart, namely the assertion that unless people feel that moral rules originate in the decree of an authority they respect and fear, they will not be motivated very strongly to obey them. And no authority could be more commanding of such fear and respect than God. As we have seen, this claim may well be true for the authoritarian character, but it would certainly not be true for those with an autonomous character structure, some of whom reject the Christian concept of God precisely on moral grounds.

But for whatever reason, the assumption seems to be that religion makes people better behaved than they would otherwise be. This assumption is, in principle, empirically testable (see Wright, 1967). For example, if children were randomly assigned to two kinds of upbringing such that the only respect in which they differed systematically was that one was given intensive religious education and the other not allowed any contact with it at all, then any differences between them in moral behaviour could be attributed to the presence or absence of religion. A more practicable, though still difficult, test would be to find two groups who differed systematically in their religious history and commitment but who were approximately matched for age, intelligence, personality type, type of parental discipline, content of moral belief, etc., and then carefully assess their moral behaviour. If no differences could be found, though it would not disprove the fact, it would certainly undermine any confidence we might have that religion was important for moral development. Unfortunately evidence of this kind does not yet exist, and it would be idle to pretend that the evidence we do possess in any way really tests the assumption. All we have are scraps of evidence in which a moral variable and religious belief and practice are correlated with each other. They have all been mentioned in

---

* It is not relevant here to discuss the converse of these claims, namely that being moral carries metaphysical implications, and that religion can be explained away as the attempt to cope with the hangovers of frustration and guilt which constitute the price we all pay for being civilized.

previous chapters, though they deserve to be summarized again briefly.

On experimental tests of honesty, those with a religious upbringing are not distinguishable from those without it. On self-report measures there is a small tendency for religious subjects to admit fewer serious antisocial acts, a much stronger tendency for them to admit fewer 'immoral' sexual acts (which may be related to the fact that they are more likely to judge them wrong), and they are much less often officially classified as delinquent. However, it is important to note what 'religious' means in these comparisons. The decisive factor appears to be not so much religious belief or early upbringing as *current* involvement in religious groups. One of the attractions of religion is doubtless its power to reduce guilt. Yet many of its beliefs imply, or at least are interpreted by people to imply, that it is good to blame oneself, and religious people cultivate a sense of sin. At the same time all sins are said to be not only sins against other people but also sins against God. All this might be expected to increase guilt feelings. There is little evidence directly comparing Christians and non-Christians on measures of guilt, but what does exist suggests that the former do tend to have more intense feelings of guilt (Peretti, 1969). As far as compassionate and humane attitudes towards criminals and other racial groups are concerned, the two groups are indistinguishable. There is some evidence that church-going adolescents are more likely to go in for acts of charitable service to those in need. Though small differences in moral reasoning have sometimes been found they are of negligible importance. Considerable and consistent differences have been found in expressed moral belief, with religious subjects of all ages taking a stricter moral tone, particularly with regard to anti-ascetic actions. However, religious belief does not stop people changing their moral attitudes.

None of this takes us very far, because there are too many possible interpretations of these findings. Any inferences we might draw must be tentative in the extreme. But the evidence does not encourage the view that in its general influence religion strengthens the conscience. This is in no way to deny that individuals have been morally transformed by their Christian convictions. It is merely to say that as far as most believers are concerned all that existing evidence shows is that Christian belief and practice influence behaviour in the direction of social conformity rather than in the direction of personal moral growth. It is worth noting that the respects in which the religious are more moral than the non-religious are by and large the same as the respects in which women, irrespective of religion, are more moral than men. As we saw, one likely explanation of the sex difference is that girls, because of their upbringing, are more strongly motivated to appear good in the eyes of others. It is not implausible to suppose that a fairly strict religious upbringing will produce just such an increased sensitivity to moral reputation and a greater sense of shame when found out in some misdemeanour. Some supporting evidence comes from the study by Grandall and Gozali (1969). These investigators gave their Social Desirability Scale to large samples of children in Catholic and non-Catholic schools in the United States, and in Fundamentalist Lutheran and State Lutheran schools in Norway. In both countries children from the more religious schools showed a significantly greater tendency to present themselves in a good light, even though this meant saying things that were not strictly true. So this interpretation may be justified. But it would be foolish to press it any further now, and it is certainly not the whole story.

Most people who urge a return to Christianity as the cure for the nation's moral ill-health, point to the apparent association between the decline in church-going over the last hundred years and what is called the 'general lowering of moral standards'. It is difficult to know how seriously to take this since the point is usually made in such general terms that many interpretations are possible. But those who do take it seriously might care to ponder the following: that it is incumbent upon those who say that moral behaviour has declined to produce evidence that there was an earlier time when standards were higher. Nor can they ignore that during the same hundred years we have seen in our society a vastly increased respect for the rights of working men, women, the sick, the mentally ill, children and the unemployed, all of which must surely rank as evidence of moral advance; that church attendance is much higher in the United States than in England yet so is the rate of crime; and that the increase of crime in England during recent decades is much more readily explained by the conditions in which people have to live in large industrial cities than by the fact that they no longer go to church.

So far I have been talking exclusively in terms of statistical trends. This is obviously superficial and fails to do justice to the complexity of religion. What is needed is an analysis of the various elements that make up the Christian religion and an examination of how each bears upon morality. Christians themselves make much of anecdotes in which the lives of individuals have been completely changed by their conversion to faith. What we must do is separate those features of Christianity which retard moral development from those that foster it. As one way of doing this, we shall take each of the character types described in the previous chapter and look at those aspects of organized Christianity which could be counted upon to attract such a person, and encourage and preserve him unchanged. But first I should stress that each of these characters can be found among unbelievers, and many of the influences to be found within organized Christianity which tend to foster certain characters would not be accepted by Christians as being truly Christian influences.

The amoral character would find little to attract him in organized religion. The only exception might be the person we called normally amoral. There have been times when the Christian church has exercised such power in society that it naturally drew to it those whose desire was the manipulation and control of others rather than the worship of God.

Factors making for the conformist character are not hard to find. In communal acts of worship, hymn singing and ceremonial, the individual layman is temporarily welded into a mass with his fellows; his loss of self-identity is hastened by music, ritual and common emotions of awe and elation. Though temporary, this is regularly repeated. The Christian churches have sometimes sought to incorporate the individual and his family into the wider religious group by segregating him from non-

Christians through church schools, keeping marriage within the faith, and as far as possible persuading him to stay with fellow believers for cultural and even professional activities. When these things happen the Church attracts and perpetuates the conformist or norm-controlled character; and the barriers set up against growing into moral autonomy are considerable.

Two main features of organized Christianity are sure to suit the authoritarian character. First the larger Christian churches are strictly hierarchical in structure (few institutions are less democratic) and they have traditionally propagated a conception of the universe in which all things from an all-powerful God through angels, saints, religious and secular authorities, men, women, children and animals have their appointed position and status. Everyone has his niche, and the rules enjoin obedience to those above and paternalistic care of those below. It is true that this hierarchical conception is much weaker than it was, but it still lingers. It appears, for example, that of all groups Catholics are most likely to think that the husband is the proper head of a family and that it is virtuous for children to obey their parents (Lenski, 1961). The second feature of organized Christianity is the profound us–them division that runs through much of its belief and thought. A Christian is different, or if he is not in fact different, he ought to be. To the extent to which Christians define their religion as the one true road to salvation, insofar as they claim to have the 'truth' and to represent God on earth, they are, whether they like it or not, committed to dividing people into insiders and outsiders, the saved and the rest, those who have faith and those who do not, and so on. Of course this division is softened by many other beliefs that cut across it (such as that all men are made and loved by God). The point here is that this classifying of people has a deep appeal for the authoritarian mind. It guarantees him a large number of people towards whom he can feel at the worst superior, at best paternal, whom he can freely condemn as materialistic, worldly, morally decadent, ignorant or misguided, and whose sensual self-indulgence he can make the object of a righteous moral crusade. It is the Christian's claim that the moral code he believes in derives from God and is for all men; the authoritarian will gladly undertake to try to impose it on others, and especially its ascetic elements.

The nearest thing to the collectivist character to be found within the Christian Church is probably the dedicated believer who works for the realization of the kingdom of God in human society. It has frequently been pointed out that the implications of Christian belief for social structure and functioning are radical, even revolutionary. Some people are converted by the vision of a Christian society, in which the reality of God is universally recognized and worshipped, and where human relationships are marked by compassion and self-control. Once captured by this vision they seek to convert others and they take what action they can, socially and politically, to bring it nearer to reality. They display the hallmark of the collectivist character, dedication to a cause which takes precedence over individuals (including themselves), over authority and over public opinion. But the vision is somewhat inflexible, and when faith in it goes, energy and purpose are lost as well.

The conscientious character is drawn primarily by the Christian doctrines of sin and redemption. Within Christianity all sins are personalized in the sense that they are said to have made necessary the death of Christ. Whenever we do wrong we need God's forgiveness. Whereas these ideas may appear to others somewhat theoretical, they strike home in a very personal way to the conscientious character. The sacraments, and especially confession, are likely to be of great importance as the means whereby his guilt is allayed. Of all the character types he is the most firmly bound to his religion and most assiduous in the performance of his Christian duties. But because his religion is so intensely personal, he is not unduly impressed by religious authorities, nor easily forced into conformity by the consensus of others; and he is not particularly anxious to convert others nor does he quickly condemn them for not sharing his belief.

All the features of organized Christianity we have mentioned so far provide a basis for morality in the individual but also prevent him from growing into full moral autonomy. The morally autonomous person is a potential threat to any institution since he will not be psychologically dependent upon it. Not surprisingly, churches have not been inclined to encourage such autonomy; yet certain central elements in the Christian faith are almost certain to foster it.

It could be said that what institutional religion does is bring the individual's relationship to his deity under the control of a central authority. Indeed this is the nature of religious power. Yet in Christianity two factors work to undermine this. The first is the character of the founder, whom all Christians are exhorted to emulate. For one of the most striking things about the Jesus of the Gospels is his independence – he went his own way, the way he felt he had to go, regardless of what others said or did. The second is the belief that every individual can get into direct touch with God through prayer and meditation. He can establish a personal and individual relationship with God which others can neither monitor nor disrupt. Moreover the attempt to sustain and develop this relationship slowly but surely transforms his personality which in turn affects every aspect of his life.

This personality transformation which follows the devoted practice of prayer and meditation together with the way of living compatible with them has been well documented within the Christian tradition. A similar process has been described in even richer detail, physiologically as well as psychologically, in Buddhism. Apart from psychotherapists like Jung and Fromm, psychologists have ignored these things (though interest is beginning – see Tart, 1969). According to religious writers, the process is one of progressive liberation from anxiety and guilt, personal ambition and envy, and from all other motives which lead to moral transgression or which conflict with concern for others and the realization of the important values in human life. They are replaced by serenity and compassion, and by a profound freedom from psychological dependence upon others. It could be argued that, despite the impediments placed in the way by their official representatives, the real point of the great religions is to produce just such a moral autonomy.

And there we must leave the matter. The upshot of the discussion is simple. There is little point in asking whether religion strengthens morality. All the character types can be religious, but they will be religious in *different* ways. The question we must ask is: What type of character does this kind of religion encourage, and is this the kind of character we wish to see encouraged?

## Education

In recent years concern about moral education appears to have increased sharply both among the general public and teachers. In one survey (N.O.P., 1969) 22 per cent of a random sample of the population gave moral training as the most important aspect of the education of boys over twelve years, and 26 per cent gave it as the second most important aspect (the figures for girls were 29 per cent and 25 per cent respectively); only training for a career was judged overall to be more important, and such things as religious education, physical education and civics came well behind. At the same time there has been a flurry of activity in this field among educational experts.* With so many minds at work on the issue now it is unlikely that I shall be able to add anything novel or significant to the debate; but the material reviewed in this book has certain general implications for moral education that may be worth voicing.

At the outset we face the question of whether school life is ever likely to be an important and enduring influence upon morality. Clearly there is no simple answer. The Hartshorne and May inquiry failed to find a greater incidence of honesty among adolescents who attended schools where special attention was given to moral training or among those who belonged to the Boy Scouts and other comparable organizations. And surely there are few teachers who in their realistic moments suppose that their moral influence goes very deep. But until we know more and until schools themselves have experimented more imaginatively in this area, we cannot say what could be done. Meanwhile there are signs that different educational conditions are associated with

*For example, Peters (1966); Wilson, Williams and Sugarman (1967); Kay (1968); and Bull (1969b).

differences in moral behaviour. On self-report and experimental tests of honesty, grammar school pupils are better behaved than those at secondary modern schools, and the upper streams are better than the lower ones in the same school (Graham, 1968; McDonald, 1969). Intelligence and social class do not account wholly for these differences; and though this still leaves an embarrassingly large number of possible interpretations, there is a real possibility that the teacher-pupil relationship is an important factor. Academically successful children are more likely to identify with their teachers, and their teachers are more likely to identify with them, for they represent for the teacher the best evidence he has that he can teach.

Though there is at present little evidence to show that the school has much impact upon the child's moral development, we can at least say something about the way its influence is mediated. If we wanted to know the nature of the moral education going on in any school our best strategy would be to seek answers to five questions: What is the nature of the relationships between staff and pupils? What actions are rewarded or positively reinforced? What actions are punished or negatively reinforced? What is the nature of the example set by staff? What kind of talking goes on in relation to morality?

The importance of staff–pupil relationships is obvious. If they are characterized by mutual hostility or indifference, the school may be actually encouraging antisocial behaviour. If their most salient features are power and control on the part of the teacher and fear and submission on the part of the pupils, then what the pupils will be learning is discretion and the avoidance of being found out, but not self-control. The more internalized moralities of the conscientious and autonomous characters depend upon relationships of mutual liking and democratic equality.

The relationship between teacher and pupil considerably influences the effectiveness of the teacher as a source of reinforcement and example. Here the important thing is how this reinforcement and example are actually seen by the pupil, and this may not coincide with what the teachers intend. It is obviously possible for a school to encourage obsequious time-serving, lying, snobbery and conceit, and to discourage truthfulness and integrity, without the staff having any clear idea of the fact.

School punishment is unlikely to lead to increased self-control in the child unless he has sufficient affection for the teacher to be partly on his side (though it will make him more careful about being found out); and if this affection exists the teacher's disappointment and disapproval are likely to be sanction enough. Of all sanctions corporal punishment is the least effective in increasing moral restraint in the offender, and it may have certain negative effects. If the teacher is mainly concerned with deterring others, however, there may be some point in such punishment. The evidence suggests that others can be vicariously conditioned by seeing an offender punished. Of course if in their view the punishment is unjust, or if there is in the school an unspoken norm which defines the staff as the enemy, then the effect will be very different.

Punishment of offenders is probably the least important factor, especially since many punishable offences at school have only tenuous moral implications. Much more important is the example set by the teacher. Obviously he will be a respectable citizen and not a criminal. But he faces a certain occupational hazard (which others face, though usually to a lesser extent). Through his authority he can control the child's response to his own behaviour. It is possible for a teacher to be rude to a child in ways in which he would not dare to be to an adult – his authority protects him from the social feedback which would otherwise inhibit him. A teacher can imperceptibly slide into the habit of more or less continually setting an example of bad manners, injustice, bullying, or even mild sadism, without knowing it, for the children have been trained to inhibit the responses which would bring home to the teacher the real nature of his conduct. I am not suggesting of course that this often happens. The important point is that because of the role he occupies in the classroom the teacher is unlikely to be fully aware of the nature of the example he is setting.

Moral education at its most conscious and deliberate takes the form of talk. Several different kinds can be distinguished. Exhortation and preaching are probably the least effective. It all depends upon whether the teacher is accepted as a natural leader by his pupils, as distinct from the occupant of a social role; that is, it depends upon whether he has any influence in shaping the norms that exist among the pupils themselves. A particular danger associated with the roles of parent and teacher is what has been called 'identification with the superego'. In his anxiety to help the moral development of his pupils the teacher may find himself recommending standards that are higher than the ones he actually lives by, and this will be seen as hypocrisy by the more perceptive of young people he teaches. The commonest form that moral education takes is discussion. This can range from, in effect, moral philosophy at one end to discussion of social problems like drugs and venereal disease at the other. The aim is primarily to inform and to encourage responsible judgement. Finally the school can provide opportunities for children to work through their own moral problems with the help of a sympathetic adult. In this situation the teacher's role has really become that of the counsellor. It seems probable that it is this kind of 'moral talk' which will have the greatest impact upon the child's behaviour.

Finally we should look carefully at the kind of self-concept our education develops in children. As we saw in chapter 3 when people's self-esteem is reduced their moral controls are weakened. This raises the interesting question of the extent to which the damage done to self-esteem by academic failure in the classroom has repercussions in the child's moral life outside it. Schools commonly hold up two identities before the child, the positive one (the 'good boy') which includes politeness to staff, hard work, cheerfulness, obedience, cooperation, and so on, and the negative one (the 'bad boy') made up of the opposites of these. It sometimes seems that children who fail to qualify for the positive identity, however much they try, end up by opting wholeheartedly for the negative one – if they cannot have fame in a competition in which the odds seem weighted against them they will have notoriety instead. Children only have an incentive to live up to the high opinion of their teachers if these teachers have a high opinion of them. Distrust is no cure for untrust-worthiness – it merely increases it. Likewise being unsym-pathetic to children who lack sympathy for others is not likely to make them more sympathetic.

All this is in a way obvious. What it boils down to is that the first step for anyone who has to take responsibility for the moral education of children should be to examine the morality of his own actions towards them. Children become moral by living in a community in which honesty and generosity are valued, which is just and which therefore supports and encourages protest against injustice which may occur within it, and so on. What is not so obvious is that we have to decide not simply whether we are going to throw the resources of the school community into making children moral, but what kind of character we wish to see emerg-ing at the end. The discussion of character in the previous chap-ter illustrates some of the main options before the educator. Whether he likes it or not he will be tending to produce one such character rather than another. It is true that genetic predisposi-tion and family background may leave so deep an imprint on character that the influence of school is superficial, even negli-gible, by comparison. But it is also the influence which is most under our control and we are obliged to use it as responsibly as we can.

Presumably schools are never actually intended to encourage the amoral character. But they may do so inadvertently, espe-cially if moral development is not thought to be their concern. Sometimes, perhaps because of dissension among the staff and the stress of coping with impossibly difficult children, the school's morale can sink so low that on balance its moral influence is more harmful than good, so that, for example, flattery is always re-warded and expedience invariably takes precedence over justice. The conformist character would tend to be fostered by a school in which children are herded together in large groups all the time and where opportunity to form individual friendships is minimal. If the staff are distant and ineffective, and follow a *laissez-faire* policy, the child ends up by being influenced mainly by peer groups in which the influence of adults is totally absent. It is not difficult to picture the kind of school which encourages the authoritarian character. The staff are remote and powerful people. In the child's eyes the principal virtue is obedience to authority. Hierarchy runs all through the school, with great emphasis upon the powers and privileges of older pupils and staff. The main lesson the child learns is that as you gain power so the rules become more adjusted to suit your pleasure and convenience, and they increasingly enable you to make use of others. Relationships of mutual respect are rare and tend to be restricted to those at the bottom of the hierarchy. English schools do not seem to be designed to produce the collectivist character though certain movements within them which stress the grouping of children for work purposes and the deliberate use of the group to change the individual might be said to be a small step in this direction. The conscientious character will tend to be the product of small schools, with small classes, where there is a lot of staff-pupil contact of a warm and friendly kind, and where high standards are set and the staff present a unanimous front over what these standards are.

The view taken here is of course that the character most worthy of cultivation is the altruistic-autonomous. Though developmentally speaking this must be an achievement of adulthood, school life may facilitate its emergence. The kind of school most likely to encourage it is one in which pupils and staff come from varied backgrounds and where there is plenty of opportunity for individual relationships to flourish, both among pupils and between pupils and staff. Relationships of this kind provide the child with an experience of the interhuman, of trust and creative personal exchange, which makes the point of moral principles seem obvious, and they form the context in which he can talk out his own moral problems and experience giving them shape and meaning (as distinct from discussing more abstract and hypothetical moral issues in a group or class situation). What he needs to find in the staff is unanimity over the importance of commitment to basic moral principles coupled with diversity of judgement over their application. Democratic moments between staff and pupils are common. What the child learns is that moral

243

issues are of the greatest importance, that they are controversial, and that they can only be settled by reasoning and the appeal to common values and never by the exercise of authority and power. And he also learns that, though he has no alternative but to live by his own standards, these standards are relative and partial, and always in need of revision.

What I have said amounts to the claim that the really valuable part of moral education occurs outside the orthodox teacher role, when the teacher is for the moment 'off duty', or in his role as unofficial counsellor. Of course school organization and all the chores that teachers are burdened with make this kind of private and individual contact difficult – but not impossible, for some teachers manage a lot of it. Its very rarity can make it that much more significant and memorable for the child. Teachers have also to shake loose from constrictive professional roles which inhibit them from being personal, and which compel them to present to the child a united, safe and usually conservative front on the really important things like values, moral rules, religion and social problems. There is evidence that teachers are not seen as fully human, by adolescents anyway (see Wright, 1962). If teachers are to exert a wider influence than just an academic one then they must be able to meet their pupils outside their normal role. There is a simple belief which underlies the whole discussion, namely, if we are to take moral education seriously, and even more if we take the autonomous character as the ideal to be pursued, then it is no use supposing that moral education is something that can be tacked on to the existing curriculum as an extra; on the contrary, all aspects of school life must be looked at in its light, and it must enter centrally into our concept of what a school is.

## Conclusion – on the Application of Psychological Knowledge

With the end of the book now fully in sight the inevitable question is what it all adds up to. Have we learned very much about moral behaviour? In the sense of factual results from empirical studies we have learned quite a lot. It is true that the scope for further research in this area is almost spectacular; but enough has been reported in earlier chapters to make a summary at this stage hardly feasible. Hopefully too we may be a little wiser about the complexity of moral behaviour. But in the sense of 'deep' truths that startle and transform our conception of human nature we have learned nothing. And this is not surprising since it is in the nature of empirical psychology that most of the time it is making precise, explicit and accurate, and establishing as knowledge through the slow accumulation of factual results, ideas that are already familiar, or of which we are at least half aware already.

Nevertheless we do not study moral behaviour just to satisfy our disinterested curiosity; we hope that one day the knowledge we acquire will be applied. Admittedly, until there is more money and opportunity for research in this field, it is questionable whether we have enough knowledge to talk at all confidently about its application. But certainly anyone who is perplexed about the moral training of his children has a right to turn to the psychologist for help. There are many areas of psychology, such as the performance of certain tasks, the measurement of certain human characteristics, the design of machines for human operators, and so on, where the psychologist can make more or less straightforward recommendations based on sound experimental evidence. Child rearing is not one of them. Here the situation is quite different and it is important to understand why.

Ethical considerations prohibit the kind of experimentation which would give the psychologist an unequivocal basis for advice on many of the problems that are brought to him. But this is not the main difficulty. When a child is physically ill the doctor can give his mother quite explicit instructions based upon careful diagnosis – for instance that she must keep him indoors for three weeks and give him four pills a day at regular intervals. The child psychologist faced with a mother complaining of her child's temper tantrums cannot be anything like as explicit. At best he can suggest a general change in policy on the mother's part – for instance that she stops being so punitive, treats his tantrums with tolerant amusement, and spends more time playing constructively with him. But the real difference appears when the mother puts the advice into practice. As far as the medical advice is concerned, normally, and within obvious limits, it does not much matter from the point of view of the child's health how the mother does it. She may be wheedling and ingratiating, dominating and punitive, brisk and businesslike, or lie and bribe in order to get her child's cooperation – whichever way it is he will get better. But as far as the psychological advice is concerned, it is crucial how the mother carries it out; indeed the advice consists precisely of the suggestion that the mother herself should change.

It would not be difficult to draw up a general blueprint for bringing up a child to have a certain kind of moral character – we have already done this after a fashion. But the great majority of the instructions would be specifying habitual styles of behaviour in the parents, the things they should consider important and unimportant, the quality of their feelings for their child, and so on. Notoriously people cannot change their attitudes to order. It is futile to advise an anxious mother to be less anxious – she simply becomes anxious about her anxiety; or to tell a father never to smack his child – it will lead to the bottling up of anger, its eventual release in actions more violent than usual, and an aftermath of guilt.

Does this mean that the psychologist has no role to play at all? Not quite. For what he can do is try not so much to give parents policies to follow, as to provide them with a new awareness of their relationships which spontaneously generates changes in attitude and feeling. He can help the parent to *see* things differently so that he naturally starts behaving differently. In effect the psychologist puts the parent into much the same position that he himself is in by sharing his knowledge and experience, and then leaving him to work out how it applies in his own situation.

Of course this presumes a higher level of intelligent cooperation than many parents are able to give. All kinds of qualifications are needed. The point that I wish to make clear is that the application of much psychological knowledge will take a different form from the application of knowledge in the physical sciences. As Bakan (1968) said, the main social value of psychology lies in people knowing about it. It is worth quoting him at length on the matter.

Yet it would be wrong for the psychologist to enter upon the larger scene in precisely the social role of the physical scientist. The knowledge of the physical scientist becomes socially significant as it is mediated, applied, and used in design processes and equipment. His knowledge of heat, or electricity, or mechanics becomes significant as it is used in making devices of which we avail ourselves without necessarily understanding the nature of heat or electricity or mechanics. The physical scientist was able to turn his knowledge into use without teaching us what he knew. But the value of understanding human functioning does not inhere in its application in the usual sense, but in its possession. This is one of the most significant results of the clinical enterprise. In order to help a person who is in psychological difficulties we work to enhance his understanding of himself and of his relationships to others. If we think in terms of traditional social roles, then the significant place in society of the psychologist will be more that of teacher than expert or technician. (Bakan, 1968)

It is entirely in the spirit of this passage that this book has been written. My intention has been not to tell parents or anyone else how children should be morally trained, but to make the reader a little more psychologically aware of the processes involved in moral behaviour. And, let it be admitted, there has also been the more daring hope that it might edge some readers towards a greater autonomy in their own moral life.

# References

ABEL, T. M. (1941), 'Moral judgments among subnormals', *Journal of Abnormal and Social Psychology*, vol. 36, pp. 378–92.

ABELSON, R. P., ARONSON, E., MCGUIRE, W. J., NEWCOMB, T. M., ROSENBERG, M. J., and TANNENBAUM, P. H. (Eds.) (1968), *Theories of Cognitive Consistency*, Chicago: Rand McNally.

ADORNO, T. W., FRENKEL-BRUNSWIK, E., LEVINSON, D. J., and SANFORD, R. N. (1950), *The Authoritarian Personality*, New York: Harper.

ALLINSMITH, W. (1960), 'The learning of moral standards', in Miller, D., and Swanson, G. (Eds.), *Inner Conflict and Defence*, New York: Holt & Co.

ALLINSMITH, W., and GREENING, T. C. (1955), 'Guilt over anger as predicted from parental discipline: a study of superego development', *American Psychologist*, vol. 10, p. 320 (abstract).

ALLPORT, G. W. (1954), *The Nature of Prejudice*, Reading, Mass.: Addison-Wesley.

ALLPORT, G. W. (1955), *Becoming*, Yale University Press.

ALLPORT, G. W. (1961), *Pattern and Growth in Personality*, New York: Holt, Rinehart & Winston.

ALLPORT, G. W. (1966), 'Religious context of prejudice', *Journal for the Scientific Study of Religion*, vol. 5, pp. 447–57.

ALLPORT, G. W. (1968), *The Person in Psychology*, Boston: Beacon Press.

ALLPORT, G. W., and ROSS, J. M. (1967) 'Personal religious orientation and prejudice', *Journal of Personality and Social Psychology*, vol. 5, pp. 432–43.

ALLPORT, G. W., VERNON, P. E., and LINDZEY, G. (1960), *Study of Values*, 3rd ed., Boston: Houghton Mifflin.

ALPER, T. G., LEVIN, V. S., and KLEIN, M. H. (1964), 'Authoritarian versus humanistic conscience', *Journal of Personality*, vol. 32, pp. 313–33.

ANDRY, R. G. (1960), *Delinquency and Parental Pathology*, Methuen.

ARGYLE, M. (1958), *Religious Behaviour*, Routledge & Kegan Paul.

ARGYLE, M. (1961), 'A new approach to the classification of delinquents with implications for treatment', in *Monograph No. 2*, California Board of Corrections.

ARONFREED, J. (1961), 'The nature, variety of social patterning of moral responses to transgression', *Journal of Abnormal and Social Psychology*, vol. 63, pp. 223–40.

ARONFREED, J. (1963), 'The effect of experimental socialization paradigms upon two moral responses to transgression', *Journal of Abnormal and Social Psychology*, vol. 66, pp. 437–48.

ARONFREED, J. (1964), 'The origins of self criticism', *Psychological Review*, vol. 71, pp. 193–218.

ARONFREED, J. (1968), *Conduct and Conscience*, New York: Academic Press.

ARONFREED, J. (1969), 'The concept of internalization', in Goslin, D. A. (Ed.), *Handbook of Socialization Theory and Research*, Chicago: Rand McNally.

ARONFREED, J., CUTICK, R. A., and FAGEN, S. A. (1963), 'Cognitive structure, punishment, and nurturance in the experimental induction of self criticism', *Child Development*, vol. 34, pp. 281–94.

ARONFREED, J. and REBER, A. (1965), 'Internalized behavioral suppression and the timing of social punishment', *Journal of Personality and Social Psychology*, vol. 1, pp. 3–17.

ARONSON, E., and METTEE, D. R. (1968), 'Dishonest behavior as a function of differential levels of induced self-esteem', *Journal of Personality and Social Psychology*, vol. 9, pp. 121–7.

ASUMI, T. (1963), 'Maladjustment and delinquency: a comparison of two samples', *Journal of Child Psychology and Psychiatry*, vol. 4, pp. 219–28.

BACON, M. K., CHILD, I. L., and BERRY, H. (1963), 'A cross-cultural study of correlates of crimes', *Journal of Abnormal and Social Psychology*, vol. 66, pp. 291–300.

BAKAN, D. (1968), *On Method*, San Francisco: Jossey-Bass.

BALDWIN, A. L. (1967), *Theories of Child Development*, New York: Wiley.

BANDURA, A. (1969a), *Principles of Behavior Modification*, New York: Holt, Rinehart & Winston.

BANDURA, A. (1969b), 'Social learning of moral judgments', *Journal of Personality and Social Psychology*, vol. 11, pp. 275–9.

BANDURA, A., and MCDONALD, F. J. (1963), 'The influence of social reinforcement and the behavior of models in shaping children's moral judgment', *Journal of Abnormal and Social Psychology*, vol. 67, pp. 274–81.

BANDURA, A., and WALTERS, R. H. (1959), *Adolescent Aggression*, New York: Ronald Press.

BANDURA, A., and WALTERS, R. H. (1963), *Social Learning and Personality Development*, New York: Holt, Rinehart & Winston.

BARNDT, R. J., and JOHNSON, D. M. (1955), 'Time evaluation in delinquents', *Journal of Abnormal and Social Psychology*, vol. 51, pp. 343–5.

BECKER, W. C. (1964), 'Consequences of different kinds of parental discipline', *Review of Child Development Research*, vol. 1, Russell Sage Foundation.

BELL, R. Q. (1968), 'A reinterpretation of the direction of effects in studies of socialization', *Psychological Review*, vol. 75, pp. 81–94.

BENNETT, I. (1960), *Delinquent and Neurotic Children*, Tavistock.

BERES, D. (1958), 'Vicissitudes of superego function and superego precursors in childhood', *The Psychoanalytic Study of the Child*, vol. 13, pp. 324–51.

BERGER, S. M. (1962), 'Conditioning through vicarious instigation', *Psychological Review*, vol. 59, pp. 450–66.

BERKOWITZ, L., and CONNOR, W. H. (1966), 'Success, failure and social responsibility', *Journal of Personality and Social Psychology*, vol. 4, pp. 664–9.

BERKOWITZ, L., and DANIELS, L. R. (1963), 'Responsibility and dependence', *Journal of Abnormal and Social Psychology*, vol. 66, pp. 429–36.

BERKOWITZ, L., and DANIELS, L. R. (1964), 'Factors affecting the salience of the social responsibility norm', *Journal of Abnormal and Social Psychology*, vol. 68, pp. 275–81.

BERKOWITZ, L., and FRIEDMAN, P. (1967), 'Some social class differences in helping behaviour', *Journal of Personality and Social Psychology*, vol. 5, pp. 217–25.

BERNARD, J. L., and EISENMAN, R. (1967), 'Verbal conditioning of sociopaths with social and monetary rewards', *Journal of Personality and Social Psychology*, vol. 6, pp. 203–6.

BERNE, E. (1966), *Games People Play*, André Deutsch.

BERRIEN, F. K. (1965), 'Japanese and American values', *Journal of Social Psychology*, vol. 65, pp. 181–91.

BERSCHEID, E., BOYE, D., and WALSTER, E. (1968), 'Retaliation as a means of restoring equity', *Journal of Personality and Social Psychology*, vol. 10, pp. 370–76.

BERSCHEID, E., and WALSTER, E. (1967), 'When does a harm-doer compensate a victim?', *Journal of Personality and Social Psychology*, vol. 6, pp. 435–41.

BIAGGIO, A. M. B. (1969), 'Internalized versus externalized guilt: a cross-cultural study', *Journal of Social Psychology*, vol. 78, pp. 147–9.

BLACK, M. S., and LONDON, P. (1966), 'The dimensions of guilt, religion and personal ethics', *Journal of Social Psychology*, vol. 69, pp. 39–54.

BLAKE, R. R. (1958), 'The other person in the situation', in Tagiuri, R., Petrullo, L. (Eds.), *Person Perception and Interpersonal Behavior*, Stanford University Press.

BLOOM, L. (1959), 'A reappraisal of Piaget's theory of moral judgement', *Journal of Genetic Psychology*, vol. 95, pp. 3–12.

BOEHM, L. (1962), 'The development of conscience: a comparison of students in Catholic parochial schools and in public schools', *Child Development*, vol. 33, pp. 233–51.

BOEHM, L., and NASS, M. L. (1962), 'Social class differences in conscience development', *Child Development*, vol. 33, pp. 565–74.

BOWLBY, J. (1969), *Attachment and Loss: Vol. I Attachment*, Hogarth Press.

BREZNITZ, S. and KUGELMASS, S. (1967), 'Intentionality in moral judgement: developmental stages', *Child Development*, vol. 38, pp. 469–79.

BRIGHAM, J. C., RICKETTS, J. L., and JOHNSON, R. C. (1967), 'Reported maternal and paternal behaviour of solitary and social delinquents', *Journal of Consulting Psychology*, vol. 31, pp. 420–22.

BROCK, T. C. and BUSS, A. H. (1962), 'Dissonance, aggression and evaluation of pain', *Journal of Abnormal and Social Psychology*, vol. 55, pp. 197–202.

BROCK, T. C., and BUSS, A. H. (1964), 'Effects of justification for aggression and communication with the victim on postaggression dissonance', *Journal of Abnormal and Social Psychology*, vol. 58, pp. 403–12.

BROCK, T. C., and DELGIUDICE, C. (1963), 'Stealing and temporal orientation', *Journal of Abnormal and Social Psychology*, vol. 66, pp. 91–4.

BROGDEN, H. E. (1940), 'A factor analysis of forty character tests', *Psychological Monographs*, vol. 52, no. 3.

BRONFENBRENNER, U. (1961), 'Some familial antecedents of responsibility and leadership in adolescents', in Petrullo, L., and Bass, B. M. (Eds.), *Leadership and Interpersonal Behavior*, New York: Holt, Rinehart & Winston.

BRONFENBRENNER, U. (1962a), 'Soviet methods of character education: some implications for research', *Religious Education*, vol. 57 (research supplement), pp. 345–61.

BRONFENBRENNER, U. (1962b), 'Soviet studies of personality development and socialization', in Bauer, E. (Ed) *Some Views on Soviet Psychology*, American Psychological Association.

BRONFENBRENNER, U. (1967), 'Response to pressure from peers versus adults among Soviet and American school children', *International Journal of Psychology*, vol. 2, pp. 199–204.

BRONFENBRENNER, U. (1970a), *Two Worlds of Childhood*, Russell Sage Foundation, New York.

BRONFENBRENNER, U. (1970b), 'Reaction to social pressure from adults versus peers among Soviet day school and boarding school pupils in the perspective of an American sample', *Journal of Personality and Social Psychology*, vol. 15, pp. 179–89.

BRONFENBRENNER, U., DEVEREUX. E. C. JR., SUCI, G. T., and RODGERS, R. R. (1965), 'Adults and peers as sources of conformity', paper presented at the Conference on Socialization and Competence, Puerto Rico, April 1965.

BROWN, A. W., MORRISON, J., and COUCH, G. B. (1947), 'Influence of affectional family relationships on character development', *Journal of Abnormal and Social Psychology*, vol. 42, pp. 422–8.

BROWN. R. (1965), *Social Psychology*, New York, The Free Press (Macmillan).

BROWN, R., and BELLUGI, U. (1964), 'Three processes in the child's acquisition of syntax', *Harvard Educational Review*, vol. 34, pp. 133–51.

BRYAN, J. H., and LONDON, P. (1970), 'Altruistic behaviour by children', *Psychological Bulletin*, vol. 73, pp. 200–211.

BRYAN, J. H., and KAPCHE, R. (1967), 'Psychopathy and verbal conditioning', *Journal of Abnormal Psychology*, vol. 72, pp. 71–3.

BRYAN, J. H., and TEST, M. A. (1967), 'Models and helping:

naturalistic studies in aiding behavior', *Journal of Personality and Social Psychology*, vol. 6. pp. 400–407.

BRYANT, H. A., DOBBINS, D. A., and BASS, B. M. (1963), 'Group effectiveness, coercion, change and coalescence among delinquents compared to non-delinquents', *Journal of Social Psychology*, vol. 61, pp. 167–77.

BUBER, M. (1965), *The Knowledge of Man*, George Allen & Unwin.

BULL, N. J. (1969a), *Moral Judgment from Childhood to Adolescence*, Routledge & Kegan Paul.

BULL, N. J. (1969b), *Moral Education*, Routledge & Kegan Paul.

BURTON, R. V. (1963), 'Generality of honesty reconsidered', *Psychological Review*, vol. 70, pp. 481–99.

BURTON, R. V., ALLINSMITH, W., and MACCOBY, E. E. (1966), 'Resistance to temptation in relation to sex of child, sex of experimenter, and withdrawal of attention', *Journal of Personality and Social Psychology*, vol. 3, pp. 253–8.

BURTON, R. V., MACCOBY, E. E., and ALLINSMITH, W. (1961), 'Antecedents of resistance to temptation in four year old children', *Child Development*, vol. 32, pp. 689–710.

BUTLER, E. W., and ADAMS, S. N. (1966), 'Typologies of delinquent girls: some alternative approaches', *Social Forces*, vol. 44, pp. 401–7.

BUTT, S. D., and SIGNORI, E. I. (1965), 'Relationships of personality factors to conceived values in male university students', *Psychological Reports*, vol. 16, pp. 609–17.

CAMPBELL, D. T. (1965), 'Ethnocentrism and other altruistic motives', *Nebraska Symposium on Motivation*, University of Nebraska Press.

CAMPBELL, E. Q. (1964), 'The internalization of moral norms', *Sociometry*, vol. 27, pp. 391–412.

CARLSMITH, J. M., and GROSS, A. E. (1969), 'Some effects of guilt on compliance', *Journal of Personality and Social Psychology*, vol. 2, pp. 232–9.

CHESLER, M. A. (1965), 'Ethnocentrism and attitudes towards the physically disabled', *Journal of Personality and Social Psychology*, vol. 2, pp. 877–82.

CHESSER, E. (1956), *The Sexual, Marital and Family Relationships of the English Woman*, Hutchinson.

CHRISTENDOM, J. A. (1938), 'Ethical standards test', in Murray, H. (Ed.), *Explorations in Personality*, Oxford University Press.

CHRISTIES, N., ANDENAES, J., and SKIRBECK, P. (1965), 'A study of self-reported crime,' in *Scandinavian Studies in Criminology*, Tavistock.

CHURCH, R. M. (1963), 'The varied effects of punishment on behavior', *Psychological Review*, vol. 70, pp. 369–402.

CLARK, J., and WENNINGER, E. (1962), 'Social class, area, sex, and age as correlates of illegal behavior among juveniles', *American Sociological Review*, vol. 27, pp. 826–34.

CLARK, J., and TIFFT, L. L. (1966), 'Polygraph and interview validation of self-reported deviant behavior', *American Sociological Review*, vol. 31, pp. 516–23.

CLECKLEY, H. (1964), *The Mask of Sanity*, 4th ed., St Louis, Mo.: 333, C. V. Mosby.

CLINE, V. B., and RICHARDS, J. M. (1965), 'A factor analytic study of religious belief and behaviour', *Journal of Personality and Social Psychology*, vol. 1, pp. 569–78.

COCKBURN, J. J., and MCCLAY, I. (1965), 'Sex differences in juvenile delinquency', *British Journal of Criminology*, vol. 5, pp. 289–308.

COCKING, R. R. (1969), 'Fantasy confession among Arapaho Indian children', *Journal of Genetic Psychology*, vol. 114, pp. 229–35.

CONGER, J. J., and MILLER, W. C. (1966), *Personality, Social Class, and Delinquency*, New York: Wiley.

COWAN, P. A., LANGER, J., HEAVENRICH, J., and NATHANSON, M. (1969), 'Social learning and Piaget's cognitive theory of moral development', *Journal of Personality and Social Psychology*, vol. 11, pp. 261–74.

COWIE, J., COWIE, V., and SLATER, E. (1968), *Delinquency in Girls*, Heinemann.

COX, E. (1967), *Sixth Form Religion*, S.C.M. Press.

CRANDALL, V. C. (1966), 'Personality characteristics and social and achievement behaviors associated with children's social desirability tendencies', *Journal of Personality and Social Psychology*, vol. 4, pp. 477–86.

CRANDALL, V. C., CRANDALL, V. J., and KATKOVSKY, W. (1965), 'A children's social desirability questionnaire', *Journal of Consulting Psychology*, vol. 29, pp. 27–36.

CRANDALL, V. C., and GOZALI, J. (1969), 'The social desirability responses of children of four religious-cultural groups', *Child Development*, vol. 40, pp. 751–62.

CRANE, A. R. (1958), 'The development of moral values in children', *British Journal of Educational Psychology*, vol. 28, pp. 201–8.

CROWLEY, P. M. (1968), 'Effect upon objectivity of moral judgment in grade school children', *Journal of Personality and Social Psychology*, vol. 8, pp. 228–32.

DANIELS, L. R., and BERKOWITZ, L. (1963), 'Liking and response to dependency relationships', *Human Relations*, vol. 16. pp. 141–8.

DARLEY, J. M., and LATANÉ, B. (1968), 'Bystander intervention in emergencies: diffusion of responsibility', *Journal of Personality and Social Psychology*, vol. 8, pp. 377–83.

DARLINGTON, R. B., and MACKER, C. E. (1966), 'Displacement of guilt-produced altruistic behavior', *Journal of Personality and Social Psychology*, vol. 4, pp. 442–3.

DAVITZ, J. R. (1969), *The Language of Emotion*, New York: Academic Press.

DEACON, W. J. (1965), 'A survey of deliquency in Somerset 1958–1960', *Educational Research*, vol. 7, pp. 215–28.

DEDMAN, J. (1959), 'The relationship between religious attitude and attitude towards premarital sex relations', *Marriage and Family Living*, vol. 21, pp. 171–6.

DENTLER, R. A., and MONROE, L. J. (1961), 'Social correlates of early adolescent theft', *American Sociological Review*, vol. 25, pp. 733–43.

DE ROPP, R. S. (1969), *The Master Game*, George Allen & Unwin.

DOLAND, D. J., and ADELBERG, K. (1967), 'The learning of sharing behavior', *Child Development*, vol. 38, pp. 695–700.

DURKIN, D. (1959a), 'Children's concepts of justice: a comparison with the Piaget data', *Child Development*, vol. 30, pp. 59–67.

DURKIN, D. (1959b), 'Children's concepts of justice: a further comparison with the Piaget data', *Journal of Educational Research*, vol. 52, pp. 252–7.

EISENMAN, R. (1967), 'Sex differences in moral judgment', *Perceptual and Motor Skills*, vol. 24, p. 784.

ELMHORN, K. (1965), 'Study in self-reported delinquency among schoolchildren', in *Scandinavian Studies in Criminology*, Tavistock.

EMPEY, L. T., and ERICKSON, M. L. (1966), 'Hidden delinquency and social status', *Social Forces*, vol. 44, pp. 546–54.

EPPS, P., and PARNELL, R. W. (1952), 'Physique and temperament of women delinquents compared with women undergraduates', *British Journal of Medical Psychology*, vol. 25, pp. 249–55.

EYSENCK, H. J. (1960), *The Structure of Human Personality*, 2nd ed., Methuen.

EYSENCK, H. J. (1964), *Crime and Personality*, Routledge & Kegan Paul.

EYSENCK, H. J. (1968), *The Biological Basis of Personality*, Springfield, Ill.: Charles C. Thomas.

EYSENCK, H. J., and EYSENCK, S. G. B. (1969), *Personality Structure and Measurement*, Routledge & Kegan Paul.

EXLINE, R. V., THIBAUT, J., BRANNON, C., and GUMPERT, P. (1961), 'Visual interaction in relation to Machiavellianism and the unethical act', *American Psychologist*, vol. 16, p. 396.

FEATHER, N. T. (1964), 'Acceptance and rejection of arguments in relation to attitude strength, critical ability and intolerance', *Journal of Abnormal and Social Psychology*, vol. 69, pp. 127–36.

FEATHER, N. T. (1967), 'Evaluation of religious and neutral arguments in religious and atheist student groups', *Australian Journal of Psychology*, vol. 19, pp. 3–12.

FELDMAN, S. E., and FELDMAN, M. T. (1967), 'Transition of sex differences in cheating', *Psychological Reports*, vol. 20, pp. 957–8.

FERDINAND, T. N. (1966), *Typologies of Delinquency*, New York: Random House.

FERGUSON, T. (1962), *The Young Delinquent in his Social Setting*, Oxford University Press.

FESTINGER, L., and FREEDMAN, J. L. (1964), 'Dissonance reduction and moral values', in Worchel, P., and Byrne, D. (Eds.), *Personality Change*, New York: Wiley.

FINGARETTE, H. (1963), *The Self in Transformation*, New York: Basic Books.

FISCHER, W. F. (1963), 'Sharing in preschool children as a function of amount and type of reinforcement', *Genetic Psychology Monographs*, vol. 68, pp. 215–45.

FITCH, J. H. (1962), 'Two personality variables and their distribution in a criminal population: an empirical study', *British Journal of Social and Clinical Psychology*, vol. 1, pp. 161–7.

FLAVELL, J. H. (1963), *The Developmental Psychology of Jean Piaget*, Princeton, N.J.: Van Nostrand.

FLAVELL, J. H. (1968), *The Development of Role-taking and Communication Skills in Children*, New York: Wiley.

FLUGEL, J. C. (1945), *Man, Morals and Society*, Duckworth and Penguin Books.

FREEDMAN, J. L., WALLINGTON, S. A., and BLESS, E. (1967), 'Compliance without pressure', *Journal of Personality and Social Psychology*, vol. 7, pp. 117–24.

FREUD, A. (1937), *The Ego and Mechanisms of Defence*, Hogarth Press.

FREUD, A., and DANN, S. (1951), 'An experiment in group upbringing', *The Psychoanalytic Study of the Child*, vol. 6, pp. 127–63.

FREUD, S. (1927), *The Ego and the Id*, Hogarth Press.

FREUD, S. (1933), *New Introductory Lectures on Psychoanalysis*, Hogarth Press.

FREUD, S. (1949), *An Outline of Psychoanalysis* (first published in 1940), Hogarth Press.

FREUD, S. (1950), 'Some psychological consequences of the anatomical distinction between the sexes', in J. Strachey (Ed.), *Collected Papers*, Hogarth Press.

FRIEDRICHS, R. W. (1960), 'Alter versus ego: an exploratory assessment of altruism', *American Sociological Review*, vol. 25, pp. 496–508.

FROMM, E. (1947), *Man For Himself*, New York: Holt, Rinehart & Winston.

FUNKENSTEIN, D., KING, S., and DROLETTE, C. (1957), *Mastery of Stress*, Harvard University Press.

GERRARD, N. L. (1964), 'The core member of the gang', *British Journal of Criminology*, vol. 4, pp. 361–71.

GIBBENS, T. C. N. (1963), *Psychiatric Studies of Borstal Lads*, Maudsley Monographs No. 11, Oxford University Press.

GIBSON, H. B. (1967), 'Self-reported delinquency among schoolboys and their attitudes to the police', *British Journal of Social and Clinical Psychology*, vol. 6, pp. 168–73.

GLASS, D. (1964), 'Changes in liking as a means of reducing cognitive discrepancies between self-esteem and aggression', *Journal of Personality*, vol. 32, pp. 531–49.

GLICKSMAN, M., and WOHL, J. (1965), 'Expressed values of Burmese and American university students', *Journal of Social Psychology*, vol. 65, pp. 17–25.

GLOVER, E. (1968), *The Birth of the Ego*, George Allen & Unwin.

GLUECK, S., and GLUECK, E. (1950), *Unraveling Juvenile Delinquency*, New York: Commonwealth Fund.

GLUECK, S., and GLUECK, E. (1965a), 'Varieties of delinquent types', *British Journal of Criminology*, vol. 5, pp. 236–48.

GLUECK, S., and GLUECK, E. (1965b), 'Varieties of delinquent types (concluded)', *British Journal of Criminology*, vol. 5, pp. 388–405.

GLUECK, S., and GLUECK, E. (1968), *Delinquents and Nondelinquents in Perspective*, Harvard University Press.

GOOCH, S., and PRINGLE, M. L. (1966), *Four Years On*, Longmans.

GORANSON, R. E., and BERKOWITZ, L. (1966), 'Reciprocity and responsibility reactions to prior help', *Journal of Personality and Social Psychology*, vol. 3, pp. 227–32.

GORDON, R., SHORT, J., CARTWRIGHT, D., and STRODTBECK, F. (1963), 'Values and gang delinquency: a study of street-corner groups', *American Journal of Sociology*, vol. 69, pp. 109–28.

GORE, P. M., and RUTTER, J. B. (1963), 'A personality correlate of social action', *Journal of Personality*, vol. 31, pp. 58–64.

GORER, G. (1955), *Exploring English Character*, London: Cresset Press.

GOUGH, H. G. (1960), 'Theory and measurement of socialization', *Journal of Consulting Psychology*, vol. 24, pp. 23–30.

GRAHAM, D. (1968), 'Moral development', unpublished research report.

GREENGLASS, E. R. (1969), 'Effects of prior help and hindrance on willingness to help others', *Journal of Personality and Social Psychology*, vol. 11, pp. 224–31.

GRIM, P. F., KOHLBERG, L., and WHITE, S. H. (1968), 'Some relationships between conscience and attentional processes', *Journal of Personality and Social Psychology*, vol. 8, pp. 239–52.

GRINDER, R. E. (1961), 'New techniques for research in children's temptation behavior', *Child Development*, vol. 32, pp. 679–88.

GRINDER, R. E. (1962), 'Parental child-rearing practices, conscience, and resistance to temptation of sixth grade children', *Child Development*, vol. 33, pp. 803–20.

GRINDER, R. E. (1964), 'Relations between behavioral and cognitive dimensions of conscience in middle childhood', *Child Development*, vol. 35, pp. 881–91.

GRINDER, R. E., and MCMICHAEL, R. E. (1963), 'Cultural influence on conscience development, resistance to temptation and guilt among Samoans and American Caucasians', *Journal of Abnormal and Social Psychology*, vol. 66, pp. 503–7.

GRUSEC, J. (1966), 'Some antecedents of self-criticism', *Journal of Personality and Social Psychology*, vol. 4, pp. 244–52.

HAAN, N., SMITH, M. B., and BLOCK, J. (1968), 'The moral reasoning of young adults', *Journal of Personality and Social Psychology*, vol. 10, pp. 183–201.

HALL, C. (1954), *A Primer of Freudian Psychology*, Cleveland, Ohio: World Publishing Co.

HANDLON, B. J., and GROSS, P. (1959), 'The development of sharing behavior', *Journal of Abnormal and Social Psychology*, vol. 59, pp. 425–8.

HARE, A. P. (1962), *Handbook of Small Group Research*, New York: The Free Press (Macmillan).

HARLOW, H. F., and HARLOW, M. K. (1969), 'Effects of various mother-infant relationships on rhesus monkey behaviors', in Foss, B. M. (Ed.), *Determinants of Infant Behaviour IV*, Methuen.

HARP, J., and TAIETZ, P. (1966), 'Academic integrity and social structure: a study of cheating among college students', *Social Problems*, vol. 13, pp. 365–73.

HARTMANN, H., and LOEWENSTEIN, R. M. (1962), 'Notes on the superego', *The Psychoanalytic Study of the Child*, vol. 17, pp. 42–81.

HARTMANN, H. (1964), *Essays on Ego Psychology*, New York: International Universities Press.

HARTUP, W. W., and COATES, A. (1967), 'Imitation of peers as a function of reinforcement from the peer group and rewardingness of the model', *Child Development*, vol. 38, pp. 1003–16.

HARTSHORNE, H., and MAY, M. A. (1928), *Studies in Deceit*, New York: Macmillan.

HARTSHORNE, H., and MAY, M. A. (1929), *Studies in Service and Self Control*, New York: Macmillan.

HARTSHORNE, H., and SHUTTLEWORTH, F. K. (1930), *Studies in the Organization of Character*, New York: Macmillan.

HATHAWAY, S. R., and MONACHESI, E. (Eds.) (1953), *Analysing and Predicting Juvenile Delinquency*, University of Minnesota Press.

HAVIGHURST, R. J., and TABA, H. (1949), *Adolescent Character and Personality*, New York: Wiley.

HEALY, W., and BRONNER, A. F. (1936), *New Light on Delinquency and its Treatment*, Yale University Press.

HEBB, D. O., and THOMPSON, W. R. (1969), 'The social significance of animal studies', in Lindzey, G., and Aronson, E. (Eds.), *The Handbook of Social Psychology*, vol. 3, 2nd ed., New York: Addison-Wesley.

HENRY, A. F. (1956), 'Family role structure and self blame', *Social Forces*, vol. 35, pp. 34–8.

HERBERT, M. (in press), *The Emotional Problems of the School-going Child*, Penguin Books.

HEWITT, L. E., and JENKINS, R. L. (1946), *Fundamental Patterns of*

*Maladjustment: the dynamics of their origin*, State Printer: Springfield, Ill.

HILL, G. E. (1935), 'The ethical knowledge of delinquent and non-delinquent boys', *Journal of Social Psychology*, vol. 6, pp. 107–14.

HILL, J. P., and KOCHENDORFER, R. A. (1969), 'Knowledge of peer success and risk of detection as determinants of cheating', *Developmental Psychology*, vol. 1, pp. 231–8.

HIRSCHI, T., and SELVIN, H. C. (1967), *Delinquency Research: an appraisal of analytic methods*, New York: The Free Press.

HOFFMAN, M. L. (1963), 'Parental discipline and the child's consideration for others', *Child Development*, vol. 34, pp. 573–88.

HOFFMAN, M. L. (1970), 'Conscience, personality, and socialization techniques', *Human Development*, vol. 13, pp. 90–126.

HOFFMAN, M. L., and SALTZSTEIN, H. D. (1967), 'Parent discipline and the child's moral development', *Journal of Personality and Social Psychology*, vol. 5, pp. 45–57.

HOMANS, G. C. (1961), *Social Behaviour*, Routledge & Kegan Paul.

HORSTEIN, H. A., FISCH, E., and HOLMES, M. (1968), 'Influence of a model's feeling about his behavior and his relevance as a comparison other on the observer's helping behavior', *Journal of Personality and Social Psychology*, vol. 10, pp. 222–6.

INDEPENDENT TELEVISION AUTHORITY, (1970), *Religion in Britain and Northern Ireland*, published by the I.T.A., London.

JAHODA, M. (1959), 'Conformity and independence', *Human Relations*, vol. 12, pp. 99–120.

JENKINS, R. L. (1966), 'Psychiatric syndromes in children in relation to family background', *American Journal of Orthopsychiatry*, vol. 36, pp. 450–59.

JENKINS, R. L. (1968), 'The varieties of children's behavioral problems and family dynamics', *American Journal of Psychiatry*, vol. 124, pp. 1440–45.

JENKINS, R. L., NUREDDIE, E., and SHAPIRO, I. (1966), 'Children's behavior syndromes and parental responses', *Genetic Psychology Monographs*, vol. 76, pp. 261–329.

JESSOR, R., GRAVES, T. D., HANSON, R. C., and JESSOR, S. L. (1968), *Society, Personality, and Deviant Behavior*, New York: Holt, Rinehart & Winston.

JOHNS, J. M., and QUAY, H. C. (1962), 'The effect of social reward on verbal conditioning in psychopathic and neurotic military offenders', *Journal of Consulting Psychology*, vol. 26, pp. 217–20.

JOHNSON, R. C. (1962a), 'Early studies in children's moral judgments', *Child Development*, vol. 33, pp. 603–5.

JOHNSON, R. C. (1962b), 'A study of children's moral judgments', *Child Development*, vol. 33, pp. 327–54.

JOHNSON, R. C., ACKERMAN, J. M., and FRANK, H. (1968), 'Resistance to temptation, guilt following yielding, and psychopathology', *Journal of Consulting and Clinical Psychology*, vol. 32, pp. 169–75.

JOHNSON, R. C., and KALAFAT, J. D. (1969), 'Projective and sociometric measures of conscience development', *Child Development*, vol. 40, pp. 651–5.

JONES, E. E., and GERARD, H. B. (1967), *Foundations of Social Psychology*, New York: Wiley.

KANFER, F. H., and DUERFELDT, P. H. (1968), 'Age, class standing, and commitment as determinants of cheating in children', *Child Development*, vol. 39, pp. 544—57.

KAY, W. (1968), *Moral Development*, George Allen & Unwin.

KEEHN, J. P. (1956), 'Unrealistic reporting as a function of extroverted neurosis', *Journal of Clinical Psychology*, vol. 12, pp. 61–3.

KEMPEL, H., and SIGNORI, E. I. (1964), 'Sex differences in self-rating of conscience as a determinant of behavior', *Psychological Reports*, vol. 15, pp. 277–8.

KINSEY, A. C., POMEROY, W. B., and MARTIN, C. E. (1948), *Sexual Behaviour in the Human Male*, Philadelphia, Pa.: Saunders.

KINSEY, A. C., POMEROY, W. B., MARTIN, C. E., and GEBHARD, P. H. (1953), *Sexual Behaviour in the Human Female*, Philadelphia Pa.; Saunders.

KIPNIS, D. (1968), 'Studies in character structure', *Journal of Personality and Social Psychology*, vol. 8, pp. 217–27.

KIRKPATRICK, C. (1949), 'Religion and humanitarianism: a study of institutional implications', *Psychological Monographs*, vol. 63, no. 9.

KLINGER, E., ALBAUM, A., and HETHERINGTON, M. (1964), 'Factors influencing severity of moral judgments', *Journal of Social Psychology*, vol. 63, pp. 319–26.

KNUPFER, G., CLARK, W., and ROOM, R. (1966), 'The mental health of the unmarried', *American Journal of Psychiatry*, vol. 122, pp. 841–51.

KOHLBERG, L. (1963a), 'Moral development and identification', in Stevenson, H. W. (Ed.), *Child Psychology*, University of Chicago Press, 62nd Yearbook of the National Society for the Study of Education.

KOHLBERG, L. (1963b), 'The development of children's orientations towards a moral order: 1. sequence in the development of moral thought', *Vita Humana*, vol. 6, pp. 11–33.

KOHLBERG, L. (1964), 'Development of moral character and ideology', *Review of Child Development Research*, vol. 1, New York: Russell Sage Foundation.

KOHLBERG, L. (1969), 'State and sequence: the cognitive-developmental approach to socialization', in Goslin, D. A. (Ed.), *Handbook of Socialization Theory and Research*, Chicago: Rand McNally.

KREBS, D. L. (1970), 'Altruism – an examination of the concept and a review of the literature', *Psychological Bulletin*, vol. 73, pp. 258–302.

KUGELMASS, S., and BREZNITZ, S. (1967), 'The development of intentionality in moral judgment in city and kibbutz adolescents', *Journal of Genetic Psychology*, vol. 111, pp. 103–11.

KUGELMASS, S., BREZNITZ, S., and BREZNITZ, T. (1965), 'The development of intentionality in moral judgment: suggestions and initial test', *Scripta Hierosolymitana*, vol. 14, pp. 82–97.

LATANÉ, B., and DARLEY, J. M. (1968), 'Group inhibition of bystander intervention in emergencies', *Journal of Personality and Social Psychology*, vol. 10, pp. 215–21.

LATANÉ, B., and RODIN, J. (1969), 'A lady in distress: inhibition effects of friends and strangers on bystander intervention', *Journal of Experimental Social Psychology*, vol. 5, pp. 189–202.

LAWICK-GOODALL, J. VAN (1968), 'The behaviour of free-living chimpanzees in the Gomb Stream Reserve', *Animal Behaviour Monographs*, vol. 1, part 3.

LEFURGY, W. G., and WALOSHIN, G. W. (1969), 'Immediate and long-term effects of experimentally induced social influence in the modification of adolescents' moral judgments', *Journal of Personality and Social Psychology*, vol. 12, pp. 104–10.

LENSKI, G. (1961), *The Religious Factor*, New York: Doubleday.

LERNER, E. (1937), *Moral Constraint Areas and the Moral Judgment of Children*, Menasha, Wis.: George Banta.

LERNER, M. J., and MATTHEWS, G. (1967), 'Reactions to sufferings of others under conditions of indirect responsibility', *Journal of Personality and Social Psychology*, vol. 5, pp. 319–25.

LERNER, M. J., and SIMMONS, C. H. (1966), 'Observer's reaction to the "innocent victim": compassion or rejection?', *Journal of Personality and Social Psychology*, vol. 4, pp. 203–10.

LEWIS, C. S. (1960), *Studies in Words*, Cambridge University Press.

LIEBERT, R. M., FERNANDEZ, L. E., and GILL, L. (1969), 'Effects of a "friendless" model on imitation and prosocial behavior', *Psychonomic Science*, vol. 16, pp. 81–2.

LINNER, B. (1968), *Sex and Society in Sweden*, Jonathan Cape.

LITTLE, A. (1963), 'Professor Eysenck's theory of crime: an empirical test of adolescent offenders', *British Journal of Criminology*, vol. 4, pp. 152–63.

LIVELY, E., DINITZ., S., and RECKLESS, W. (1962), 'Self-concept as a predictor of juvenile delinquency', *American Journal of Orthopsychiatry*, vol. 32, pp. 159–68.

LOEVINGER, J. (1966), 'The meaning and measurement of ego development', *American Psychologist*, vol. 21, pp. 195–206.

LONDON, P., and BOWER, R. K. (1968), 'Altruism, extroversion and mental illness', *Journal of Social Psychology*, vol. 76, pp. 19–30.

LONDON, P., SCHULMAN, R. E., and BLACK, M. S. (1964), 'Religion, guilt and ethical standards', *Journal of Social Psychology*, vol. 63, pp. 145–59.

LORENZ, K. (1963), *On Aggression*, Methuen.

LOUGHRAN, R. (1966), 'A pattern of development in moral judgments made by adolescents derived from Piaget's schema of its development in childhood', *Educational Review*, vol. 19, pp. 79–98.

LURIA, Z., GOLDWASSER, M., and GOLDWASSER, A. (1963), 'Response to transgression in stories by Israeli children', *Child Development*, vol. 34, pp. 271–80.

MACAULAY, J. and BERKOWITZ, L. (Eds.) (1970) *Altruism and Helping Behavior*, New York: Academic Press.

MCCORD, J., and CLEMES, S. (1964), 'Conscience orientation and dimensions of personality', *Behavioral Science*, vol. 9, pp. 19–29.

MCCORD, W., and MCCORD, J. (1960), 'A tentative theory of the structure of conscience', in Wellner, D. (Ed.), *Decisions, Values and Groups*, Pergamon.

MCCORD, W., MCCORD, J., and ZOLA, I. (1957), *The Origins of Crime*, Columbia University Press.

MCCORD, W., and MCCORD, J. (1964), *The Psychopath*, Princeton, N.J.: Van Nostrand.

MCDONALD, L. (1969), *Social Class and Delinquency*, Faber & Faber.

MACKINNON, D. W. (1938), 'Violation of prohibitions', in Murray, H. (Ed.), *Explorations in Personality*, Oxford University Press.

MCMICHAEL, R. E., and GRINDER, R. E. (1964), 'Guilt and resistance to temptation in Japanese- and White-Americans', *Journal of Social Psychology*, vol. 64, pp. 217–23.

MCMICHAEL, R. E., and GRINDER, R. E. (1966), 'Children's guilt after transgression: combined effect of exposure to American culture and ethnic background'. *Child Development*, vol. 37, pp. 425–31.

MACRAE, D. (1954), 'A test of Piaget's theories of moral development', *Journal of Abnormal and Social Psychology*, vol. 49, pp. 14–18.

MALEWSKA, H. E., and MUSZYŃSKI, H. (1970), 'Children's attitudes to theft', in Danziger, K. (Ed.), *Readings in Child Socialization*, Pergamon.

MALLER, J. (1934), 'General and specific factors in character', *Journal of Social Psychology*, vol. 5, pp. 97–102.

MALMQUIST, C. P. (1968), 'Conscience development', *The Psychoanalytic Study of the Child*, vol. 23, pp. 301–31.

MASLOW, A. H. (1962), *Towards a Psychology of Being*, Princeton, N.J.: Van Nostrand.

MASLOW, A. H. (1970), *Motivation and Personality*, 3rd ed., New York: Harper.

MEDINNUS, G. R. (1959), 'Immanent justice in children', *Journal of Genetic Psychology*, vol. 94, pp. 253–62.

MEDINNUS, G. R. (1962), 'Objective responsibility in children: a comparison with Piaget's data', *Journal of Genetic Psychology*, vol. 101, pp. 127–33.

MEDINNUS, G. R. (1966a), 'Age and sex differences in conscience development', *Journal of Genetic Psychology*, vol. 109, pp. 117–18.

MEDINNUS, G. R. (1966b), 'Behavioral and cognitive measures of conscience development', *Journal of Genetic Psychology*, vol. 109, pp. 147–50.

MEDINNUS, G. R. (1967), 'Identification, conscience development, and sex appropriate behavior', *Human Development*, vol. 10, pp. 18–21.

MIDDLETON, R., and PUTNEY, S. (1962), 'Religion, normative standards, and behavior', *Sociometry*, vol. 25, pp. 141–52.

MIDDLETON, W. C., and FAY, P. J. (1941), 'Attitudes of delinquent and nondelinquent girls towards Sunday observance, the Bible and war', *Journal of Educational Psychology*, vol. 32, pp. 555–8.

MIDLARSKY, E, and BRYAN, J. (1967), 'The development of charity in children', *Journal of Personality and Social Psychology*, vol. 5, pp. 408–15.

MILGRAM, N. A., and RIEDEL, W. W. (1969), 'Developmental and experimental factors in making wishes', *Child Development*, vol. 40, pp. 763–71.

MILLER, G. A., GALANTER, and PRIBHAM, K. H. (1960), *Plans and the Structure of Behavior*, New York: Henry Hold.

MILLER, G. A., and MCNEILL, D. (1969), 'Psycholinguistics', in Lindzey, G., and Aronson, E. (Eds.), *Handbook of Social Psychology*, vol 3, 2nd ed., New York: Addison-Wesley.

MILLER, W. B. (1958), 'Lower class culture as a generating milieu of gang delinquency', *Journal of Social Issues*, vol. 14, pp. 5–19.

MILLS, J. (1958), 'Changes in moral attitudes following temptation', *Journal of Personality*, vol. 26, pp. 517–31.

MISCHEL, W. (1961), 'Preference for delayed reinforcement and social responsibility,' *Journal of Abnormal and Social Psychology*, vol. 62, pp. 1–7.

MISCHEL, W. (1966), 'Theory and research on the antecedents of self-imposed delay of reward', *Progress in Experimental Personality Research*, vol. 3, New York: Academic Press.

MISCHEL, W., and GILLIGAN, C. (1964), 'Delay of gratification, motivation for the prohibited gratification, and response to temptation', *Journal of Abnormal and Social Psychology*, vol. 69, pp. 411–17.

MORRIS, C. (1956), *Varieties of Human Value*, University of Chicago Press.

MORRIS, R. R. (1965), 'Attitudes towards delinquency by delinquents, nondelinquents and their friends', *British Journal of Criminology*, vol. 5, pp. 249–65.

MOSHER, D. L. (1966), 'The development and multitrait-multimatrix analysis of measures of three aspects of guilt', *Journal of Consulting Psychology*, vol. 30, pp. 25–9.

MOSHER, D. L. (1968), 'Measurement of guilt in females by self-report inventories', *Journal of Consulting and Clinical Psychology*, vol. 32, pp. 690–95.

MOULTON, R. W., BURSTEIN, E., LIBERTY, P. G., and ALTUCHER, N. (1966), 'Patterning of parental affection and disciplinary dominance as a determinant of guilt and sex typing', *Journal of Personality and Social Psychology*, vol 4, pp. 356–63.

MURPHY, L. B. (1937), *Social Behavior and Child Personality*, Columbia University Press.

NAJARIAN-SVAJIAN, P. H. (1966), 'The idea of immanent justice among Lebanese children and adults', *Journal of Genetic Psychology*, vol. 109, pp. 57–66.

NASS, M. L. (1966), 'The superego and moral development in the theories of Freud and Piaget', *The Psychoanalytic Study of the Child*, vol. 21, pp. 51–68.

NATIONAL OPINION POLL (1969), *Moral and Religious Education: What People Want*, commissioned by the British Humanist Association.

NELSON, E. A., GRINDER, R. E., and BIAGGIO, A. M. B. (1969), 'Relationships among behavioral, cognitive-developmental and self-report measures of morality and personality', *Multivariate Behavioral Research*, vol 4, pp. 483–500.

NELSON, E. A., GRINDER, R. E., and MUTTERER, M. L. (1969), 'Sources of variance in behavioral measures of honesty in temptation situations', *Developmental Psychology*, vol. 1, pp. 265–79.

NOWELL-SMITH, P. H. (1954), *Ethics*, Penguin Books.

NOWELL-SMITH, P. H. (1961), 'Morality: religious and secular', *Rationalist Annual*, pp. 5–22.

NYE, F. I. (1958), *Family Relations and Delinquent Behavior*, New York: Wiley.

NYE, F. I., and SHORT, J. F. (1957), 'Scaling delinquent behavior', *American Sociological Review*, vol. 22, pp. 326–31.

O'LEARY, K. D. (1968), 'The effects of self-instruction on immoral behavior', *Journal of Experimental Child Psychology*, vol. 6, pp. 297–301.

PALMER, J. W. (1965), 'Smoking, caning, and delinquency in a secondary modern school', *British Journal of Preventive Social Medicine*, vol. 19, pp. 18–23.

PARNELL, R. W. (1958), *Behaviour and Physique*, Edward Arnold.

PEARLIN, L. I., YARROW, M. R., and SCARR, H. A. (1967), 'Unintended effects of parental aspiration: the case of children's stealing', *American Journal of Sociology*, vol. 73, pp. 73–83.

PECK, R. F., and HAVIGHURST, R. J. (1960), *The Psychology of Character Development*, New York: Wiley.

PERETTI, P. O. (1969), 'Guilt in moral development: a comparative study', *Psychological Reports*, vol. 25, pp. 739–45.

PETERS, R. S. (1958), *The Concept of Motivation*, Routledge & Kegan Paul.

PETERS, R. S. (1966), *Ethics and Education*, George Allen & Unwin.

PIAGET, J. (1932), *The Moral Judgment of the Child*, Routledge & Kegan Paul.

PIAGET, J. (1967), *Six Psychological Studies*, New York: Random House.

PILIAVIN, I. M., HARDYCK, J. A., and VADUM, A. C. (1968), 'Constraining effects of personal costs on the transgressions of juveniles', *Journal of Personality and Social Psychology*, vol. 10, pp. 227–31.

PILIAVIN, I. M., RODIN, J., and PILIAVIN, J. A. (1969), 'Good samaritism: an underground phenomenon?' *Journal of Personality and Social Psychology*, vol. 13, pp. 289–99.

PITTEL, S. M., and MENDLESOHN, G. A. (1966), 'Measurement of moral values: a review and critique', *Psychological Bulletin*, vol. 66, pp. 22–35.

PORTEUS, B. D., and JOHNSON, R. C. (1965), 'Children's responses to two measures of conscience development and their relation to sociometric nomination', *Child Development*, vol. 36, pp. 703–11.

PRESSEY, S. L., and KUHLEN, R. G. (1957), *Psychological Development through the Life Span*, New York: Harper and Row.

QUAY, H. C. (1964), 'Dimensions of personality in delinquent boys as inferred from the factor analysis of case history data', *Child Development*, vol. 35, pp. 479–84.

QUAY, H. C. (1965), 'Personality and delinquency', in Quay, H. C. (Ed.), *Delinquency: Research and Theory*, Princeton, NflJ.: Van Nostrand.

QUAY, H. C. (1966), 'Personality patterns of preadolescent delinquent boys', *Educational and Psychological Measurement*, vol. 26, pp. 99–110.

QUAY, H. C., and BLUMEN, L. (1963), 'Dimensions of delinquent behavior', *Journal of Social Psychology*, vol. 61, pp. 273–7.

QUAY, H. C., and HUNT, W. A. (1965), 'Psychopathy, neuroticism and verbal conditioning', *Journal of Consulting Psychology*, vol. 29, p. 283.

RABIN, A. I., and GOLDMAN, H. (1966), 'The relationship of severity of guilt to intensity of identification in Kibbutz and nonKibbutz children', *Journal of Social Psychology*, vol. 69, pp. 159–63.

RANDOLPH, M. H., RICHARDSON, H. and JOHNSON, R. C. (1961), 'A comparison of social and solitary male delinquents', *Journal of Consulting Psychology*, vol. 25, pp. 293–5.

REBELSKY, F. G., ALLINSMITH, W., and GRINDER, R. E. (1963), 'Resistance to temptation and sex differences in children's use of fantasy confession', *Child Development*, vol. 34, pp. 955–62.

RECKLESS, W., DINITZ, S., and KAY, B. (1957), 'The self component in potential delinquency and potential nondelinquency', *American Sociological Review*, vol. 22, pp. 566–70.

RECKLESS, W., DINITZ, S., and MURRAY, E. (1956), 'Self concept as an insulator against delinquency', *American Sociological Review*, vol. 21, pp. 744–6.

REISS, A. J. (1952), 'Social correlates of psychological types of delinquency', *American Sociological Review*, vol. 17, pp. 710–18.

REISS, I. L. (1967), *The Social Context of Premarital Sexual Permissiveness*, New York: Holt, Rinehart & Winston.

REST, J., TURIEL, E., and KOHLBERG, L. (1969), 'Level of moral development as a determinant of preference and comprehension of moral judgments made by others', *Journal of Personality*, vol. 37, pp. 225–52.

RETTIG, S., and LEE, J. (1963), 'Differences in moral judgments of South Korean students before and after the Korean revolution', *Journal of Social Psychology*, vol. 59, pp. 3–9.

RETTIG, S., and PASAMANICK, B. (1969), 'Moral codes of American and Korean college students', *Journal of Social Psychology*, vol. 50, pp. 65–73.

RETTIG, S., and PASAMANICK, B. (1962), 'Invariance in factor structure of moral value judgments from American and Korean college students', *Sociometry*, vol. 25, pp. 73–84.

RETTIG, S., and PASAMANICK, B. (1964), 'Differential judgment of ethical risk by cheaters and noncheaters', *Journal of Abnormal and Social Psychology*, vol. 69, pp. 109–13.

RETTIG, S., and SUIHA, J. B. P. (1966), 'Bad faith and ethical risk sensitivity', *Journal of Personality*, vol. 34, pp. 275–86.

RICHEY, M. H., and FICHTER, J. J. (1969), 'Sex differences in moralism and punitiveness', *Psychonomic Science*, vol. 16, pp. 185–6.

RIESMAN, D. (1950), *The Lonely Crowd*, Yale University Press.

ROBERTS, A. H., and ERIKSON, R. V. (1968), 'Delay of gratification, Porteus Maze Test performance, and behavioral adjustment in a delinquent group', *Journal of Abnormal Psychology*, vol. 73, pp. 449–53.

ROKEACH, M. (1960), *The Open and Closed Mind*, New York: Basic Books.

ROKEACH, M. (1968), *Beliefs, Attitudes and Values*, San Francisco: Jossey-Bass.

ROSE, E. J. B. (1969), *Colour and Citizenship*, Oxford University Press.

ROSENHAN, D., and LONDON, P. (1968), 'Character', in London, P., and Rosenhan, D. (Eds.), *Foundations of Abnormal Psychology*, New York: Holt, Rinehart & Winston.

ROSENHAN, D., and WHITE, G. M. (1967), 'Observation and rehearsal as determinants of prosocial behavior', *Journal of Personality and Social Psychology*, vol. 5, pp. 424–31.

RUMA, E. H., and MOSHER, D. L. (1967), 'The relationship between moral judgment and guilt in delinquent boys', *Journal of Abnormal Psychology*, vol. 72, pp. 122–7.

RUOPPILA, I. (1967), *Attitude differences between young and advanced University and College students*, Finland: Jyvaskyla University Press.

RUTHERFORD, E., and MUSSEN, P. (1968), 'Generosity in nursery school boys', *Child Development*, vol. 39, pp. 755–65.

SANFORD, N. (1956), 'The approach of the authoritarian personality', in McCary, J. L. (Ed.), *Psychology of Personality*, Grove Press.

SARBIN, T. R. and ALLEN, V. L. (1969), 'Role theory', in Lindzey, G., and Aronson, E. (Eds.), *The Handbook of Social Psychology*, vol. 1, 2nd ed., New York: Addison-Wesley.

SCARPITTI, F., MURRAY, E., DINITZ, S., and RECKLESS, W. (1960), 'The "good" boy in a high delinquency area: four years later', *American Sociological Review*, vol. 25, pp. 555–8.

SCHACHTER, S., and LATANÉ, B. (1964), 'Crime, cognition and the autonomic nervous system', *Nebraska Symposium on Motivation*, University of Nebraska Press.

SCHALLING, D., and ROSEN, A. (1968), 'Porteus Maze differences between psychopathic and non-psychopathic criminals', *British Journal of Social and Clinical Psychology*, vol. 7, pp. 224–8.

SCHOFIELD, M. (1965), *The Sexual Behaviour of Young People*, Longmans and Penguin Books.

SCHOPLER, J., and BATESON, N. (1965), 'The power of dependence', *Journal of Personality and Social Psychology*, vol. 2, pp. 247–54.

SCHWARTZ, S. H., FELDMAN, K. A., BROWN, M. E., and HEINGARTNER, A. (1969), 'Some personality correlates of conduct in two situations of moral conflict', *Journal of Personality*, vol. 37, pp. 41–57.

SEARS, R. R., MACCOBY, E. E., and LEVIN, H. (1957), *Patterns of Child Rearing*, Evanston, Ill.: Row Peterson.

SEARS, R. R., RAU, L., and ALPERT, R. (1966), *Identification and Child Rearing*, Tavistock.

SHELDON, W. H. (1949), *Varieties of Delinquent Youth*, New York: Harper.

SHELTON, J., and HILL, J. P. (1969), 'Effects on cheating of achievement anxiety and knowledge of peer performance', *Developmental Psychology*, vol. 1, pp. 449–55.

SHORT, J. F., RIVERA, R. J., and TENNYSON, R. A. (1965), 'Perceived opportunities, gang membership, and delinquency, *American Sociological Review*, vol. 30, pp. 56–67.

SHUEY, A. M. (1966), *The Testing of Negro Intelligence*, New York: Social Science Press.

SIEGMAN, A. W. (1961), 'The relation between future time perspective, time estimation, and impulse control in a group of young offenders and in a control group', *Journal of Consulting Psychology*, vol. 25, pp. 470–75.

SIEGMAN, A. W. (1966a), 'Effects of auditory stimulation and intelligence on time estimation in delinquents and nondelinquents', *Journal of Consulting Psychology*, vol. 30, pp. 320–28.

SIEGMAN, A. W. (1966b), 'Father absence during early childhood and antisocial behavior', *Journal of Abnormal Psychology*, vol. 71, pp. 71–4.

SILVERMAN, I. W. (1967), 'Incidence of guilt reactions in children', *Journal of Personality and Social Psychology*, vol. 7, pp. 338–40.

SOCIAL SURVEYS (GALLUP) POLL LTD (1964), *Television and Religion*, London University Press.

SOLOMON, R. L. (1964), 'Punishment', *American Psychologist*, vol. 19, pp. 239–53.

SOLOMON, R. L., TURNER, L. H., and LESSAC, M. S. (1968), 'Some effects of delay of punishment on resistance to temptation in dogs', *Journal of Personality and Social Psychology*, vol. 8, pp. 233–8.

SPIRO, M. E. (1958), *Children of the Kibbutz*, Harvard University Press.

SPITZ, R. A. (1958), 'On the genesis of superego components', *The Psychoanalytic Study of the Child*, vol. 13, pp. 375–404.

SPRANGER, E. (1928), *Types of Men*, Tuebinger: Max Niemeyer Verlag.

STAFFORD-CLARK, D. (1965), *What Freud Really Said*, MacDonald and Penguin Books.

STAUB, E. (1970), 'A child in distress: the influence of age and number of witnesses on children's attempts to help', *Journal of Personality and Social Psychology*, vol. 14, pp. 130–40.

STEIN, A. H. (1967), 'Imitation of resistance to temptation', *Child Development*, vol. 38, pp. 157–69.

STEIN, E. V. (1969), *Guilt: Theory and Therapy*, George Allen & Unwin.

STEIN, K. B., SARBIN, T. R., CHU, C., and KULIK, J. A. (1967), 'Adolescent morality: Its differentiated structure and relation to delinquent conduct', *Multivariate Behavioral Research*, vol. 2, pp. 199–210.

STEIN, K. B., SARBIN, T. R., KULIK, J. A. (1968), 'Future time perspective: Its relation to the socialization process and the delinquent role', *Journal of Consulting and Clinical Psychology*, vol. 32, pp. 257–64.

STEPHENSON, G. M. (1966), *The Development of Conscience*, Routledge & Kegan Paul.

STEPHENSON, G. M., and WHITE, J. H. (1968), 'An experimental study of some effects of injustice on children's moral behaviour', *Journal of Experimental Social Psychology*, vol. 4, pp. 460–69.

STOTT, D. H. (1950), *Delinquency and Human Nature*, Carnegie United Kingdom Trust.

STUART, R. B. (1967), 'Decentration in the development of children's concepts of moral and causal judgment', *Journal of Genetic Psychology*, vol. 111, pp. 59–68.

SUGARMAN, B. (1970), 'Good samaritans at school: a study of altruistic attitudes among early teenagers', unpublished report, Farmington Trust, Oxford.

SULLIVAN, C., GRANT, M. Q., and GRANT, J. D. (1957), 'The development of interpersonal maturity: applications to delinquency', *Psychiatry*, vol. 20, pp. 373–85.

SVERI, K. (1965), 'Group activity', in *Scandinavian Studies in Criminology*, Tavistock.

SZASZ, T. S. (1961), *The Myth of Mental Illness*, New York: Hoeber-Harper.

TART, C. T., (Ed.) (1969), *Altered States of Consciousness*, New York: Wiley.

TAYLOR, L. (1968), 'Alienation, anomie and delinquency', *British Journal of Social and Clinical Psychology*, vol. 7, pp. 93–105.

TERMAN, L. M., and ODIN, M. H. (1947), *The Gifted Child Grows Up*, Stanford University Press.

THORNTON, A., WEBB, R., and WEIR, K. (1964), *Students' Views on Morality and the Law*, unpublished report, Oxford University.

TIDMARSH, W. M. (1964), 'The development of moral judgments', unpublished B.A. thesis, Leicester University.

TOBY, J. (1957), 'The differential impact of family disorganization', *American Sociological Review*, vol. 22, pp. 505–12.

TOMEH, A. K. (1968), 'Moral values in a cross-cultural perspective', *Journal of Social Psychology*, vol. 74, pp. 137–8.

TSUBOUCHI, K., and JENKINS, R. L. (1969), 'Three types of delinquents: their performance on the MMPI', *Journal of Clinical Psychology*, vol. 25, pp. 353–8.

TURIEL, E. (1966), 'An experimental test of the sequentiality of developmental stages in the child's moral judgments', *Journal of Personality and Social Psychology*, vol. 3, pp. 611–18.

TURNER, W. D. (1948), 'Altruism and its assessment in children', *Journal of Abnormal and Social Psychology*, vol. 43, pp. 502–16.

UGURAL-SEMIN, R. (1952), 'Moral behavior and moral judgment of children', *Journal of Abnormal and Social Psychology*, vol. 47, pp. 463–76.

UNGER, S. M. (1962a), 'On the functioning of guilt potential in a conflict dilemma', *Psychological Reports*, vol. 11, pp. 681–2.

UNGER, S. M. (1962b), 'Antecedents of personality differences in guilt responsivity', *Psychological Reports*, vol. 10, pp. 357–8.

UNGER, S. M. (1964), 'A behavior approach to the emergence of guilt reactivity', *Journal of Child Psychology and Psychiatry*, vol. 5, p. 85–101.

VAN DEN DAELE, L. (1968), 'A developmental study of the ego-ideal', *Genetic Psychology Monographs*, vol. 78, pp. 191–256.

VOGLER, R. E., MASTERS, W. M., and MORRILL, G. S. (1970), 'Shaping co-operative behavior in young children', *Journal of Psychology*, vol. 74, pp. 181–6.

WALKER, R. N. (1962), 'Body build and behavior in young children', *Monographs of the Society for Research in Child Development*, vol. 27, no. 3 (serial no. 84).

WALLACE, J., and SADALLA, E. (1966), 'Behavioral consequences of transgression: 1. the effects of social recognition', *Journal of Experimental Research in Personality*, vol. 1, pp. 187–94.

WALSH, R. P. (1967), 'Sex, age and temptation', *Psychological Reports*, vol. 21, pp. 625–9.

WALTERS, R. H., and PARKE, R. D. (1967) 'The influence of punishment and related disciplinary techniques on the social behavior of children: theory and empirical findings', *Progress in Experimental Personality Research*, vol. 4.

WALTERS, R. H., PARKE, R. D., and CANE, V. A. (1965), 'Timing of punishment and the observation of consequences to others as determinants of response inhibition', *Journal of Experimental Child Psychology*, vol. 2, pp. 10–20.

WARD, W. D., and FURCHAK, A. F. (1968), 'Resistance to temptation among boys and girls', *Psychological Reports*, vol. 23, pp. 511–14.

WATTENBERG, W. W., and BALISTRIERI, J. J. (1950), 'Gang membership and juvenile misconduct', *American Sociological Review*, vol. 15, pp. 744–52.

WHITEMAN, P. H., and KOSIER, K. P. (1964), 'Development of children's moralistic judgments: age, sex, IQ, and certain personal-experimental variables', *Child Development*, vol. 35, pp. 843–50.

WHITING, J. W. M. (1959), 'Sorcery, sin and the superego', *Nebraska Symposium on Motivation*, University of Nebraska Press.

WHITING, J. W. M., and CHILD, I. L. (1953), *Child Training and Personality*, Yale University Press.

WILSON, J., WILLIAMS, N., and SUGARMAN, B. (1967), *Introduction to Moral Education*, Penguin Books.

WOOTTON, B. (1959), *Social Science and Social Pathology*, George Allen & Unwin.

WRIGHT, D. (1962), 'A comparative study of the adolescent's concepts of his parents and teachers', *Educational Review*, vol. 14, pp. 226–32.

WRIGHT, D. (1965), *Attitudes towards the Church in Wellingborough*, Vaughan College Paper No. 9, Leicester University.

WRIGHT, D. (1967), 'Morality and religion: a review of empirical studies', *Rationalist Annual*, pp. 26–36.

WRIGHT, D., and COX, E. (1967a), 'Religious belief and coeducation in a sample of sixth form boys and girls', *British Journal of Social and Clinical Psychology*, vol. 6, pp. 23–31.

WRIGHT, D., and COX, E. (1967b), 'A study of the relationship between moral judgment and religious belief in a sample of English adolescents', *Journal of Social Psychology*, vol. 72, pp. 135–44.

YOUNG, J. Z. (1964), *A Model of the Brain*, Oxford University Press.

# Index

# INDEX

# INDEX